Family Web

Family Web

A STORY OF INDIA

Sarah Hobson

JOHN MURRAY

Printed and bound in Great Britain by
REDWOOD BURN LIMITED
Trowbridge & Esher
0 7195 3477 1

For Tony, who loves India,
this book is from our sharing

Contents

Illustrations

PLANS

All the photographs were taken by the author except the family in the fields, for which thanks to Kevan Barker. Also my grateful thanks to Chris Connors who drew the Plans and the Family Tree.

Family Tree

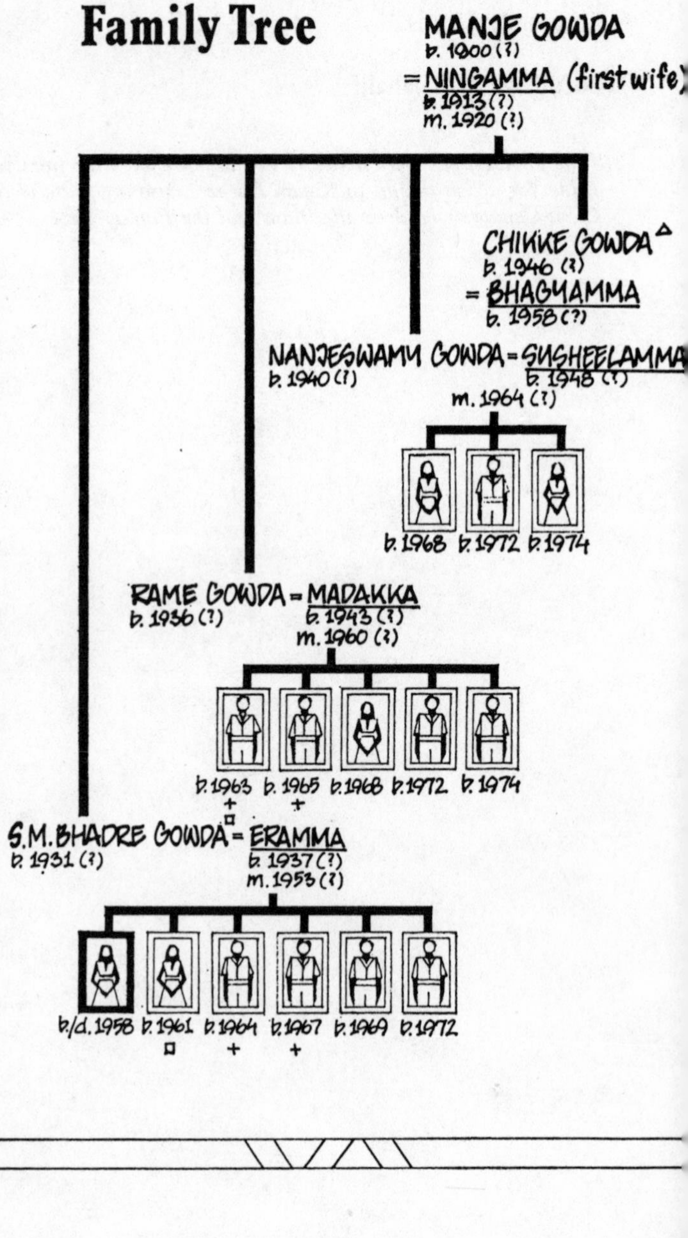
MANJE GOWDA
b. 1900 (?)
= NINGAMMA (first wife)
b. 1913 (?)
m. 1920 (?)
CHIKKE GOWDA △
b. 1946 (?)
= BHAGYAMMA
b. 1958 (?)
NANJESWAMY GOWDA = SUSHEELAMMA
b. 1940 (?)
b. 1948 (?)
m. 1964 (?)
b. 1968
b. 1972
b. 1974
RAME GOWDA = MADAKKA
b. 1936 (?)
b. 1943 (?)
m. 1960 (?)
b. 1963 + □
b. 1965 +
b. 1968
b. 1972
b. 1974
S.M. BHADRE GOWDA = ERAMMA
b. 1931 (?)
b. 1937 (?)
m. 1953 (?)
b./d. 1958
b. 1961 □
b. 1964 +
b. 1967 +
b. 1969
b. 1972

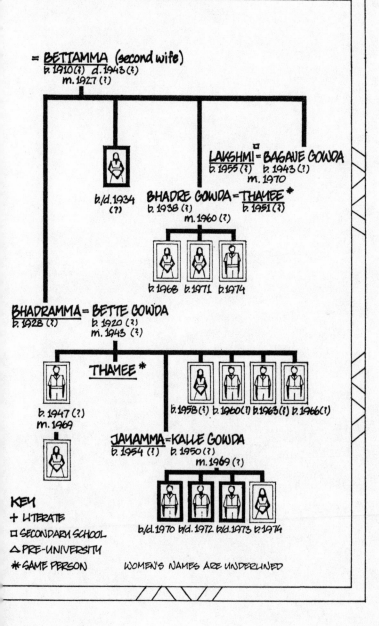

= **BETTAMMA** (second wife)
b. 1910(?) d. 1943(?)
m. 1927 (?)

b./d. 1934
(?)

LAKSHMI = **BAGANE GOWDA**
b. 1955 (?)   b. 1943 (?)
m. 1970

BHADRE GOWDA = **THAYEE** *
b. 1938 (?)   b. 1951 (?)
m. 1960 (?)

b. 1968   b. 1971   b. 1974

BHADRAMMA = **BETTE GOWDA**
b. 1928 (?)   b. 1920 (?)
m. 1943 (?)

THAYEE *

b. 1947 (?)
m. 1969

b. 1958 (?)   b. 1960 (?)   b. 1963 (?)   b. 1966 (?)

JAYAMMA = **KALLE GOWDA**
b. 1954 (?)   b. 1950 (?)
m. 1969 (?)

b./d. 1970   b/d. 1972   b/d. 1973   b. 1974

KEY
+ LITERATE
□ SECONDARY SCHOOL
△ PRE-UNIVERSITY
* SAME PERSON   WOMEN'S NAMES ARE UNDERLINED

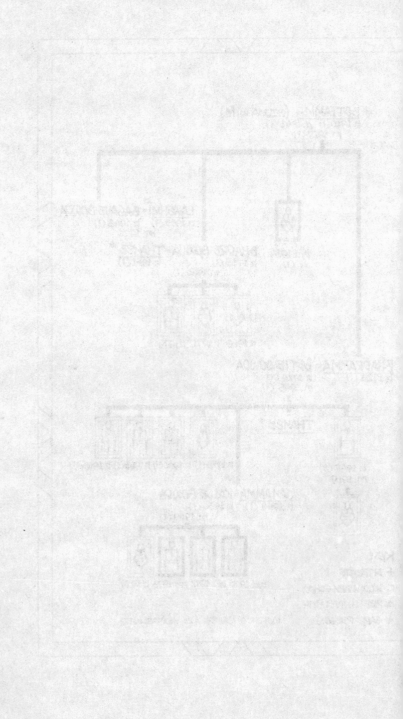

Author's Note

While I was trying unsuccessfully to gather material for a book in Iran, I received a letter from my husband Tony asking me to join him on a project in India. He said we could work together and that I might find another book. I cabled back sharply, 'Ready to join project in any capacity but no book thanks stop resent you organise my choice stop'. Four months later I admitted to him with a touch of defiance that I'd become so involved I wanted to write the story of the family we were studying.

My aim in this book is to act as a mouthpiece through which members of this family can express their hopes, their ambitions, their feelings, and the difficulties which face them. When living with the family, I quickly learnt how articulate even the women could be: they knew in their own terms exactly what their life was about.

But the family was not always willing to talk, and I found myself drawn into their lives as an individual in order to gain their confidence. To remain as objective recorder was even more difficult once I was sharing their confidence, though any idea of helping them proved poignantly inadequate. I have therefore included my relationship with them in the story in order to show the difficulties which must face any outsider wishing to enter a community whose codes and structure rest more on the need to survive than on humanistic principles.

Finding the family

We met the family through a chain of contacts and advice. The initial project was for Tony to make a documentary film* which explored village attitudes to fertility and family planning. We spent a month in Delhi talking to family planners, officials, and academics, then drew up a blueprint for the kind of family we

---

* '3900 Million and One' – produced and directed by Anthony Mayer, co-produced by Oxfam and the BBC, distributed by Concord Films Council, Nacton, Ipswich, Suffolk.

wanted to study, preferably in the south since so many projects
and studies were concentrated in the more cosmopolitan north.

We journeyed through Madhya Pradesh, researching and visiting
villages, then went on to Bangalore in Karnataka State, to be
kindly helped by a number of people: the social anthropologist,
Prof. M. N. Srinivas, and his wife; Mr. Jayanna, of All India
Radio, whose agricultural programmes reached many villages;
Kitu Krishnaswamy; Srikanth and John Staley of Oxfam. They
all introduced us to different groups and different villages.

We also went to Krishnapatna, a small decaying temple town
eighty miles from Bangalore, where Mr. Koulagi, a Gandhi
follower, runs a school for physically and socially handicapped
children of all castes. It was he who introduced us to Manje
Gowda's family in a village five miles away, and he who asked
them to agree to a study since they fulfilled some of our require-
ments: a joint family in which several women were pregnant, one
of whom was soon to deliver; a family which depended on the land
for its survival; a family which came from a poor background, cut
off from development activity; yet a family which had wrought its
own economic change, enabling a minimum choice in attitudes;
and a family with one son in town to highlight the urban-rural
conflict. It was unusual that they lived in a one-caste village, and
it was unrepresentative since they were the most powerful family
in the village – but we responded to them as people and wanted
to work with them. They in turn accepted our request to study
them, partly with excitement at the prospect of being on film,
partly because of a promised fee. They also accepted the idea of a
book mainly because books to them were a sign of education, a
commodity they envied.

Working methods

Tony returned to Bangalore to gather the unit and finalise
details for filming. I began research on my own. For the first two
weeks, I lived in Krishnapatna, walking to and from the village
each day with an interpreter. During my three months in the
village, I was helped by three people. The first, Thimme Gowda,
came for a week to help out. He was from the same caste as the
family and was therefore accepted with less suspicion; then
Varalakshmi, of the Vaishya community, who though she came

from Bangalore had worked with villagers before; and finally Venkamma, a Brahmin whose humaneness and keen mind meant she crossed the barrier of caste with ease.

I am very grateful to all three, but in particular to Vara and Venkamma, who put up with much discomfort and many difficulties: both were strictly vegetarian while the family was nonvegetarian; both required daily baths while the family bathed once a week; both were used to strict rules of diet and cooking. The family helped wherever it could with special cooking facilities, hot water, and privacy, though in the end the interpreters moulded into the family ways. The tolerance of everyone was remarkable.

I am very aware that without the cooperation of Vara and Venkamma, my communication with the family would have been greatly reduced. They had a difficult task in muting their own personalities in order to convey my thoughts, questions, and reactions, while trying to gain at the same time the confidence of the family. Regretfully, I have kept their role in the book to the minimum in order to save confusion, but where they altered a situation, I have said so. I give them my sincere thanks for their patience and hard work.

While living with the family, I used a concealed tape-recorder to record more than sixty hours of conversation. I have been dependent for their translation on Laxmi Chadrashekar: I am indebted to her for her sensitive, intelligent, and professional work, and for the hundreds of hours she has spent in transcribing often highly complex and indistinct dialogue. We have worked on the English version together, but her command of English literature and her experience of village life in the same part of India have provided a rare combination: she has given me many invaluable insights.

I feel that these conversations are the most important element of the book, for it means that the family has expressed itself in its own words and not in my interpretation of what each person said and felt. At the same time, they have proved the greatest hazard, for the family's speech was often unhurried and repetitive, often to the point of obscurity. It has been difficult to include as much of the transcripts as I had hoped, and they are therefore, to some degree, misrepresentative.

I have tried always to use the family's translated words when-

ever revealing an attitude; I have also used extracts in isolation
in order to give more emphasis. This means the endless questions
and answers which often were needed to prompt their thoughts
have not been included. But I have attributed no comment or
thought to any of the family unless proven by the tapes or by
notes written at the time.

Inevitably, something is lost in translation, but I have not tried
to compensate by characterising their dialogue. Nothing can
replace their intonation – the soft high mumblings of the old man,
the harsh muttered curses of the old lady, the exclamations of
Jayamma – but I hope their individuality will come through their
words nonetheless.

Double inverted commas (") indicate direct translation from
tape; single inverted commas (') indicate material from notes
made by me at the time or summarised on tape. If anyone wishes to
refer to my notes or tapes, I should be very happy to let them.

I spent one day a week in Krishnapatna typing additional
material from notes made hastily in the village. I tried to avoid
writing in front of the family for they were suspicious of recorded
information. I wrote down those things of which they were proud,
such as the number of cattle, the acres of land, the value of a crop;
but for anything more intimate, I disappeared into the bushes or
went for a walk away from the village where I could write unseen.
By the end of my stay, my supposed weak bladder was a joke
among the women.

For all places, I have used fictitious names to prevent identification; in the case of Nanjeswamy Gowda and S. M. Bhadre
Gowda, I have avoided the use of 'Gowda' for convenience and
easier recognition. The women do not have such an appendage.

Acknowledgements

I would like to thank Giryjamma and Surendra Koulagi for
their generous and warm hospitality in providing a base in
Krishnapatna which I quickly came to feel was home, and where
the handicapped children taught me much about self-sufficiency.
My warm thanks also to Jayamma, Venkamma's sister, who
returned with me to the village a year later; to Mr. Channabasappa
and Asim Chaterjee, the liaison officers for the film unit, who
worked for the Ministry of Health and Family Planning in

Author's Note

Bangalore and Delhi respectively, and who both provided enthusiasm, knowledge, and time; to Mr. Channabasappa for his superb work as mediator with the family men; to the many officials and scholars in Delhi, Bangalore, and Mysore, who offered advice and information; to David Watkinson who so skilfully printed the photographs; and to my mother, who helped check the proofs.

Once more, I am indebted to friends for their constant encouragement: Bryan Bennett, sane rationalist and counsellor; Colin Thubron, delicate critic and skilled writer; Morton Paley, close friend and mentor, all of whom gave so much time and lucid comment. But most of all to Tony, on whom I was dependent for support, sympathy, and patience, and whose understanding helped me through the loneliness of writing. It has been extraordinary to share with him not only the experience itself, but the interpretation of such an experience. Through him, I reached the family.

Finally, with deepest feelings, I want to express my thanks, my apologies, my remembrance to the family which took me in, fed me, cared for me, tolerated me, revealed their lives to me, trusted me, mistrusted me, and finally accepted me. And to Jayamma, the most deprived of them all, who opened her heart.

1 Early Days

'They think you're from the police,'* said the man who was walking beside me. He had emerged from a dip in the land as though he had been expecting me.

'Who?' I asked.

'The family. Manje Gowda's family. And others. They think you've come to take away one of their sons.'

'No, no,' I said, 'I'm only a visitor from England.'

'Visitor? England?' he said with a blank look.

'My country. I've come to learn. You know, studies.' He didn't know. 'Information,' I said, struggling for a word which would mean something.

'Investigation?' he asked, suddenly worried, though his face remained impassive.

'No, no, nothing like that. Why should I want to do that?' But I knew instinctively I had worsened the problem of getting to know the village and some of the families who lived there.

"Do you know the family?" I asked, wondering how he had heard of me.

"I'm related."

"How?"

"We're all related. My father and Manje Gowda were first cousins. My mother and Manje Gowda were brother and sister. My mother and father were first cousins. We're all related."

'But you live with them?'

'No.'

'You work with them?'

'No.'

'You live in the same village?'

'Yes.'

'You can show us the way?'

'Yes.'

We walked on along the track kicking up the dust in the dry heavy air. The man's feet were bare, his soles flattened and

*See Author's Note p. xvi regarding use of inverted commas.

cracked beneath stick-like legs; he wore torn baggy shorts and a white cotton vest. Thimme Gowda, my interpreter, and I both wore shoes; our shirts were new and crisp and we sweated in the heat. We crossed a tiny field planted in wavering rows of wilted millet seedlings: a path was worn through the middle regardless of plants or property. This was the way to the village and always had been.

Another man of about thirty-five crossed the path in front of us with a wooden plough balanced on his shoulder. He had a handsome, sensual face and his black hair was greased smoothly into casually drooping waves; his shorts were bright from white and orange stripes; and his vest outlined the contours of a well-formed chest. He was Nanjeswamy Gowda, one of the sons of the family.

I greeted him: he nodded brusquely and hurried on.

"We've come to meet your family," I called.

"My father's at home," he replied.

"Aren't you coming home now?"

"Oh, I'll come," he said, but turned in the opposite direction from the village.

'He's scared,' said the cousin. 'All the family are scared.'

'But why? I've only been once before. How do they know what I want?'

'They know; everyone knows in the village, too.'

'And you?'

He did not answer, and his face showed no expression in its tight mouth and sunken cheeks. Only his eyes were wary. He swung back his arms from muscled shoulders and took the lead as the path narrowed, forcing us into single file as we crossed a dry river bed whose banks were sand and rock.

The land around was wide open to let in the burning sun. A buff colour, the earth was spotted with spiky bushes and streaked with innumerable paths like streamers of cloud in the sky. To the right, the paths ran into a forested cliff which darkly guarded one side of the plain; behind, the ground rose up in a funnel to a precipitous tumble of rock which guarded the small and decaying town of Krishnapatna.

It was from Krishnapatna that we had come. We had walked five miles along a dusty track which passed through empty landscape – it was almost as though we were leaving aside our contact

2

with modern life, so quiet and remote was the road. Our feet made the only sound, scrunching on the dry soil. We kept glimpsing the village ahead, its squat roofs tightly knit together. There seemed no contact between town and village. No buses or cars came this way, nor even a creaking bullock cart. We met one man walking beneath his black umbrella, but otherwise there was no one.

Now at last, after a two-hour walk, we were on the edge of cultivation. Paths ran everywhere, dividing the land into square plots where the soil was packed into hard dry lumps, a dusty brown beneath the flimsy veil of pale green shoots. The sides of the plots were banked to capture the rain when it came, if it should come, to water the waiting crops: millet and paddy, pumpkins and sorghum, a field of yellow chrysanthemums. Away to the left, rising above the mirage, were the green heads of coconut palms on their sloping slender trunks.

Far in the distance the plain swept on and on, its surface broken only by hillocks of rock, and the dusty road wandering through. But close to, the village was half-hidden by two great mango trees whose fruit was beginning to ripen. The fields seemed private and enclosed, the place surprisingly empty; the village itself released no sound.

'And the family, do they live well?' I asked.

Not turning, our guide answered, 'They live well. Who wouldn't with six sons?'

'Six?'

'Only four of them live in the house. The other two are in town.'

'And how many daughters are there?'

He shrugged.

'But the four sons have wives?'

'Yes, they're all married. They all live together.'

'And how do the wives get on with each other?'

'There might be some quarrel between the women.' He clicked his tongue knowingly. 'But the old lady solves all that kind of thing. She makes sure they live in peace, she arranges everything. Each wife cooks for a month, they take it in turns to cook.'

'Then what do they quarrel about?'

'Oh petty things, what else? If one mother takes too much milk for her child, won't the others complain? Or if one mother beats another's son? They quarrel over food, they don't like each other's

3

cooking. Won't women always quarrel over petty things?'

We passed a square water tank where women were filling pots four hundred yards from the village: they had climbed down shallow steps and were waiting their turn with a babble of chatter which stopped the moment they saw us. The water was low, muddy, and thick with insects: as each woman approached, she wiped the surface with her hand then plunged in the pot to swallow the liquid; she scooped in the last few handfuls, levered the pot on her head, and resumed the path to return to the village.

We approached Palahalli past a solitary temple whose slabs of whitewashed stone were like a primitive monolith; as we grew closer we heard at last the noises of a village: the women and children, the clanking of metal, the loud call of a man. The houses were squat and disordered, set back from the road in a huddle, but the red clay tiles and red mud walls gave a richness of texture which seemed to match the red ploughed fields beyond. It was only a small village of twenty-five houses or so, but, unusually, all its inhabitants belonged to the same caste, Gangadikara Vokkaliga. Vokkaliga means cultivator, and probably derives from 'vokka', meaning 'to thresh the grain out of ears'; its men bear the name of Gowda, and are mostly peasant agriculturalists.

The Gowda community lives mainly in South India, in the state of Karnataka which was once Mysore. Their language is Kannada, rooted in Dravidian and written down with its own alphabet from the fifth century B.C. The Gowda have their own customs for marriage, birth, puberty and they are different from many castes in allowing their widows to remarry, in burying their dead, and in encouraging adoption for those without children.

We entered the village past a well whose mouth was boxed with granite, where women were drawing water with the help of a pulley; they covered their heads hastily at the sight of a man and a female stranger. Their faces were hooded as though by cowls but they watched us warily as we passed. On the right was a large new house – the largest in the village and certainly the smartest, though it had an air of neglect and all the windows were shuttered. Perhaps the landlord was absent? We left the main track and crossed a wide flat bridge where two men were smoking: they sucked at their tobacco, turned slowly to watch us pass, but showed no reaction.

Early Days

The street was narrow and short, running uphill gently to a line of granite slabs which blocked the path like tombstones beneath an impassive sky. Most of the houses had covered verandahs at platform level with steps to a door and shuttered windows; but one house – more of a hovel – had only a grass thatched roof sagging on flimsy walls. A woman came to the door, a baby on her hip, a daughter at her sari; she leant against the frame, jogging the child and chewing betel. Her teeth and gums were stained red, her oiled hair was dishevelled, her sari torn, her hands cracked, her face sharp and watchful.

I had heard many things of Indian village life, mainly from urban people – some good, some bad, much of it ill-informed: the ignorance of the peasant, his secrecy, his virility, his superstition, his prejudice. Or else a villager was mere statistics, in political plans or development programmes. It was the normal rift between city and village society, exaggerated to some degree by the segregation of caste. None of it worried me much except the constant reference to the difficulties of any outsider penetrating a closed community: the villagers resented intruders, they never disclosed their secrets, but remained politely aloof, and misled people on purpose.

Manje Gowda's house stood at the widest part of the street: an impressive house whose verandah was made from massive blocks of granite plastered with red cement. Three carved pillars supported the porched roof, and a lavish doorway glistened with silver paint. At least, it was lavish by village standards, and I felt the need to see things in village terms. By western standards, the house was a bit of a shack, though solid enough to withstand storms, and pleasantly inviting. We walked up the steps, removed our shoes, and stood waiting at the door. Our guide called into the house, then turned and walked away.

An old woman came to the door. "Welcome," she said, "enter, enter." She bowed deeply, pulling the end of her sari across her mouth. She was barefoot, a small wiry woman with a waspish voice and fanatical eyes.

"Come in, come in," she called, dropping the end of her sari to show a grinning mouth pulled back over horsy teeth.

The hall we entered was long and spacious: down the centre was an oblong washing area surrounded by granite pillars and

5

open to the sky. Light poured in to give the feeling of cloisters, for the rest of the room was shadowed. On one side was the cattle area; on the other, the living area with its wooden beds, two wooden chairs, and one narrow bench. Four doors led into small dark rooms, the private part for the family.

The house seemed a little desolate with its bare floor and bare mud walls but at least it was cool and simple. I stood awkwardly gazing about me.

"Sit there on the cot," instructed the old lady, pointing to a high wooden bed near the door. It was like a dais with its front open for audience, to be used only by men. The head of the house, Manje Gowda, was huddled on top in a blanket, an old man with a shrewd, shrivelled face: his lips were thin over toothless gums, his cheeks hung over his jaw bone. Grunting a little, he man-oeuvred both legs over the edge of the cot and slid mumbling to the floor.

"Don't move, please don't move," I said, "we'll sit somewhere else."

"Don't pay any attention to him," said the old lady, grinning. "You can sit on the cot in comfort." She motioned her husband aside and told us to climb up. But we crossed to a bench and sat down. The old man joined us and squatted at our feet as a sign of respect to his guests. The sun streamed down near him.

"We'll sit here," he muttered. "There's enough light here."

I tried to sit on the floor with him, but he looked sourly at me and told me to sit on the bench.

"Shall we put on the water for coffee?" asked the old lady. She seemed annoyed that we had rejected the cot.

"No, it's alright, thank you," I said. "We don't want anything."

"You can drink something here," she said, half-heartedly.

"We had everything before coming."

"Make it," ordered the old man.

She shuffled away into one of the rooms and emerged with a handful of coffee which ostentatiously she had covered with her sari, as a sign of her careful cleanliness. It was a torn sari, and faded: it hung from her waist in crumpled pleats to swing round her skinny ankles. She smiled at us, almost openly, but suddenly her face hardened as she noticed the crowd at the doorway: several women had entered and were huddled together, their

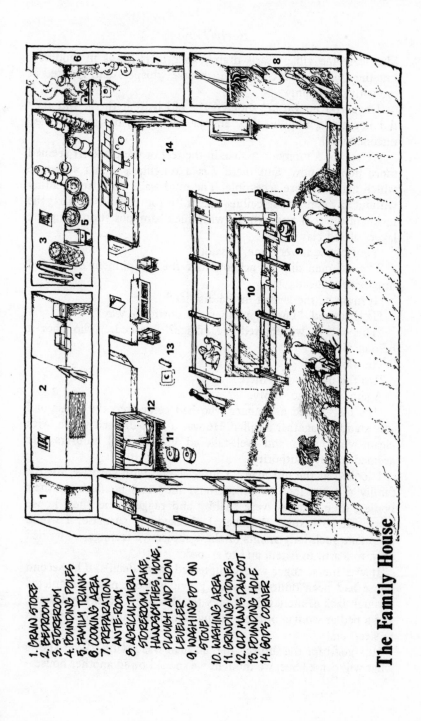

1. GRAIN STORE
2. BEDROOM
3. STOREROOM
4. POUNDING POLES
5. FAMILY TRUNK
6. COOKING AREA
7. PREPARATION
   ANTE-ROOM
8. AGRICULTURAL
   STOREROOM, RAKE,
   HANDAXE, HOE,
   PLOUGH AND IRON
   LEVELLER
9. WASHING POT ON
   STOVE
10. WASHING AREA
11. GRINDING STONES
12. OLD MAN'S DAY-COT
13. POUNDING HOLE
14. GOD'S CORNER

The Family House

identical blue village saris draped over their heads in modesty; but they talked to each other in hoarse whispers and glanced at me with suspicion.

'Have you no work?' shouted the old lady at them. But they did not move, nor did they answer back. The old man seemed unconcerned.

We sat for a moment to take in the feel of the place. It seemed more homely now, and there was a roughness in its structure which made it more accessible. The mud walls were freestanding without any connecting ceiling except for some planks in part; the inside of the roof was strutted with thick bamboos supporting the layers of red clay tiles.

'Your house is very fine,' I said.

The old man did not acknowledge the compliment but stared impassively ahead.

'It must be the largest in the district?'

He shrugged. 'There's another one down the way.'

'The one as we entered the village?' I asked. 'Who does it belong to?'

He was silent.

'Do the owners live there?'

Again he did not reply.

'It's his,' called a stranger who had come into the house and was standing against a pillar. He was a well-dressed youth with clean white shirt and well-tailored grey flannel trousers. He seemed to have authority.

I looked at the old man. 'Yours?' I said with surprise, for the family did not look so prosperous: they had no flesh on their bodies, their clothes were shabby and ragged, and their house displayed no luxury. But then I checked my surprise: I would not make such judgements or show subjective feelings – I wished only to learn, to listen, and to record.

It was the stranger who volunteered more details. The second house had been built nine years previously but never completed through lack of money. Now only the sheep and goats lived there, and a pedlar woman of the weaving community used the verandah to sleep on.

'It's good for the future,' the old man was saying. 'Who knows what will come? See, we thought we should build another house –

it's better to do whatever comes into your mind. If you leave something till tomorrow, it'll never . . .'

"We've got to occupy that house before the ninth year," interrupted the old lady knowingly, though nine years had passed already. "Otherwise the house will never be blessed. We'll live here, and we'll live there. We'll build a washroom there. Mm. We're going to build a water store, yes, that's what we're going to do." And talking to herself, she wandered into the kitchen to start preparing coffee.

"It's been good," said the old man nodding. "We've done all this." He lifted his arm feebly and pointed at the clay tiles. "See, we used to have a thatched hut."

"Even now we don't have enough to eat," called the old lady, her grating voice easily audible over the kitchen wall. "Do you think what we grow is enough? We don't have spare to sell, we have to buy in extra. It's always been like that."

"Part of it we grew, and part of it we bought," repeated the old man. "But somehow life goes on. At a level. Somehow we carry on."

"Why did you change the thatching?" I asked. "Wasn't it very costly?"

"It didn't cost much," shouted the old lady. "The villagers . . ."

But the old man interrupted and started to talk in a high monotonous voice, his head tilted on one side. He was frail, and sometimes he stopped to cough up phlegm.

"One day," he said, "I took the bullock cart and went to the forest. See, there's this man who's a forest officer." He emphasised the word 'officer'. "This officer stopped the cart in the forest – see, I'd gone to cut some grass for thatching – he caught me and wouldn't let me go. And he said, 'Why have you come here, what reason do you have to come to the government forest?' He went on and on about this and that. And I said, 'Swami, we're poor people, we're collecting a bit of grass to thatch our small hut. We haven't cut down a tree or anything. I'll go away. If you say, 'Don't come', then I won't come again.

"Then he said, 'That can't be, we can't let you come.' So I said, 'If you say I shouldn't come, I won't come. What else is there to it?' Then he said, 'Alright, since you've come today, I'll let you go. But don't come back again.'

"I went back to the village at once. Somehow I was feeling a tightness in my chest. I came back and that very day I took the same cart and went off to get clay for tiles. I got the tiles made. I made ten thousand tiles for this house, and arranged to build this house. That very day. It was fifteen years ago. See, we had some wood on our land also. Timber. We bought some more and arranged to build this house we're sitting in now."

"It didn't cost much," shouted the old lady again. "The walls were done by the villagers: we only paid them their meals. We fed fifty or sixty every day. They dug it all, they built it all. We used the wood from the banyan tree, we used it for wooden beams. And we got the bamboos in the bullock cart from a village four miles away."

The conversation ceased as we heard a horn in the distance. It got louder and louder, approaching the house up the street. A man climbed the steps and stood blowing a conch in the doorway. The sound was like a fog-horn, but softer, sadder, as though calling one's soul to the sea or sky, not trumpeting others to keep away. The man wore a thin turban of cream-coloured cotton which fitted his head like a bandage. A long sallow face swayed above a cream shirt; delicate fingers with long nails cupped the swaying shell. He stood in the doorway and waited, calling, calling on the conch. Then he dropped his hands to his side and held out a small copper basin which was strapped to his shoulder with string.

The old lady emerged from the kitchen and emptied some millet into his basin; she bowed and the holy man bowed in return. He stood waiting for more. The old lady turned her back abruptly and picked up a besom of coconut stalks to start sweeping the floor. The holy man stood for a moment longer, then turned and moved away.

The old lady used sharp movements, brushing the same place three times before stepping forward, her legs straight, her bottom bent. She mumbled to herself as she worked. "There's a man we call the Coconut Sapling Man. He said, Put your signature here, Ajji, I'll give a note to your son. But I said, Sir, I won't do it, I've never done it. Then he said, No, you don't have to bother about that, Ajji, I'll write a note and give it to you. You show it to your son. This has to be done."

The old man was staring into his lap, nodding his head gently, so she swept round him briskly. She tapped the floor impatiently, and called out, "Hey, Thayee, is it ready? Bring the coffee at once."

A girl of twenty-four or so walked out from the kitchen with two glasses. She wore an old cotton sari, once bright emerald but now faded to the tired green of cut grass. She walked barefoot with her legs apart, the knees not touching, to support better the weight of her pregnant stomach. The crinkled material was stretched over the bulge and baggy breasts to her shoulder, where it twisted up round her head in a hood.

I smiled and said hello when she handed me the coffee, but she kept her eyes lowered. Her bottom lip pouted slightly, not from any sulkiness but from the contours of her face. The long wide cheeks ran in a sweep to a narrow chin pushing the wide lips out almost in surprise. She was pretty, with dark bright eyes and a flat straight nose which flared at the end. She wore a jewel in her left nostril: tiny crystals set in gold which was soft against the gleam of her pale brown skin.

She watched me sip the coffee with a questioning look.

'It's good,' I said. 'Thank you.'

She returned to the kitchen and soon I could hear the sounds of her husking paddy.

'Where are your sons?' I asked the old man.

'They're in the fields as they should be,' he answered.

'When will they be home?'

'They come when they've finished their work.'

'And your daughters?'

'Will daughters stay at home?'

'How many daughters do you have?'

'One,' said the old man. 'My . . .'

'None,' said the old lady firmly. She had been watching hawk-like as the old man answered our questions, eager to interrupt yet knowing that as a woman she should not converse with strangers.

'No daughters?' I asked.

'No daughters,' confirmed the old lady.

'And who was the one who brought me coffee?'

'She's Thayee,' said the old man. 'She's my daughter's daughter – the granddaughter of this house.'

'She's a daughter-in-law of the house,' said the old lady. 'She married into our family.'

'She married my son,' said the old man.

'She married his son,' said the old lady. 'See, she married her own uncle.'

It seemed a little confusing so I asked their permission to draw up a family tree: I knew it would also produce a lot of unguarded information. But the old man and old lady could not agree on the details. Each named the sons in different order with different ages. The old man talked of a daughter who had died; the old lady spoke only of four sons; the old man added two more sons and a daughter, and the old lady deducted another two who were living in the town. I tried to match the sons with their wives, and then add in the children, but this only increased my confusion.

The stranger near the door had been listening in silence, but he unfolded his arms and came to squat near us.

"See, there were two wives," he explained quietly. "The old man took a second wife."

"You have to marry and get children," said the old man defensively. "It was only later that the first wife had four sons."

"Four," chanted the old lady. "My four sons."

"The second wife had two sons and then she died."

"Died."

Formerly in the Gowda community it was common practice for a man to take another wife if the first could bear no children. Barrenness was a woman's curse; why should a man suffer too? But if the old lady had borne four sons, where was the need for another wife?

"I married her when I was twenty-five," said the old man nodding towards the old lady. "She was very young, about seven years old. She couldn't do the housework and we didn't have the nuptials, so she went to live in her mother's house. Times were hard. I was the only son. How could I work the land alone? There was no one to help: my mother had died when I was very young, and my father couldn't afford to marry another wife. He brought us up, the two girls and me. And then both my sisters were married, so I was the only one left in the house. Who was there to do all the housework?

"I waited five years for my wife to mature so that she could come to my house. But still she didn't mature. Then everyone in the village said I must marry again. I myself was having to carry water, and who could do my cooking? I needed someone to help in the house. So I took a second wife. *She* was eighteen. She bore me two daughters, though one of them died; later she had two sons. Then my first wife matured and bore me four sons. But I tell you, I wasn't looking for children.

"We all lived together for fifteen years – the two wives, my six sons, and a daughter. There weren't any quarrels: one wife worked in the fields, the other did the housework. Then the second wife died, leaving her two sons and her daughter; and this woman brought up all the children and got them married and everything."

"Yes, we lived in the same house, about ten or twelve years," said the old lady without emotion.

"Then she lost her stomach," said the old man. His face also displayed no emotion.

"You mean while having a child?" I knew that infant mortality had always been high in villages until western medicine was introduced on a wide scale.

"No, no, she wasn't pregnant. It was some time after the child was born. She said she didn't feel well. After that she started losing her stomach. Loose motions. She died of that."

Perhaps it was cholera? The old man didn't know—they hadn't brought in a doctor, for how could a poor family pay for any treatment?

The second wife intrigued me, and the relationships it threw up of step-sons, step-brothers, and blood sons, all in the same household. What did the old lady really think of her rival? And had the old man chosen his second wife out of a need for sex, or did he view both his wives merely as vehicles for work and bearing children?

In theory it seemed that the old lady's side of the family possessed the power and status: there were more sons and grand-sons, who as men could wield influence, especially since some were educated; there were two sons in town, an achievement which brought great respect from others; and she herself was alive to protect and nurture their interests. Yet both families had lived together since the second wife's death more than thirty years before. I wondered if there was harmony between step-brothers and step-mother.

"Was she much older than you?" I asked the old lady, hoping she'd talk a little.

"Hn," she nodded.

"Did you get on well together?"

"Hn," she nodded.

"It must have been difficult sometimes though?"

She did not answer, and the old man closed his eyes.

I looked at the stranger questioningly, but he stared at his lap and started to play with the ends of his shirt, pinching them into folds, then opening them out like a fan.

The old lady scooped up a circular basket and balanced it on her head. "We don't have time to stay at home," she said, crossly. "I came from the fields just now. I have to run back and chase the birds away."

"The birds will eat up the sorghum," the old man said.

"They eat up the sorghum. I've tied two calves there. I must go. I haven't eaten my lunch yet."

I stood up.

"We'll have to go also," I said.

The old man nodded. "Go and come," he said.

"Yes, go and come tomorrow," said the stranger.

The old lady picked up a sickle near the door and led us out of the house: she ignored the stranger and threaded her way through the neighbours who were still clustered at the doorway.

I put on my shoes outside.

"Who was the man answering some of our questions?" I asked.

'Who? Oh yes, that man. He's . . . he's the old man's grandson. He's the brother of Thayee. He's . . .' Her voice trailed off.

'Does he live in the house?'

'Oh no! He's only the son of the old man's daughter. And even now there are quarrels.'

'Quarrels?' I said, too sharply, for she suddenly seemed to check herself.

"There's always a quarrel in this house," she said in a friendly way. "See, the women keep fighting. I scold them and they shout at me in return, 'You old hag, who do you think you were born of? Were you born to your father? Aren't you a bastard?' Yes, they say all that. And they fight over anything. But do you think I'll let them go without scolding if they haven't swept the floor, if they haven't washed the dishes, or if they don't come to the fields? See, I told one of them to bring some food to the fields, but did

The old lady prays to the gods for protection

The old man, his head freshly shaved, takes his weekly bath

she come? She didn't come. And you think I'll let her go without scolding?"

The old lady walked stiffly down the street, her eyes moving sharply from side to side to see what was going on.

"See, nobody does any work. Does anyone take the cattle? Does anyone take out the sheep?"

Turning into the main street, she walked to the family's second house, opened the front door, and let out a flock of sheep.

"Ayee, Saroji! Saroji!" she shouted, brandishing a stick, till a small girl of six ran up the steps. "Hey, child, why aren't you out in the fields? Take the sheep at once, and don't come back till evening."

Without a word, the girl took the stick from her grandmother and brandished it at the sheep, forcing them to move slowly out of the village. The old lady bent to the ground – I thought to pick up twigs till she moved towards my feet.

'No, no,' I said, stepping hastily back. 'You don't have to touch my feet.' Such self-abasement appalled me – I felt it was she who should receive my respect as the female head of her house who had given us hospitality.

She groped again for my feet. I took her arms gently and made her straighten up. Perhaps I had given insult by refusing to accept her obeisance and by touching her so intimately, but I knew I did not want to become part of any hierarchy for it meant the manipulation of power over those in a lesser role. I was not interested in power: I had no wish to change the family's lives.

The old lady grinned and told me to come back the following day. Then she turned and hurried after the sheep, her body hunched forward, her mouth working silently. All were quickly lost in a dip of the land, so Thimme Gowda (my interpreter) and I swung north in the hot sun for the long walk back to Krishnapatna. It seemed quite natural to walk ten miles a day in order to be with the family, especially since they had to do it themselves whenever they went to market. It gave me no hardship, except for the blisters, since I loved the heat and the feeling of freedom as I walked through open landscape with its rarefied light and raw contours. It was also a useful period to reflect on the day's events, and to discuss with Thimme Gowda the meaning of certain actions.

15

I was hopeful of the future: the family had been helpful and seemingly open, though God knows what they had thought of me. At least Thimme Gowda was of their caste and provided some sort of link. My main problem was recording the information. I was hesitant to write notes in front of the family unless they specifically gave permission – they were bound to be suspicious, since writing to them usually meant government forms, notes of debt, interest demands, and electricity bills. And they could not read to check my notes. I did have a tape-recorder hidden in my bag which none of them had noticed, but there were problems of changing the cassette over once the tape had run out. Each side lasted an hour, and their explanation, say, of the family tree, had lasted nearly three hours. It was therefore a question of multiple function – memory, tape-recorder, and written notes – which provided an evening's work of transcription. I got to bed after midnight.

The use of the tape-recorder worried me. It was a devious way to betray their privacy. And yet I felt it important that they should speak in their own words. However well an interpreter might translate, and however accurate my notes, it could not compare with a word-for-word translation of what they actually said. When a human studies other humans, objectivity is impossible: with tapes, there might be the chance of some accuracy on the family's thoughts and the techniques of their survival. You might say that the family's story is not worth the telling if it depends on secretive means for gathering information. I would say that the tape-recorder and tapes were only a smaller part of a much larger intrusion: myself.

2 Retreat

Krishnapatna clings to the side of a rocky promontory which sweeps down to the plain in layers of tumbled stone. From a distance the town is concealed by massive boulders so that only a tiny pinnacle is seen where the hill temple, tiered with thousands of carved figures, raises its pale grey *gopuram* to the gods. It is only a small town, remote and inaccessible, yet within its confines are fifteen temples, eight shrines, and thirteen holy tanks. For it was here in the twelfth century that Ramanuja the reformer lived for twelve years, preaching the Vedanta and bringing the beliefs of the Sri Vaishnava community to a wider cross-section of people. He believed strongly that religion was not meant for the priestly élite alone but that God was accessible to all devotees whatever their caste and occupation: in a society governed by gradation, he rejected caste and the restrictions which surrounded it.

Despite such radical origins, the sect in Krishnapatna has calcified with ritual, and the priests have withdrawn into their Brahmin caste, isolating themselves from society. Today their power is declining since religion is losing its hold. Once thousands of pilgrims came to the temples, bearing their gifts and money: the priests were all-powerful and often enormously wealthy. Now pilgrims come in numbers only at major festivals, but it is not what it used to be and the offerings are smaller. Many of the priests have left, unable to make a living according to their expectations, and those who remain quarrel among themselves over rights and duties and money: the maintenance of hierarchy has become more important than the development of spiritual virtue.

The town also decays: within the last twenty years its population has halved. Its community of weavers has largely moved to other towns since patronage for fine cloth has disappeared with the priests. No other commerce has replaced the business of religion – Krishnapatna lies on the road to nowhere, so any who come must return, for few come to stay. The houses are empty and neglected, their windows barred against thieves; along the narrow

17

main street, stalls sell stale sweets, bruised fruit, and dusty boxes of batteries. Only the old and young are seen in any number: the others leave if they can, taking a bus from the outskirts, since no buses enter the town – the streets are too narrow, the ground rough with bouldered paths and deep gutters. Lanes dawdle in the heat, their steps climbing to the sky, their granite blocks whitened by the sun: a priest mounts the steps one by one, leaning on his knee, his head bald except for a pigtail falling from the crown.

We were walking through the town on our way to the village, towards the steps beyond the temple that led down the mountain to the plain below. We bought some sweets and tobacco for the family, and one of the traders gave me a flower for my hair. Then we were out in the open, where the street widened to relinquish tatty living, the end of barter and common bustle. Pale blue ashrams, cream, ice green, with pillared verandahs and delicate balconies marked the beginning of holy land where others were cautious to go. But here also neglect seeped through the buildings: some of the windows were boarded, the heavy doors were bolted to protect against pollution from other castes entering. These were Brahmin houses, decaying in grand isolation. An ox bequeathed to the temple by a prosperous devotee chewed at the weeds on a doorstep; inside, a fat Brahmin read his daily newspaper beneath a whirring fan, and with a mouthful of mango he called for more coffee and some morsels to eat before lunch.

The wail of a trumpet poured into the street, demanding attention, declaring itself to the soul. Drums ingeminated the rhythm, tattooing the call of religion; a pale chant of priests discorded. A procession turned into the street, lurching and staggering forward. About thirty priests balanced across their bare shoulders a grid of huge bamboos the size of telegraph poles. Mounted on a dais was the hallowed figurehead: a tiny head of gold suffocated by garlands; a body sunk into a skirt billowing with yards of cloth. She nestled against a cobra's head, its lead hood raised, its fangs alert, swaying beneath a canopy of tassles.*

---

* For some Hindus, the snake is a symbol of sex and fertility and is worshipped in complex ceremonies (the cobra particularly appears frequently in mythology). For the village family, the snake represented danger, power, and the need for placation; for the town family, the cobra was king – it was a town snake; all others were mere country snakes.

Retreat

This was Devi, the goddess of earth, the giver of life, the provider of fertility: two priests protected her face, fanning it free from flies and sprinkling it with cold water. Brahmin men and women emerged from their houses to watch: they prostrated themselves on the dusty ground as the wobbling procession passed. But the villagers scarcely stopped as they walked through to the market. They glanced with curiosity, attracted by the music and the smell of burning incense, yet this was not their god, and these were not their priests performing unknown rituals – most of the villagers worshipped Shiva and knew little about other gods. But they did understand the remoteness of priests as representatives of religion: their fat bellies and stocky bodies wrapped from the waist in delicate cloth, the striped symbols painted across their well-oiled chests, the strange hairstyles, the perpetual chanting in a language they did not know. Any relationship villagers might have with priests was more economic than religious, supplying goods or services to the town sanctuary, and labour to temple lands. Maintenance of caste was more important to the priests as a means of bolstering religious authority; even today, the shadow of an 'untouchable' meant contamination for the priests of Krishnapatna and complex procedures for purification.

An attendant wrapped in orange cloth stood guard at the doorway to the temple clutching a holy pennant. He bowed as the chief priest – bronzed, waxen, muscled, with hook nose and shaved head – strode in. But the moment he saw me approach, his hands twitched with anxiety, and he gesticulated for us to keep away.

We left the god to its dark interior and followed the building round its colonnaded sides. Above on the roof were nubile women carved with grapefruit breasts, and lithe gods with bejewelled bodies surveying the physical world from delicately ornate niches.* The profuseness of Hindu sculpture, its liberality and fullness, reflects the polytheism of godheads within the religion itself, a religion which allows such variation that hundreds of sects exist – sects which allow a man to express his individualism

---

* One of the family women, Bhadramma, told me much later: 'When I go to the temple, I see the God. I see the priests also. What else is there? Perhaps I see a few of the sculptures also. But I don't know what they mean. Only educated people know. Such things are only for them.'

without impinging on others, so that tolerance and respect can grow between men.

But such metaphysical musings were out of place as we moved through the harsh landscape away from the temple town. The village ahead had a separate identity, based on practicality: it was the survival of the body rather than the soul and had little to do with priests. The long walk seemed to cut one away from anything false or superfluous: by the time we reached the village we had forgotten the town and were thinking of crops and water.

Today I felt more comfortable: I knew the way to Palahalli, the weather was cooler, and I was no longer anxious about the family, for they had been hospitable and only slightly suspicious. But when Thimme Gowda and I entered the house, no one greeted us or welcomed us. They seemed purposely to ignore us. The old man was standing in the sunken area swamped in strands of sunlight as he said his weekly prayers. Smoke curled upwards from the joss-stick he was holding, its smooth spirals broken intermittently by the quavering of his hand. He began to revolve, his face lifted to the light, his eyes closed, his lips mouthing a supplication for the god Shiva to provide and to protect. The old lady was breaking twigs and pushing them into the fire beneath a huge brass cauldron where water was heating for baths. Near the kitchen, a daughter-in-law cleaned paddy, tossing it up from the front of the basket and catching it at the back; but the moment she saw us, she scooped up her work and hurried into the darkness of a back room.

We stood with embarrassment near the door until Thayee, the old man's granddaughter, invited us to sit down. I tried to give her the sweets and tobacco but she frowned and nodded towards the old lady.

'You must give them to our mother. She's the head of our house.'

I offered them to the old lady, but she nodded towards the old man.

'Isn't he the head of our family?' she asked. But she grasped the packets and hid them under her sari without a word of thanks.

We sat on the floor, but no one spoke. The old man finished his prayers, settled in one corner, and arranged the folds of his lungi around his fragile thighs. Thayee served him food on a freshly plucked banana leaf: he ate some rice, then scooped up the watery buttermilk on his fingers and drained it into his mouth. When he had finished, he turned and stared at me.

"Who's she?" he asked.

I felt bewildered that he did not recognise me.

"She's the one who came yesterday," said the old lady.

"No, is it?"

She laughed scornfully. "Oh ho, do you think you can see? Aren't you too blind? See, she's wearing different clothes, that's all that's different. Do you think she'd stay in the same clothes like you? Do you?" She herself was still in the same blue sari.

It was true I had changed, after the dust and sweat, but the clothes were very similar: a printed long cotton skirt and a plain coloured shirt hanging loose. Only the colours were different, softer today, less urban. But perhaps it was not so much bad memory as fear on the old man's part which made him fail to recognise me. I learnt later that the family had been threatened by others in the village, either from anger or jealousy, and that rumours were running wild: I had come to take one of their sons, I had come to take some of their land, or at least to exact some taxes. No one knew where I came from, no one knew who I was. And today, because the family had asked me to come, they could not turn me away, so they suffered me in silence and got on with their duties. The old lady called one of her grandsons into the sunken granite washing area, unbuttoned his shirt and shorts, and pulled them off roughly. The child stood passively until she started to pour steaming water from the brass cauldron in potfuls over his head; he burst into tears and tried to struggle away. But the old lady gripped him hard and scrubbed his body with soap and a pumice-stone.

'Do the children bath every day?' I asked.

No one replied. I repeated the question, louder, but still no one replied. The child was gulping frantically between his screams, as the water streamed over his head swilling away the soap.

'Is it always the old lady who washes the younger children?'

This time Thayee answered in a whisper. 'We bathe them every three or four days, whoever . . .'

The old lady shot her an angry glance which silenced her immediately.

We must have sat for twenty minutes in uneasy silence. Only the old man muttered to himself, "Let them take a son to England. Let them take the youngest son who's not married. What if they do take him? They'll give him food. He can be happy there instead of scratching the earth in this jungle. What do we have here? Only the earth to scratch at."

Then a man entered the front door and the family forgot its restraint.

"Oh Ningappa," said the old man and old lady together. "You've come at the right time for coffee. Thayee, bring some coffee for Ningappa."

The family had pointedly not offered me coffee, and did not do so now.

"No, I won't drink any," said Ningappa, climbing onto the old man's cot as though it were his right. No one had offered such a seat but he seemed unabashed and wrapped a blanket round himself. I discovered later that Ningappa lived in the neighbouring village and earned his food as a storyteller. He moved from village to village reciting poems and stories, passing on gossip, collecting the latest news. He knew the most prosperous houses and so visited them often; he knew also that Manje Gowda's house wanted to prove it was prosperous so would always be good for some coffee.

"Why don't you drink coffee?" asked the old man.

"Drink it," urged the old lady. "It's made with cow's milk."

"That's good," said Ningappa with a nod to indicate he'd take coffee. His face was the perfect caricature of a rascal, with his shifting eyes and beaky nose and endlessly wrinkled skin. His mouth seemed set in a permanent grin to reveal two of his front teeth missing, and the rest of them stained brown from tobacco.

"These days," he said, "you can't get anything like you used to."

"You could get things then, in those days," said the old lady. "Can you get them now? You could get thirty seers of millet for one rupee. Is it like that now? For coarse rice alone, it's two and a half rupees."

"Yes, times have changed," said Ningappa, philosophically. "There's no contentment now. There's more trouble, more complication."

"Complications!" exclaimed the old man. "In those days we

didn't have all these troubles. There's no peace now. There's nothing but talk, talk . . ."

"We've had to shrink our stomachs and instead fill our mouths with words," said the old lady. "There isn't enough to eat now the family's bigger. A family is like an ocean. You've seen it. How do you bring up everyone? There are guests to feed, this aunt, that cousin, the mothers of our daughters-in-law. When we were doing coolie work, somehow we were quite happy. Oh what can you say about those days? Even though they were hard, they were comfortable."

"The country has changed, the rulers have changed." said the old man.

Thayee came out of the kitchen and gave Ningappa his cup of coffee. He drank it noisily, blowing first on the hot liquid.

"Is it good?" asked the old lady.

Ningappa nodded.

"The rains aren't good now," said the old man. "We can't do much on the lands."

"They're no good," said the old lady. "The rains aren't good. And what else is there? So we worry, saying, 'Why did it happen like this, why isn't there any rain? There's no rain at all. The tank's not full, the well's not full, why is it like this?' There's nothing else. Of course we eat rice, or millet, we don't go without eating yet. But we worry constantly at the lack of rain. How will the children live in the future? How will they manage? We haven't seen our loans repaid so what will happen? Yes, we have to do everything."

Everyone sat in gloomy silence, till the old man said, "You must give us a story now, Ningappa."

"Yes, tell us what we must do," urged the old lady.

It was a suitable day for religious songs in Manje Gowda's house. Today was Monday, and every Monday the old man shaved, bathed, and offered prayers to the gods before taking a meal. He was the head of the house, so he should approach the gods. Shiva, Lakshmi, Vishnu – they were important gods deified by all Hindus. Bhadreswamy, Manjunatha, Dikkadamma – they were the lesser, household, gods who the family felt gave them special protection. These three had been the household gods of Manje Gowda's parents, and their parents, and their parents, and so on right back for hundreds of years.

And the old lady, she said prayers on Mondays too. She didn't have to, but she wanted to. She liked to do as her husband did. Sometimes she wouldn't bathe till late afternoon or evening, when no one was in the house. Then she would say her prayers after which she could finally eat. Some of the grandchildren were made to pray with her.

Ningappa cleared his throat ostentatiously and began to sing in a loud, croaking voice:

> "Where are you going, my little sister? Come
>   with me this side,
> For this is the only way to the world of truth.
> Walk over the roads and through the forest and
>   come, come with me:
> Learn the road which leads to the knowledge of
>   detachment.
>
> "Where are you going, my little sister? Come this
>   way with me,
> This is the only way to the world, the world of truth.
> Look at the child, how he lies in the arms of
>   the lotus petals;
> Caress him in your arms and listen to his words."

"I don't recite anything which has to do with worldly affairs," said Ningappa. "If it's philosophical, then I'll say it. Philosophical in the sense that it's related to holy men. I can't tell stories about Once Upon A Time. Mine are only about the soul, and cooking in the body, and other things. 'Oh Life! You have seen the illusory web of lust, anger, pride, and jealousy. Oh Life!'" he said, closing his eyes and lifting his eyebrows with pain, "'Whatever times you might have survived, you cannot escape the coming death.'"

With his eyes still closed, he slid his hand into his pocket for some tobacco; but when he could not find it, he opened one eye like a hawk for an instant and swiftly pulled out the packet.

"Can a frog resting in the shade of a snake's hood live forever?" he asked dramatically, while rolling a cigarette. "But if you build a tank or plant a flower garden, then you can attain salvation."

He leant forward earnestly. "Eh, Gowda," he called to the old man, "have you got a match?"

Through the front door came Susheelamma, a tall elegant girl of twenty-five or so. She was carrying water in large brass pots – one on her head and one held against each hip either side of her pregnant stomach. Gracefully, she bent her knees, keeping her back straight, and passed beneath the lintel with only an inch to spare. The granddaughters ran to help unload but spilling some of the water received a smack in reprimand. The old lady re-kindled the fire beneath the big brass pot, and started a running commentary while she worked. "Hey, where's the axe for cutting these sticks?" she called, in a high querulous voice. "It's not in our house now. I don't know who's taken it. It was in someone else's house. They took it." She glanced at the women and children to see what they were doing. "Hey, child, go and wash your hands," she ordered. "Thayee, don't use that for pounding. What about the cooking? We could have made coffee for everyone. But she curdled the milk. See, I'd kept it to one side. I could have used it for coffee. But now there's no milk. Hey, child, fetch some sticks for the fire. The flames are burning now. I'd kept some milk in the morning, so that we could make coffee for everyone. Eh, Susheela, have you eaten your *rotti* today?"

Ningappa frowned and stopped his recital. "Don't make such a noise," he shouted, and drew himself up haughtily, casting aside the blanket. Nobody paid any attention. He raised his voice a little. "You can't learn all these things without a guru," he said. "There's a group, a few of us get together and that's the group. Children of the guru, that's what we are. Every month we go and see our guru on the day of the new moon and the day of the full moon. We worship and serve God. Hundreds of people come together."

The old man was dozing, but he woke with sudden interest. "Tomorrow's a full moon. Will you meet tomorrow?"

"We're not getting together this time. It'll be on the new moon day instead, fifteen days from tomorrow. Hundreds of people will come. Even women. In the night."

"In the night?"

"In the night. See, this mind, which they call a monkey . . ."

"Is it a monkey?" asked the old man, puzzled.

25

"No, it's not a monkey. See, Shiva is in this house, he's in your body also. If you break the tip of a thorn, he's in that also. He's sitting in this house, all over. If you keep this house clean, the whole world will be here in your body. See, this mind that's been called a monkey is like a bird wherever it flies. It's a bird. I am the whole world; man is the whole world."

He spoke with finality, and gathering up the blanket, he wrapped it round his head and lay down to sleep.

"The whole world," echoed the old man.

The old lady was still talking to herself. "There's no milk in anybody's house. He went and asked in everyone's house. Hey, Saroji ... no, it's Sudhamani, hey, child, run and see next door whether they've got some milk. She's curdled it. See, I'd kept it aside for coffee."

But the child did not move, and the old lady forgot to remind her. It was strange how the women and children, though working so closely together, barely seemed to communicate; or if they spoke, it was to tell one another what to do.

Ningappa's snores intruded, reminding the old man and old lady that they were alone with me, for they stopped their musings and concentrated on their work. The old man picked up a branch of harvested pulses to strip off the long black pods. Perhaps it was calculation, perhaps it was simply discomfort at being idle when others were working, but I squatted beside the old man, picked up one of the branches and copied his actions.

'No, no, you can't do that,' said the old man and the old lady simultaneously. I dropped the branch, worried that I had given offence by touching their food.

'A guest can't work in our house,' they said.

'But I'd like to help. I do it at home in England.'

'No, no,' they said. But when I picked up the branch again, they did not protest. I started to pod the pulses with pleasure, ejecting the yellow peas onto a pile on the floor: I liked using my hands and I knew the importance of learning their tasks if I was to understand something of their lives.

It seemed only natural to talk while we worked, to reminisce of earlier times when life had been much harder, when the family had been very poor.

"We used to do coolie work then," said the old man, quietly.

"We used to do coolie work," said the old lady loudly, bustling up to us with a small bowl for the pulses. "We worked for other people."

"Did you grow enough to live on?"

"Oh no," said the old lady.

"We used to do coolie work also," repeated the old man. "Only now God has been . . ."

"Only now, after my eldest son grew up," continued the old lady. "We shouldn't lie just because we're like this today. We've done coolie work also. For one anna, for half an anna a day. We've even carried fuel."

I had seen the village women carrying bundles of fuel to Krishnapatna that morning – not mere twigs but branches of wood six feet long strapped together with string or grass and balanced on the head. Their faces were sweating but they never stopped for a rest: they had to sell the wood as fuel for cooking to some of the weavers and high-caste Brahmins for one or two rupees, then walk back to the village to start the day's work.

"When did things start getting better?"

"Since about fifteen years," answered the old lady. She was sweeping up the husks on the floor with her hands.

"Fourteen or fifteen years," added the old man.

"After the children grew up?"

"Yes, yes." He pulled out the delicate pods from between the prickly leaves, starting first at the top then working downwards, swivelling the branch evenly. He was squatting against his heels, his knees bent to his chin, his arms stretched round his calves holding the plant out in front of him. Twice he showed me how to pod more efficiently, his nimble fingers scoring them out like bullets. My efforts improved, but not to his standard.

"God has been somehow . . . in our house . . . now . . ." struggled the old man.

"Oh you keep quiet," whispered the old lady hoarsely. She picked up all the husks and crossing the room to the cattle area threw them onto the floor as fodder.

The old man stopped for some tobacco, swinging the weight of his body onto his bottom, relaxing his spine in a curve. Feeling beneath his shirt, he pulled out a packet of *bidis* – local tobacco wrapped in a brown leaf. He scratched at the box of matches and

27

waved the stub in his mouth trying to catch the flame. Between smokes, he extended his arm lazily across his knee, holding the *bidi* backwards between thumb and forefinger, and gazing blankly across the room; the light was falling behind him in streams of rectangular bars.

"Dada," I asked, "you're so old, why do you still work?"

"Oh, what to do? I don't do any big jobs, I do only small things."

"He does only small things," shouted the old lady. She came and stood over me. "See, in your country, you must be happy," she said almost accusingly. "See how your belly's covered! But for us, life is difficult. We don't have enough to eat. You must write down that there are so many people. But how do you know what's inside, what the difficulties are? Have you seen what trouble we have? How can you know? We have to do everything. But we can't work. Aren't we old?"

"We can't sit quiet," said the old man. "Must feed the cattle. The pods have to be opened and the husks fed to the cattle. We keep doing such things."

The rest of the men were out in the fields except for Nanjeswamy, the old lady's third son whom we had met briefly the day before: he sauntered into the house and sat on the bench above us. He watched us through lowered lids, his head bent, his fingers idly tapping his knees.

"Why do you bother to do that?" he asked of my work.

"I like it," I said.

He smiled.

"Have you been ploughing?" I asked.

"Isn't there always work?" he replied.

"So what work have you been doing?"

"My work? They want me to work in the field, they expect me to hire labourers – I have to do this and that, here and there. There are so many demands. No clothes for tomorrow, no millet to eat. If there's an emergency, I'll get up round five or six. Otherwise if I'm very tired it might be a bit later. How can you ask the Goddess of Sleep to come or go at a certain time? You can't say you're going to get up at a particular time. Who can say it? No one can."

He was interested in Thimme Gowda, my interpreter, for

Thimme came from the same sub-caste as the family but had been to university and now had a job in a town. He was a Gowda who had made good, and Nanjeswamy was impressed. But soon he grew bored, and, yawning, stretched himself out on the wooden bed near the kitchen door. He listened idly to the old lady as she hovered about him explaining how she had made us welcome, and how she had answered all our questions. She went on and on, repeating herself until Nanjeswamy interrupted abruptly.

"What's it to do with you?" he said. "Keep quiet and get on with your work."

"I was just saying . . ."

"Shut up!" he shouted. "Who are you anyway? Women should never talk so much."

"Oh alright," grumbled the old lady, "what have I said?" And to compensate for her scolding, she turned and yelled at one of the children. "Hey, you, get off and take the mat next door. And where's the sickle gone?"

Complaining to herself, she picked up a basket and wandered out of the house.

Nanjeswamy turned to us and smiled with winning charm.

"You must have your meal here," he said.

"Yes, do it, have it, have it here," echoed the old man.

"They've prepared curry. You must eat it."

Without waiting for our reply, Nanjeswamy got up and spread a rush mat near the kitchen door. Thayee came out at his curt command, holding a pot of water: she stood at the edge of the sunken area waiting for me to approach. I offered to take the pot but she silently poured a thin stream of water in which I should wash my hands. When I straightened with dripping hands, she motioned me down again and told me to wash my face and mouth; then she told me to raise my skirts to the knee so she could splash my feet. She bent to rub the dirt from my toes but I backed away in embarrassment that a woman should be subservient to me. She looked at me with puzzlement.

Thimme Gowda repeated the ritual and we sat down cross-legged on the mats. Thayee rinsed two stainless steel plates and placed them in front of us. She went backwards and forwards from the kitchen to fetch the food: balls of millet like small haggis, liquid curry, salt. She bent forward to serve me and showed me how to put a wooden stick under one side of the plate to tilt the liquid into a pool; she taught me how to break off a piece of millet, dip it in the liquid and toss it into my mouth. Then at Nanjeswamy's order she retired to the kitchen and stood watching me round the doorway.

I began to chew.

'Swallow, swallow,' she said, bursting into giggles.

I tried to gulp but the lump stuck in my throat. I brought it up again and chewed despite her protestation.

'The millet will stick in your teeth, the millet will stick in your teeth,' she cried.

I broke off a smaller piece and taking a deep breath gulped it whole. Thayee laughed and clapped her hands in praise.

'Look, look,' she cried, 'see how she breaks it off. See how she swallows it. Is it good? Do you like it?'

I felt my throat contracting.

'Delicious,' I said, smiling.

She smiled back.

Then she brought us rice, more curry soup, and finally rice with buttermilk. She laughed a lot, especially when I looked at her. But the moment Nanjeswamy glanced at her, or Thimme Gowda said something, her mouth straightened and she lowered her eyes.

At the end of the meal, she offered me water again for washing.

'Thank you,' I said quietly. 'I loved your cooking.'

She nodded. The first communion had been offered and accepted.

The street leading to the family house (top right, beside the goat)

Inside the family house (from bottom left, clockwise): the open granite washing area; the front door; the grinding stone; the old man's cot and a spare bed; the entrance to the bedroom; a bench for visitors. In the centre, the pounding hole.

3 Family Power

It was already 9.30 in the morning but it seemed early. The light was pale and the ground was still cool; a breeze bumped our faces and the sunlight spattered the ground between the shade of clouds. Only the old man had come to the fields and was scratching the earth in solitude.

"In spite of all my spitting," he muttered, "those bastards don't bother, they never bother. I told that widow's daughter so many times, and she still hasn't bothered."

He was squatting on the ground, inching forward on each haunch as he weeded a patch of onions.

"No, you can never sit down," he said. "Life's not for sitting down. Life says, 'Work, you must work.' I can't see properly and my back's bent with pain but I have to work. What else can one do? We'd lose everything otherwise."

He stabbed angrily at the ground with the short stick he was holding, disregarding our presence as though we didn't exist. It didn't matter: it was such a beautiful morning to sit on a rock with the sun in our faces, breathing the pure air, watching the distant hills, with only the ripple of wind in the bushes to accompany the old man's mumblings. I no longer felt so intrusive, for by its very size the joint family had a natural capacity to contain people – perhaps it also brought flexibility and compatibility so that people of diverse character could live together in harmony while gaining support from each other. Any solidarity must give solace when life is insecure.

In the distance one of the women approached, trailing a buffalo and calf behind her, a basket of washing on her head. She was tall and well built; she walked slowly, swinging her hips leisurely to keep her head on one level; she pushed her pregnant stomach forward to relieve some of its weight in the motion of walking. It was Susheelamma, the second daughter-in-law of the house and wife of Nanjeswamy.

Susheelamma did not know when she would deliver: she

31

thought it might be anything from one month to six weeks. Her husband was even more vague and said we must ask his wife or his mother, then stated she had only two weeks to go. Susheelamma looked ill but she still had to work: in the village, women work till delivery though the load decreases as the time comes close. If a woman sits idle, they say no blood can circulate, and then delivery will be hard. Only afterwards does a woman rest, for several weeks or several months according to the wealth of the family – she has to regain her strength after the loss of blood in birth.

Susheelamma was handsome, her body gracefully proportioned with full hips and breasts; she was also sexily languid, dropping her arms over her stomach, bending her head to close her eyes and to pout her mouth. Her face was soft and submissive and her brown eyes lacked curiosity.

She crossed a tilled field and stopped at some rocks near the onion field; she tied up the two animals and pushed her way through some bushes to find fodder for the cattle. The noise attracted the old man.

"Why are you tying it there?" he called. He screwed up his eyes in an effort to see. "Hey, what animal have you brought?"

"The buffalo and its calf," said Susheelamma.

"Did you bring it over those people's fields?"

"How else? Could I have come any other way?"

"But they've sown there. What will they say? You should have come round the other side. You should have tied it in the hollow. Oh, they've sown seeds on that land, why did you bring it that way? Let mud fall into your mouth."

"What do you expect me to do with such a load on my head?" retorted Susheelamma.

"You're answering back?" said the old man, his voice rising; but he choked in the middle of his words and began to cough painfully. He shifted his legs uncomfortably and turned back to his work.

Susheelamma moved the buffalo and its calf nearer the old man as provocation. He looked up with fury.

"Why tie the buffalo there?" he shrilled. "What can it graze there? You should have left it at home on its arse. Why did you drive it here? Where's the place to tie it? You whore, you'll bring ruin on your children, you barren woman. Go on, take the animal back. Leave your work here and take it back to the house."

32

Susheelamma ignored him. She squatted in the onion patch far from the old man.

"These women," he said, "they'll only bring evil on the house, and the house will never prosper. It's only evil. No prosperity. Look, she just brought the buffalo and dumped it here."

The sun streamed down on his crouched back so he wound a white cotton towel round his head as a turban to ward off the heat. The back of his neck was bare and tiny white hairs glistened in the sun; he kept scratching his chin with annoyance at the thin downy stubble. The old man worked methodically, rarely stopping for rest, but his arthritic fingers kept dropping the weeds he had just pulled out of the ground.

Susheelamma stopped frequently. Her stomach was uncomfortable, suspended as it was between her rising thighs. She shifted frequently, placing her hands beneath her stomach to release its weight for a moment. As the morning grew hotter she pulled her sari across her head as an eyeshade and with its loose end wiped the sweat from her upper lip.

Half an acre of land was planted with onions and garlic: it had been levelled into a terrace above a bank of rocks which dropped steeply to a pool of calm clear water more than a hundred yards wide. Reflected in the surface was the duck-egg blue of sisal plants contoured by tawny stubble and lined by the patchwork of sky. The plot was a grid of tiny beds through which ran shallow gullies to carry the water for irrigation: an imperceptible gradient meant that water lifted by hand from the pool could flow freely down the network, to be splashed by hand across each bed.

The family had bought the one acre plot for about a thousand rupees; they had taken advantage six years ago of the distress of a Brahmin named Rama Rao whose family had divided through quarrels and squabbles. As the head of the family, Rama Rao had kept this plot: he saw its potential beside the water and was ready to clear the ground himself. He felt he could make it prosper. But he did not consider the debts outstanding at the time of his family's division and when creditors started pressing he was forced to sell the plot. Manje Gowda's family was the only one to put in an offer or rather the only one which could raise the money to buy it.

Manje Gowda's family had now cleared more than half an acre, and this was the first crop. It had to be watered twice a week and weeded once a month. Weeding was women's work; watering was for the men; spreading manure was also the women's duty though the weight of the load was more suited to men. And the old man? He did women's work now that he was so old, so weak, and nearly blind. But he had to keep on working since every hand helped. And he was the head of the family – how could he sit at home?

The rest of the women arrived – the daughters-in-law of the house. Thayee came first in her faded green sari, calling out loudly about the food I had eaten; she was followed by two others, who squatted near Susheelamma, each taking a bed to weed. They worked quickly and deftly, a gang of women so used to work that they did it without comment and seemingly without effort. Their hands were gnarled and rough, the skin of their feet was cracked, the skin of their faces was starting to wrinkle, and their bodies had thickened from child-birth; and yet they had the youth of supple limbs and they chattered together like girls.

They giggled when I approached to squat near Thayee: I rolled up my shirt sleeves and tucked up my skirt between my knees. The soil was damp, almost slimy, from the water recently splashed across it; but grasping a stick, I leant forward.

"Wait," called the old man quietly. He pressed his palms against the soil, then lifted them to his closed eyes, touching the eyelids gently. He did this three times as a mark of respect to the soil. "Mother Earth, bless us," he said on my behalf.

I scuffed the top of the soil and eased out a weed. All the women were watching.

"See how she pulls out a weed," they laughed.

"How can she work like that?"

"Why doesn't she squat like we do?"

I worked steadily, grasping the weeds in my right hand before throwing them onto a pile between the beds. Suddenly one of the women shouted:

"See, see, she's pulled out one of the greens!"

"Pah! Pah!" cried the others in derision.

"The greens?" I queried.

"See, we'd planted such a lot of herbs, and we can't see many now," said Susheelamma, the wife of Nanjeswamy and the one who had brought the buffalo.

34

"There are no herbs at all."

"What sort of seeds were they?"

"One of them is called coriander," called the old man. "You can smell it. Just pull it out and smell it. You'll know then." He pulled one out and getting up stiffly brought it over for me to smell. "But I can't see it properly," he said pathetically, holding it close to his eyes. "Oh, I can't see."

The women worked hard, moving from bed to bed so that the plot soon looked like a chessboard with squares of red from upturned soil or smoothly pale from mud. The moment they slackened their pace, the old man was at them with his croaking, goading voice, supervising their movements as though they were only beginners.

The women were kind to me: they pointed out the herbs, they pulled out some of the weeds to help me through my patch, and they showed me how to gather my skirts to stop them trailing in the dirt yet still to remain decent. It was like wearing a pair of trousers with a bundle of cloth wrapped into a ball on the lap.

Perhaps on reflection it wasn't kindness but efficiency which prompted them: I was the newest member of their workforce and had to be taught the traditional methods. But they did show concern over the mud on my hands and kept asking why I worked. It must have seemed odd to choose to do it: they themselves had no choice. I felt ashamed. My hands were white and plump compared to theirs; my blouse seemed too revealing beside the folds of their saris; and I had to keep stopping for rest. I was slow in my work, unused to the method and unexercised, so that my hands fumbled against the plants. I was also uncomfortable. I stood up to stretch and then tried to work bending down from the waist but my back soon hurt and I had to force my aching thighs to resume a squatting position.

It was hard to make out the relations between the women for there was little reaction between them. The eldest must have had most authority. She was a shrewish woman of thirty-one with thinning hair and tiny limbs and a coarse, scolding voice. She worked beside the youngest, correcting her all the time:

'You've left too many weeds; you must loosen the earth round the plants; why do you work so slowly?'

The youngest listened passively but did not change her pattern of work, nor did she quicken her pace. She was a beautiful girl of nineteen who seemed remote and aloof. Once or twice I caught her staring at me, but she dropped her eyes immediately; and once when I purposely worked beside her, she whispered in English, "Baa baa, black sheep."

Susheelamma, the wife of Nanjeswamy and the second daughter-in-law of the house, worked in isolation: she did not give nor did she receive any orders. But for some reason the old man harassed her mercilessly. He blamed her for the number of weeds, he blamed her for the lack of herbs, he blamed her for the thinness of the onions planted. He went on and on, until Susheelamma lost her temper and told him to get out.

"Oh ho, listen to you," he mocked. "Look at you! Look at all you women sitting there with your bottoms stuck together. Look, who planted this bit? Is that the way to plant?"

"Did I plant it? Was it me?" shouted Susheelamma.

"If it wasn't you, then who did?"

"See! See how he abuses me!"

"Why did you come here then? Did you come here to wipe your face in the mud?"

"You say that in front of these learned people . . ."

"Huh! Resting your bottoms on each other!"

"Do they talk like this in other parts?"

"I'll slap you across the face if you talk too much."

But Susheelamma continued to talk and the old man continued to curse, and neither seemed to tire. The argument stopped only when Susheelamma gathered her basket of clothes and walked away to the pool, swinging her hips defiantly and disregarding the old man's commands to finish her work on the onion plot.

"They don't care how it's done," muttered the old man. "Who else will work like me until their ribs are broken?"

One of the hardest tasks was to dispel assumptions which came from my own half-knowledge about the structure of Indian rural society. I had read a number of studies, but the variabilities within caste, language, religion, and culture were frequently so numerous as to make comparison misleading. A Bengali is not a Madrasi; a Rajasthani blacksmith has little to do with a Kerala Christian apart from the shared experience of their recent political history and the effects of the Hindu religion. Of course such studies helped me to be more aware of possible kinship structures and patterns of defined behaviour but they frequently failed to reveal the human pressures of life and the role of the individual within a specific predicament. I was also a little suspicious of how data had been collected, especially relating to women when a man had been doing the study. Formal questioning by representatives of authority, whether health worker, teacher, or academic researcher, can elicit misleading statements.

Both to understand the family as humans and to examine the means of access were of primary importance to me, but I had first to break down my own prejudices. When interpreting any statement, my own values and experience were bound to intervene however much I wanted to control them. My judgements and understanding sprang from a Western classical culture where my democratic, ex-Christian ethic asked for justice and information. Yet accurate information was only one of the luxuries I had to quickly forgo: the statements of the family were indications of attitude and subjective interpretation rather than reasoned fact. And my interpretation of their information was a hazardous route to take, whether the subject was land or money or women or even something as simple as food.

Language itself was a problem. Their vocabulary was sometimes limited, especially for abstract concepts; yet sometimes it was rich as with agricultural terms, and then the interpreter did not always understand. There was also the problem of colours, numbers, weights: their 'red' covered my red, scarlet, and yellow; their four or five meant two or three; their eight or nine meant a few; their measurements were sometimes positively known, sometimes only guessed at.

Even if they had the vocabulary, they were often inarticulate, repeating words, changing the subject, forgetting to put in a word to identify the topic. Even close, repetitive questioning did not always produce a clear answer.

"Did you know your mother's mother?" I asked Thayee once, thinking I'd find out something about the old man's second wife.

"I don't know," she answered. "I believe I'd been born. Even then I don't know."

"Was she alive at the time of your marriage?" I asked again.

"No, I don't know. I believe she died."

Was her vagueness from lack of memory, or because she didn't want to answer the question, or because she wasn't sure what answer I wanted to hear?

"How long ago did she die then?"

"I believe she lived for twelve years after her marriage."

"So your mother and her brothers were quite young then."

"My husband was quite big."

"Does he remember her?"

"Yes, he and my mother remember everything."

"Was your mother married when she died?"

"Yes." Thayee paused. "Oh, no. My mother wasn't married."

"Then how could you have been born?"

"My mother wasn't married I believe."

I was lucky with Nanjeswamy. He wanted to talk; he did talk, and in so doing he revealed more than I could have asked, for he seemed at ease with information, was able to express it clearly, and had opinions about events within the family. He was eager for our company – a handsome man whose somewhat surly face relaxed into smiles of encouragement. He had an answer for everything, even without a question, and spoke with surprising frankness. At first we sat in the family house so that he could keep an eye on the women.

"I was so angry this morning," he said. "Everything should be done with order – I can't stand it when it's not. See, the women should wash the children's faces. But this morning no one bothered to wash my son's face. My wife, Susheelamma, was lying down, she said she couldn't sweep or anything, she was feeling very bad. I thought, Well, she's pregnant, I'll keep quiet. So I called one of the others and said, 'Come here, clean my son's face.' And do you know, she answered back? 'Does your wife do all these things for *our* children?' she said. I was angry. 'Did I say my wife does it?' I asked. 'All I said was that everyone must do it, everyone must look after the children.'"

He got up to pace along the hall, kicking a piece of twig in anger that no one had swept the floor. He looked as though he wanted to shout out orders but was restraining himself with an effort because of the guests he was entertaining. He lit a *bidi* and casually puffed out the smoke.

"Do the wives often neglect your son?" I asked.

He shot me a glance to see what I meant by the question. He smiled, knowingly.

"I'm not complaining because she didn't wash *my* son's face. But he had a running nose, there were flies on his face. If people like you come home, what would you say? You'd say, 'What filthy people these are.' It's like that now, cleanliness is important. We ought to keep the children clean. I'm not saying the women should do it to *my* son or *my* daughter – I just say there should be no discrimination. And I don't let my wife get away with it either. I don't care what the women think of me. I'll tell them whatever I feel like saying. What can they do to me? Can they hang me for it? Let them. I'm not scared. Everyone has to die sometimes. Because you're alive today, I'm talking to you; but if fate had taken you yesterday, we wouldn't be talking here. Because God keeps you strong, and you still have some days left in life, that's why you're here."

"But you say you're scared of the women?" I asked. "Surely they're scared of you."

He laughed callously. "The women must do what I say, or else I get really angry. And when I get angry I don't mind anything. I don't mind beating, if there's need. It might be my wife, my mother, or my children."

"You beat your wife?" I asked, surprised not so much that he should beat her as that he should admit it.

"Oh yes, I beat her," he said casually. "Once she served me food without washing the plate first. I wanted to hit her, but a guest was there. Now it's different – I wouldn't beat her, not while she's pregnant. And as for the other women, we only beat them when they've done wrong. It's the same with the children. It's the only way they learn. That's what it's like in a joint family. My brothers can beat my wife and children, and I can beat theirs."

It was obvious Nanjeswamy had the privilege of power. Not that he abused it, oh no! He was the one who worked, there was always so much to do. The others just wandered about, and this caused all sorts of problems. *He* didn't want the family to divide; *he* was keeping the family together; *he* advised and helped the family; because of him the family had grown strong and prospered. He gave his brothers no chance for complaint. His wife, his children, himself – none of them stayed at home, no one could accuse them of not doing their share of the work.

Yes, he was the manager of the family, he supervised and took care of the money. Of course he worked in the fields, but there was so much work looking after the money. Yes, he managed it all – at least in the village. His eldest brother, S.M. Bhadre Gowda, he was the one in the town, he had a job as accountant there.

"Everyone shivers when he comes," said Nanjeswamy. "We all hide in some corner. Even I don't smoke or anything in front of him. See, our improvement is all the result of his efforts. If he'd gone away on his own, nobody would have known which Palahalli Manje Gowda's house was. But he tells us what to do, he says, 'It's not enough if I'm alright, the whole family should improve.' *I* help the family also, but he's had education."

Although S.M. Bhadre Gowda had taken over the control of family affairs in 1959, it was Nanjeswamy who had the title of Manager. His position seemed inexplicable, for he was only a younger son who had no education and no particular qualities. The rest of the hierarchy was traditional: the old man was titular head of the family; the eldest son in town, S.M.B., deserved responsibility because of his work and education – why should Nanjeswamy be chosen for the village?

'You see, I'm very bold,' he said, 'and I've got the capacity to do things. I can make contact with people and I've got lots of energy. I can think, work, talk, try out new things. So the family has given me responsibility – it was God who made me clever.

'It's a responsible job managing money. Those who manage money never have a *paise* for themselves. I always account for everything, and even when there's a profit – say from selling a pair of bullocks – I'll always keep an account. But I don't have money myself even though I'm handling it. Whoever takes on the financial burden just borrows from one to pay back another.

'Look,' he said, showing his pocket book scribbled with figures and lists. 'I keep strict account of everything, it's all written down. I can't write myself, but I get someone to do it for me.'

His latest shopping list detailed a box of matches, some cloth for a new shirt, coffee, sugar, and joss-sticks. Every week he showed these accounts to his eldest brother, but he didn't inform the others. How could he? There was so much to tell to so many of them. But he always told his parents of everything he'd done, and they could tell his brothers if anyone wanted to check them. No, his brothers couldn't read but they could always ask someone to do it for them.

'Money!' he said. 'There's never any left. I borrowed two thousand rupees* from someone. Out of that there's nothing left. I borrowed it to buy a buffalo. People trust me, they know I pay money back. I'm telling you, I can go to the village and get hold of five hundred rupees – right now if you want. They'll give it, they'll give it to me.'

It seemed strange that he could command such sums, but perhaps it was merely boast: he certainly liked his power and the thought of controlling the money. He also liked to have our exclusive attention. Once we tried to talk with the old man and a neighbour, but Nanjeswamy sat guard on the wooden bed. Within half an hour he was pacing angrily in front of us, his mouth turned down, his expression sulky at this lack of regard for himself. Only when we asked him to show us the lands and his projects was he enthusiastic and swinging a transistor in his hand he led us out of the house.

We passed the neighbouring coffee house where tinny music played from a cheap radio while men sipped their coffee: they chatted idly of the lack of rain, the wilting crops, the cost of rice and paraffin. Some were broodingly silent, wild-looking with their tattered clothes and dishevelled hair as they hunched themselves round their knees.

'Nanjeswamy,' called one, 'don't you take coffee here?'

'I've urgent business,' he answered.

'Yes, yes,' said another. 'Nanjeswamy's always occupied with something.'

'He has to take care of his guests.'

'Yes, he has to take care of his guests.'

'Doesn't he give them coffee?'

'He wouldn't stop here for coffee.'

'Why would he drink with us?'

---

* When I was there, 18 rupees was worth about £1, so 2000 rupees was equivalent to £111.

Family Power

Ignoring their comments, Nanjeswamy walked on down the street – a few steps ahead of us so that no one could mock him further for mingling with suspect strangers. The village was busy now: a man was chopping wood with slow swings of his axe; some women were tying chrysanthemum heads into an endless garland; others sat at their doors to watch the world go by while they sorted dried chillis or plaited their daughter's hair. They shouted and gossiped within their own households but rarely communicated beyond their own territory.

'Sitting idle?' called Nanjeswamy to one of the women who turned out to be his cousin.

She covered her face with her sari. 'What can we do without rain?'

'*We* have plenty to do. With our well, we have plenty to do.'

Near the family's second house, the potter was unloading clay from a cart. He bowed as Nanjeswamy approached and nervously wiped his hands on his shirt. He looked a forlorn man, with sunken eyes and bony nose above a tight-lipped mouth.

'Haven't you finished yet?' asked Nanjeswamy, brusquely.

'N-no, swami.' His voice was high and he smiled with fawning subservience.

'Well, hurry. We need the cart in the fields.'

'Y-yes, swami.'

'And get some rope for the bullocks.'

'Y-yes, swami.' He climbed onto the cart and feverishly tried to heave lumps of clay larger than he could manage.

'Now,' barked Nanjeswamy.

He climbed down again and disappeared into the house.

The potter had been brought to the village by Manje Gowda's family to tile their first house. Now he spent half the year making his tiles to sell to surrounding villages, and the other half earning some cash as a coolie. He desperately needed money to pay off the massive debts he had run up when his son had been seriously ill.

'We even had to pawn my wife's jewelry,' he explained later. 'And we had no food to eat. I could only find work looking after the sheep at twelve annas a day. What could we do with that? We had no food. No food. But the old lady – the old lady of the family – *she* knew we had nothing. I wasn't going to ask her. I wouldn't beg like that. She just sent millet to us.'

42

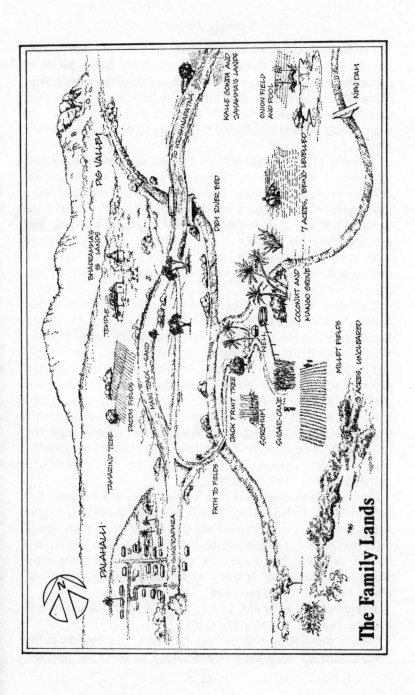

The Family Lands

PALAHALLI

PIG VALLEY

SHADRAMMA'S LANDS

TO KRISHNAPATNA

KALLE GOWDA AND JAVAMMA'S LANDS

ONION FIELD AND POOL

NEW DAM

TEMPLE

TAMARIND TREE

PADDY FIELDS

MAIN TRACK - SAND

DRY RIVER BED

COCONUT AND MANGO GROVE

7 ACRES, BEING LEVELLED

TO SHIVARAPURA

PATH TO FIELDS

JACK FRUIT TREE

WELL

SORGHUM

SUGAR-CANE

MILLET FIELDS

3 ACRES, UNCLEARED

Family Power

The family had helped in other ways: they allowed him to store his materials without charge at the back of the family house in return for a few days' work and the free repair of their roofs. And Nanjeswamy was always using him to run around doing jobs. Not that the potter minded – he must have been glad for any patronage since he had no land and owned no house and belonged to a lower caste.

The rest of the village was Gowda, all agriculturalists whose plots spread out round the village. We passed through some on our way to the family lands: a few were full of weeds, some were neatly planted, and some seemed carelessly tended. It was hard to tell the status of the owner, for only irrigation, bullocks, and machinery are the symbols of real prosperity, and none of these were evident, only an old man trailing his plough behind an ill-matched pair of skinny cows which probably weren't his anyway.

The plots were small because of the traditions of inheritance where the sons divided the land into many equal pieces. Each family therefore had several portions scattered in different places which made the working difficult and caused much loss of time.

The path continued through dense holdings, past a woman plucking sorghum from plants which crackled like brown paper, past lines of pulses curling beneath the millet, and up onto a green bank which overlooked the family's land. The fields suddenly were larger, the crops thicker, the leaves greener. Only marginally, but enough to be noticeable. The layout was also more spacious, with wider paths, grassy slopes, and a large tree giving shade to a pair of gleaming black bullocks.

Manager Nanjeswamy hurried forward: this was his land, the family's land, the land which he managed. He clicked his tongue with appreciation as he passed the pair of bullocks, then swung right past some egg-plants and beckoned us to follow. There, in a hollow, was a well, its huge granite walls soaring down to the water some thirty feet below. It was a perfect circle, thirty feet across, with a broad flat stone surround.

Nanjeswamy was proud. It was his work, his creation, which had inspired such a beautiful thing.

"When we were digging the well," he said, "my brother in the ɔwn wanted it twenty-five feet wide. But I sat down and thought.

I thought, we're six brothers and we've got a lot of land. There ought to be enough water to cope with those six people.

"We had about forty labourers – hired diggers – so I told them to go on digging, to make it fifty feet wide. Yes, fifty feet wide! I'd answer to my brother if he should object, and I told them to carry on.

"Then my brother came. 'Why have you made it so wide?' he asked.

" 'Compared with a smaller well,' I said, 'this one holds much more. The land will get more water.'

"He said: 'It's better if it's small.' But I said, 'No, I want it bigger. If it's wide, there'll be lots of water; if it's small, there'll be less.' 'Go ahead,' he said. He told me to carry on.

"Then we began to build the well. How could it best be done? Everyone said the main problem was that the walls might cave in. So I decided to use small blocks of granite – other people use much bigger ones, but I felt they should be two feet wide. I stood over the workers all the time and told them which stones to use each time. 'It'll be stronger if you use this stone or that stone,' I said. I made stone steps for people to climb up and down. And I'm going to put an iron railing round the top to stop the children falling in. And I'll put a gate so we can get to the steps. It'll be very convenient.

"All this was my idea. I calculated everything myself to make it really strong. Now if any official comes, or any visitor comes, he says, 'Yes, what an excellent well this is. Yes, Mr. Nanjeswamy Gowda, we haven't seen a well like this anywhere. It must be worth at least thirty or forty thousand rupees.' "

The well had increased the reputation of the family and made them seem the most prosperous in the village. It was the only well in the village which had stone steps, a stone surround, and an electric pump. To see so much water at this barren time! Some people were talking of famine in one of the regions nearby, but here, here there was water: slimy green water, perilously near the bottom, but still water which could feed the crops and ensure something to eat for the year.

In 1970 the well was finished and a diesel pump installed. In 1972, with the help of a loan from the Government, the family brought electricity to the fields and installed an electric pump.

Family Power

The pump house stands next to the well, with tiled roof and whitewashed walls, and over the door is a plaster plaque reading '1972'; inside, down three steps, is the machine and a wooden bed for those who guard it at night.

With irrigation from the well the family could now grow cash crops and guarantee some income: sugar-cane, rice, coconuts. They could also increase the yield of their own subsistence crops of rice, millet, and sorghum. For Nanjeswamy, the greasy metal and wheels were a symbol of current success rather than future security. With a grin, he pressed the red button to start up the engine. We ran outside and followed a pipe at head level to its terminus: water exploded into a rusty chute; it gushed along a channel, filling the cracks of dried earth, brushing aside the dead leaves, and swamping the spindly weeds.

Nanjeswamy pushed his way through a bank of tall leaves whose stems were fed by water. This was the triumph, this was the sugar-cane, with its mass of sword-shaped leaves and pinkish thick stalks: it was rich, fertile, and spoke of money. Two cullings from the same crop . . . it would bring more than ninety tons . . . for as much as one hundred and twenty rupees a ton!

The mango grove was sweet smelling and richly green with slashes of filtered sunlight: coconut palms stretched upwards to capture the heat for their khaki fruits while through the grove like geisha figures fanned the leaves of banana plants, their widely drooping arms cut to brown ribbons and their bunches of fruit hanging like chandeliers. A breeze sprinkled the tree, dappling the sand with shadow.

At one end a granddaughter skidded between the giant leaves flapping her dress like a fairy. She was meant to be guarding the sheep, but since they were grazing calmly, she had started to play a game. She was only a child of six or so, with delicate face and timid smile, who was barely as big as the sheep. Near her, a man sat in the shade paring a stick with his knife. It was Basave Gowda, the youngest son by the second wife: the moment he saw Nanjeswamy he scrambled to his feet and started shooing the sheep.

"I've just been d-doing the p-pumpkins," he said.

Nanjeswamy ignored him and marched on through the glade.

"It's hot," I commented, smiling.

He nodded, shyly.

"Here, take this." He pulled a lime from his pocket and handed it to me. "You'll need it," he said. "You can make sherbet and drink it."

"Shall I eat it now?"

"You can open the skin and eat it if you want. It's good for the heat. It's very cooling. You must squeeze it." He took out another and crushed it between his palms; he licked his fingers and then rubbed the juice on his eyelids.

"When you feel thirsty," he said, "it's nice to make sherbet with lime. Keep it, keep it. Does a man become poor by giving? If we help others, we'll also benefit. See, our life is to grow and to give: we don't just want to do everything and eat it ourselves. That's not the village way." He sighed. "But Bangalore. That's everything for us. If I have an ambition, it's to see that town – that is, if I have any ambition at all. I haven't been there, no, I'm not the one who goes about."

Nanjeswamy reappeared and angrily looked at the limes.

'Is that the thing to give our guests?' he asked.

'I thought they c-could make sherbet.'

'Sherbet? And where could they get the sugar? Get them some fresh coconut,' he snapped.

Basave Gowda walked to a palm and gingerly clasped the trunk; he inched his way upwards, his gangly legs feeling the rungs of the bark, and disappeared into the foliage some forty feet up. Two coconuts dropped to the ground with a thud. Nanjeswamy shaved off the tops with a sickle and piercing a hole handed us each one to drink. The juice was warm, pungent, and very sweet; and when he cracked open the shell, the flesh was milkily translucent, quivering like a jelly, to be scooped out with a spatula carved from the fibrous shell.

I felt a sense of luxury and ease as we sat in the dappled sunlight. We seemed far from poverty and the crude demands of life with a coconut in our hands. Coconuts were God's fruit, God's gift to man, for they gave juice and food, and could be harvested all through the year; they also required no labour, no special care, and could each be sold for cash, while all the parts of the palm could be used at home for brooms, matting, and fuel. But Basave

Family Power

Gowda and Nanjeswamy did not cut a coconut for themselves: as part of the joint family they could not eat unless everyone else had a share. At least that is what they claimed, though they accepted without hesitation the portion I gave of mine. Perhaps it was that as step-brothers they were wary of any criticism.

The mango grove and palm trees occupied an acre. The plot was part of the original land inherited by the old man. As the only son of an only son he had received all fifteen acres – a large amount for a village farmer. But without labour and without money, what good were fifteen acres? He could work only a part and even that was barren, without water, without wells, and only a wife to help.

The old man had not at first devoted himself to the land: he departed for several months at a time to buy and sell cattle, walking for a week or more from one cattle fair to another. He started with a buffalo, bought with borrowed money, and within a year or two he was buying three at a time. He must have walked miles and got to know the country for he could still remember the routes to Ponnampet, Gonikoppalu, Periapattan, and Chitradurga.

But then he returned home, for the family were growing up and he could use the sons on the land. They cleared the rocks and scrub, they tilled and ploughed and furrowed, and sowed and reaped their harvests to last them another season. But sometimes there was drought, and sometimes there was famine, and then they had only gruel to drink made from millet and water.

The story of the family was a story of rare chance: with God, luck, determination, shrewd calculation, call it what you will, the family had changed and prospered. If the old man had had brothers, the land would have split into small pieces; if the old man had not had sons, the land would have lain barren as the old man had known it; if S.M. Bhadre Gowda in the town had not had education and advised on development; if the family had not stayed together to provide a free work force; if the brothers had been lazy – so many possibles adding up to a positive which suddenly turned to prosperity.

It had started the year they rebuilt the house, discarding the ignominious thatch. The old man and his eldest son decided to plant some trees: eighteen mango saplings, eighteen banana plants, eighteen coconut palms – three each for each son. They dug a hole near the river bed and watered the grove weekly.

They also bought more land, with help from the eldest son who worked in the agricultural government office: they acquired three acres from the government for fifty rupees an acre; then later they bought another three acres for only ninety rupees. This land for thirteen hundred rupees, but the sons had refused to more than a mile from the house. But land was land and the more they had the safer they were.

They had made one mistake. They had bought some barren land for thirteen hundred rupees, but the sons had refused to work it: it was so much like a jungle that the pigs and deer ate anything anyone planted. So the old man gave it away. He gave it away to his sister who lived in a nearby village. She was as poor as he was, but her sons were prepared to use it. Now the plot was worked, the soil was rich and red: it was scored by lines of ploughing ready for planting millet.

The family had asked their cousins to give a portion back but since it was worth so much now, they hadn't offered an inch.

"*How* much did you pay?" I asked Nanjeswamy.

"About thirteen hundred rupees."

"So how could you afford to give it away?"

"Oh, we only gave part away. The rest we sold for fourteen hundred rupees."

"To whom?"

"To them. Our cousins. We gave them half and sold them half."

They also had one success – apart from the well, of course. They had bought some land near the mango grove, about seven acres in all, up on a small rise. The soil was always dry, for the rain ran straight off the top down to the lower ground. But soon it would all be irrigated, for the government was building a small dam which was meant to help all the village – indeed the project belonged to the village, since it provided much of the labour; but the idea belonged to the family since they'd put in the application signed by eight other families. It was these families who knew they would benefit most, for their land lay along the intended channel of water. With irrigation, the family's plot would be worth at least twenty thousand rupees, though Nanjeswamy put it at seventy thousand. They had paid only four thousand.

"We bought it from the village accountant," said Nanjeswamy cheerfully. "He came to us and said, 'See, I'll be ruined, I've got to pay so much money back to the bank. They'll make me suffer. They'll take my land away. They're troubling me so much. Do something. Save me.' He came and held my brother's hand, and said, 'You must save me somehow.' And so we bought the land. We didn't really want it then. Everyone was saying, 'What can you do with such barren land?' We did him a favour really. We paid a lot of money."

It hadn't been hard to learn about the family lands, for Nanjeswamy was always willing to show me round the fields, to take me to see the well, to explain over and over again which parts were irrigated, which newly levelled, which recently purchased. His facts were usually consistent, and usually tallied with what the old man said, or one of the other brothers on the few occasions I met them, but Nanjeswamy seemed purposely to avoid them.

Their land was their life, and its demands dictated their routines: I was therefore happy to go to the fields, to try and work where I could; besides, it was good to get out of the house, away from the old lady and her constant harassment of the women. It took days, however, for Nanjeswamy to show me the dry lands beneath the rocks where the temple stood, near the bend in the road to Krishnapatna. These six acres were part of the original lands inherited by the old man, but unlike the sugar-cane plot, they had never prospered. They were stark reminders of early days, where the lumps in the soil were so hard and stony that they were broken by foot to protect the ploughs. Here the family grew paddy, but the rains were so fickle and the soil so poor that the crop was invariably thin. A tamarind tree offered better prospects, concealing its fruit in the feathery branches and protected by vicious thorns. Bitter, sweet, and sour, the fleshy pods were turning brown, ready soon for plucking to be dried and stored for cooking.

I loved that tamarind tree for its mixture of guarded fruitfulness, and because it had stood there for so long and seen the family grow. It had seen the old man in his youth, agile, thin, an orphan; it had taken in two wives and given them fruit for cooking; it had watched the number of sons increase as they came to the land to work; and now it was watching a labourer working the soil on his own.

Family Power

The family labourer had been employed a couple of years, earning ninety rupees a month with food. His main responsibility was to clear the channels for irrigation, but he also ploughed, levelled, or planted, according to Nanjeswamy's command. I suppose the security was something, but he seemed pitifully poor: his body was very emaciated, and he begged for tobacco, snuff, anything, with out-held, pleading hands. To the family, despite his tatty appearance, he represented power and prosperity: who else in the village of Palahalli could afford a full-time labourer?

4 The Women

I first got to know the women when my interpreter Thimme Gowda left and I had the day to myself. I wandered towards the village without a particular plan; then with sudden instinct I slipped away from the road, skirted the open scrubland along a narrow ravine so that no one could see me, clambered through a line of boulders and emerged near the pool of water which lay beneath the onion field. The four women were there alone, tucked near a bush on the edge of the plot, gulping large mouthfuls of millet as part of their midday meal: they seemed relaxed without the presence of men and the old lady, for each sat casually with one knee raised against a shoulder and her sari carelessly loose. They were surprised to see me and hastily covered their hair; but they beckoned and called me to join them. Thayee took out some bowls of food from under an old cloth which kept off the flies and dust.

'I'll fetch a banana leaf,' she said, standing up, though the nearest tree was half a mile away.

'No, no, I've brought my own,' I protested, and undid a package of leaves and laid them out as a plate. I offered them some of my *idli* – small flat rice cakes – but they refused; I offered again but still they refused; I placed some on their plates and they laughingly tried to resist by pushing my hand away. They in turn offered rice which I refused. They tried again and finally insisted.

'Why don't you give me millet?' I asked, for I knew they had only a little rice which they kept for the end of the meal.

They were puzzled. Why should I want to eat millet? Millet was peasant food, not eaten by those who had money. But when I said I liked it and wanted it, they gave me a small handful. We looked at each other and began to eat. They smiled at the lack of rhythm in my fingers while trying to pick up the food; I smiled at them for pleasure of the day and for sharing food with them.

When we had finished we washed our hands over our plates from a pot of water brought from the house. I did not clean myself properly so Susheelamma took my hand and washed away the sticky millet. Then we drank water, pouring it down our throats without letting the pot touch our lips. We passed it from one to another, clutching the neck in our clean left hands, tilting the base with our right elbows.

Thayee lay back against a rock and picked her teeth with a stick. Susheelamma yawned and pulled a thorn from her foot. They all looked tired with dark rings round their eyes but they seemed to have a resilience, an almost passive acceptance which perhaps carried them through the long hours of work. I found it difficult to separate them as individuals for unlike the men they seemed to suppress their characters. It was expedience not choice; it was conditioning not calculation; and it enforced conformity: if Susheelamma strutted like Manager Nanjeswamy she would surely get a beating; if Thayee talked too freely she would be reprimanded. After all they were only the women who had been brought to the house as daughters-in-law: the house was not theirs; the land was not theirs; even their sons belonged to the house and not to them.

But now was a time for relaxation. Susheelamma leant forward and groped inside my shirt; I hesitated; she pulled from under her own sari a black bead necklace, the sign of a married woman. From it hung two gold discs given at the time of marriage by her own parents and by her parents-to-be; there was also a gold charm, glass beads, two safety pins, and a cotton thread tied round it to protect her from harm in pregnancy.

I pointed to my wedding ring of silver: they were uninterested and lifted my hair to look at my ears. No gold earrings? No jewelled nosering? And where were my bangles? No married woman went without bangles.

Wrinkling her nose at the quality, Thayee rubbed my skirt between her rough hands: why was I wearing cheap cotton like them? And why a skirt which looked like a petticoat, and a shirt which only men wore? But my hair, that was the worst, I had made it so short – had I cut it for a vow, or gone on pilgrimage to ask for a child? After all, I didn't have a child after two years of marriage.

Thayee undid the bun at the back of her head and took out a black hairpiece made from synthetic fibre. Her own hair reached past her shoulders in thin greasy strands. She liked long hair, it was nice like that, just as a woman should have it: she washed it once a week and coated it with castor oil to darken the colour and cool the head.

Susheelamma pointed shyly at my breasts. Did I . . . ? Giggling, she quickly showed the strap of her bra. I opened my shirt wider: elastic straps, embroidered flowers, it wasn't like her badly fitting bodice of thin faded cotton, but it was something we both had, something which made us the same.

Taking my turn, I showed the top of my pants, and they slipped their fingers down the waist of their saris to show they did not wear any; I touched the tattoo marks which were dotted over their arms and faces: some were single spots the size of drawing-pin heads, others were single flowers or neatly worked geometrics. Didn't it hurt, I asked, hissing with pain and pretending to cry. They laughed and laughed. Yes, it hurt a bit but nothing much – the man with the needle didn't come any more to the village, he hadn't been for years. It was more expensive and more trouble to get it done in the town, so no one bothered much now, the children had hardly any.

I touched their hair which was thick with oil; I made them undo their silver belts which held their saris in place; I asked them to show me their fabric pouches tucked secretly into their waists and we counted out the money each woman had. There were only a few coins so they put out their hands for more: as I had none, I pulled some hairs from my head and laid them on their palms. They weren't sure what to think, but they asked to look at my legs. Mine were white and hairy beside theirs which were smooth and bony: I felt envious and embarrassed. I don't know what they thought.

They returned to work lethargically and looked at me in amazement as I started to weed with vigour. I wanted to help them finish the plot for there was only a small patch left; but they seemed uninterested in such a goal and kept telling me to relax. What was it to them if the plot was finished or not? And as if to emphasise the point, Susheelamma and Thayee wandered away to the pool to rinse out some shirts and pants. When I finished, I stood up and walked towards them. The senior daughter-in-law of the house, Madakka, with one commanding movement gestured for me to stay. I did not dare disobey; but I suddenly lost confidence in translating her response. What had she meant? Was it to show her authority; or would I somehow pollute the water? Perhaps all the women were so suspicious – despite our tentative intimacy – that she was the one with responsibility to keep me in control.

The arrival of a female interpreter, Vara, made it easier for me to talk with the women. Or rather I should say, less difficult to begin to talk with the women. Apart from their own reticence and the problem of finding a common bond, the greatest barrier was inaccessibility. The women were closely guarded: by some unspoken system, one of the men was usually with them, or at least the old lady. Whether it was because I had arrived, or was normal practise, I do not know. Probably a bit of both.

Manager Nanjeswamy was the worst: he followed us round everywhere, watching our reactions, listening to every question. He felt he was doing a favour, giving us so much time; and he grew petulant whenever we said we no longer needed his help. Once we gave him the slip by pretending we were going to wash at the well. As a man, he was forced to leave us in privacy. So we headed for the millet fields, where we knew the women were working. They were clearing stones from empty plots on high ground far from the village in preparation for rain when ploughing could begin. It was hard, piling stones in baskets and carrying them away to be emptied: the women's faces were sweating. Sometimes the stones were so big that two women had to carry them. I helped by loading the baskets but I did not offer to lift them. I knew I could not manage.

Susheelamma was resting on the edge of the field, languid as ever. She sighed as Vara and I came to rest with her and complained of the pains in her stomach. Round her thumb was a cotton bandage holding in place a poultice of crushed leaves and lime to ease a septic boil. Ningappa, the philosophical storyteller, had lanced it that morning with a safety pin sterilised with saliva.

'I had the same thing before, for a month on my foot,' she said. 'I had to use a rope to carry my foot about. Oh, it was so sore, so sore, I could hardly bear it. I cried. I wanted to die. I kept the whole house awake at night. It was worse than having a baby.'

She gazed at us mournfully. "What's there for us? Aren't we born peasants? What is there which isn't hard?"

"But at least with pregnancy you have some rest?"

"When we're pregnant, we don't do much work – plant paddy, bring fuel, carry food, not too much. But we have to fetch water also."

"And the baby's due soon?"

She shrugged. "What do we know? Maybe two, maybe three weeks."

"How long ago was your last bleeding?"

"Do we keep count of such things?" she laughed.

"So you never know from month to month when your bleeding might start?"

"We don't learn such things. Who is there who'll tell us?"

"Your mother?"

"No."

"Your sister?"

"I have no sister."

"Then how did you know what would happen when you first matured as a child?"

Susheelamma smiled at the memory. "When I was fourteen, my family thought I'd begun. There must have been a stain on my clothes – I don't know what I'd sat on, it must have been some cow's urine. But everyone thought it was blood. They cried, 'She's matured, she's matured, she has it, she's got it. You must give her the leaves, you must give her the leaves immediately.' So my aunt, the neighbours, all of them came and made them give me the leaves."*

She spoke in a high soft voice, slightly nasal and monotonous. Its tone was passive and unstressed, the words almost whispered.

"In our caste when a girl starts bleeding, they put her in a corner and give her coconut leaves to lie on. They boil chick peas

---

* Formerly in this caste when a girl reached puberty, she was put outside the house in a construction of green leaves erected by her maternal uncle. She was considered unclean. On the third day she took a bath and was fed special foods provided by her maternal uncle, or if she was married, by her husband's family. Most of these customs remain, but now for economy and convenience the girl is confined inside the house behind a screen and presented with token leaves.

and oil from freshly crushed seeds; they add dried coconut and jaggery, then give it all to her. They also give her rice in the afternoon. Again rice in the evening. They say, 'You've got to eat this now or else your health will suffer.' I don't really know why we eat these things, it's just that we've always done it."

She changed her position, turning her body so that her stomach rested against her knee.

"In our caste, girls are treated like this for three months after they mature. But I didn't know what was happening, I didn't understand what it was all about. No one had told me anything, and it was only a year later when I started to bleed properly that I knew what it was. But I don't think the food they gave me . . . I don't think it was good for me."

The other women joined us and were curious to know what happened when I bled. They found it hard to understand that there were no rules, that I could choose to have a bath or change my clothes, that I could even continue to cook. They themselves were not allowed near the kitchen or the corner of the gods for the first two days but on the third day they had a bath and resumed their duties as normal. A washerman from the next door village washed their polluted saris; the torn strips of sari, used to hold the blood, were washed by the women themselves.

In India, the pollution of death, birth, and menstruation dictate elaborate rituals, the highest executants of which are the orthodox Brahmins of the priestly caste. With them, when a woman starts her periods, she must stay in a room in semi-darkness and not walk about the house; she may not sleep on a bed for it cannot later be cleansed properly; for three days she may not enter the kitchen; she must not be seen by older women who have already bathed and are cooking. Until she has finished bleeding she must use separate water and eating vessels; she cannot worship, she cannot touch cooking pots or people, and at the end she must take a cold bath to wash away impurities.

There is a story that Shiva the Destroyer cut off one of the heads of Brahma the Creator in an attempt to limit his power. But the sin stuck to Shiva and when he returned home his wife was deeply distressed. She decided to take the sin onto herself so that he could be purified, and from that time on all women suffered bleeding once a month as an expression of the sin.

The Women

The village women were not concerned with such refinements: they had no time for elaborate ceremonies, even though they knew of them. They could describe the pollution of touching; they could talk of separate vessels – but they had a bath, changed their clothes, didn't cook for a day: wasn't that enough? Theirs was a practical outlook derived from working all day; theirs was the view of those who work closely with the earth. They did not feel polluted – they rarely used the word.

But they knew all too well the word 'work' and its demands on their time and energy. They had to get up at four in the morning to grind millet for the day's cooking, two women to a stone for more than two hours. Then there was breakfast to prepare with millet-bread and coffee. Some of the women cleared out the cattle dung and carried it off to the fields; there was water to fetch and fuel to chop, the children to dress, and always a pile of clothes to wash, and sewing and sorting and husking, not to mention the work in the fields. They did not individually have definite roles or specific tasks to fulfil, but each was aware through experience what work she was meant to be doing. Nor did they question their daily routine, for such duties were immutable through custom and tradition, and the need for division of labour. They might complain, they might resist, but they also knew that the men had the heaviest work of ploughing and watering and levelling.

The women were driven so hard in the house that they preferred to work in the fields, unless they were duty cook. They all liked cooking – not that they chose what to cook, or took out the stores, for that was the old lady's job together with checking each stage of the preparation and tasting the final results. Cooking was more technique than imagination, but nonetheless there was rivalry: a good cook was a woman who succeeded in mixing the millet evenly, who cut vegetables neatly, who grated the coconut in tiny shreds, and who knew which species to grind to the perfect consistency. But the old lady could never find praise: 'Why have you made so much millet?' she would howl, or, 'Why have you made so little?'

The old lady was constantly scolding and cursing, driving them on to more work. Her grey greasy curls swung out from her head in a frenzy, her hunched shoulders and scrawny limbs displayed a martyred energy – nobody else did any work, she had to do it all, but wasn't she old, wasn't she tired, shouldn't the old have respect? Her mouth would suddenly draw back, snorting with anger at something; and then just as suddenly her expression would slump in passivity, her eyelids drooping, her mouth half open, and the strings of her throat relaxing. And then she would start again, her face pulled back in a hideous mask as she goaded the women to work.

Only the languid, heavily pregnant Susheelamma was given any respite: the old lady seemed to favour her, just as the old man seemed to pick on her – not, I suspect, because of her own qualities, but because she was an auxiliary to Manager Nanjeswamy.

He came to find us the moment he realised we were no longer at the well. We could hear his voice calling across the lands, loud and arrogant, and then we saw him picking his way daintily along the path, his sandalled feet treading lightly, his head nodding jauntily. He cupped his hands to his mouth, and burst into song. All the women except Susheelamma scrambled back to work. They knew where authority lay.

Manager Nanjeswamy was dressed in a new cotton shirt, mustard-coloured and immaculately crisp; he stood on the bank, hand on hip, smoking a *bidi*. He surveyed the land and piles of stones; he frowned. Susheelamma continued to sit. Nanjeswamy smiled at her, discreetly, slyly. Nobody said a word.

'Saramma knows how to work,' he said. 'And yet she's only a stranger.'

'What work am I doing?' I asked, sourly.

Nanjeswamy ignored me. 'But you women do *nothing*.'

'And you?'

He looked at me with amazement that I could be so insolent.

'Perhaps you'd better beat me for my boldness?' I mocked, half in apology.

The women laughed gleefully, then smothered their mouths with their hands. Nanjeswamy was furious.

'Let your mouths rot,' he cursed. But he was pricked into action. Standing astride a small boulder, he picked it up in one swoop and hurled it off the plot; then another, and another, casually showing his prowess. He took care not to dirty his new shirt and stopped sometimes to supervise. He supervised all the women but never approached his wife.

'It must be easier for you as the manager's wife?' I whispered to Susheelamma.

She looked at me with surprise and genuine innocence. "If he's the manager, then he's the manager – how does it affect me? Ayor! If they see him doing anything extra for me, they curse and scream."

'But now you're sitting idle while the others have to work.'

'That's only because I'm pregnant. I never get extra rest otherwise.'

'And what's to stop him buying you extra things? Nobody else need know.'

"I *can* ask for little things but when there are lots of people they get jealous – that's why I don't ask for more. See, he buys me some of the things like cloves, *jayikayi*, and herbs. Like that if I ask for little things."

I found it hard to determine whether she spoke the truth or whether her frank simplicity concealed a clever cunning which gave her an advantage over the other women. They could be friends, they could be enemies, it was difficult to tell as they worked without expression under her husband's command. Only the youngest showed some feeling, when she looked at us relaxing: her mouth tightened and she frowned almost tearfully.

The daughters-in-law of the house had no choice in their lives, and no right to make decisions, whether in household matters or something more personal. If they wanted to go to the doctor, they had to have permission from their husbands or the old lady or preferably the Manager; if they wanted to go to market, or to see their own mothers, they had to have permission. And that was frequently denied them. They did not even choose the colour and shape of their clothes, for Manager Nanjeswamy bought them without consultation. Once there had been a row when he gave his wife a fine olive sari bordered with gold and blue while the others received the ordinary green ones which all the villagers wore. None of the women had spoken to him for days.

By contrast, Bhadramma, the old man's only daughter, was freer. She could make her own decisions, choose what to wear, organise her own routine, partly because her husband was old and incapable of running the household, partly because of her personality and not sharing her house with others. She had an imposing presence – proud, erect, honest – with a touch of flamboyance in her orange blouse and the display of jangling bangles she carried on each wrist – silver, glass, plastic of all colours, forming a solid band six inches deep. She looked young, unscarred by seven children, yet within her face was wisdom which perhaps had come from suffering; her eyes revealed a tenderness, and the delicate structure of her bones showed a sensitivity. But she was not sentimental or precious – her mouth was full and sensuous and frequently broadened into a powerful smile.

She came in the late afternoon to the fields, swinging past the rocks and scrub in silhouette, a strong image against the sun, calling cheerfully to the women. She walked past Nanjeswamy. He purposely ignored her.

Bhadramma was part of, yet separate from, the joint family: as the eldest of all the children, she had helped to look after her brothers when the family had been so poor; and after the death of her mother, she assumed even more of a caring role. But then her marriage had come. She remembered it very clearly. Her in-laws had paid for everything: her own family at that time was so poor that they couldn't give even gruel. There was nothing, nothing. She was lucky to get a husband.

On her nuptials, she moved to the neighbouring village about five hundred yards away. Technically she became part of another family. In reality, she was still involved. She wanted to be involved, however much tradition proclaimed her exclusion and despite any jealousies between herself and the old lady. She only hinted at them.

She was still poor now, with debts of more than eight thousand rupees, but worse, there was no one to work the fields. At least in her father's house there were so many men to do the work. But she, whom did she have? Her husband no longer worked, her eldest son was away in town, how much could the young ones do?

I felt an immediate bond with Bhadramma, she was so alert and alive, and also unafraid. She squatted determinedly beside me – wasn't I hot, wasn't I tired, look at my hands, they were getting so dirty, there was no need for me to work. But she knew immediately why I was working. She said it. 'You want to work so you can know us better.' We laughed that she knew the truth. But she also knew that I genuinely enjoyed the work.

The Women

She had heard about my activities – whom I had met, the work I had done in the fields – but she wanted to know more of my family, the country I came from, the place where I lived. We both wanted to know of the other.

Manager Nanjeswamy stood glowering on the bank.

'Ayor, woman,' he called to Bhadramma. 'Haven't you any not move her, and to prove he felt no slight to his masculine work? Go to your own lands – you can talk to the birds instead of disturbing this field.'

'Why should you give me orders?' she challenged.

'Aren't you one of the family?' he jeered. But he knew he could not move her, and to prove he felt no slight to his masculine authority he nonchalantly strolled from the field.

The women continued to work in silence as if the Manager's influence were still with them. It was Bhadramma who interrupted.

'Sharda, Shara, come here, here,' she called, and burst into laughter at the difficulty of my name. She delved into her sari and pulled out some betel leaves, nuts, and a tiny tin of lime: her gums and teeth were stained brick red from constantly chewing the mixture and she wanted to teach me its pleasures.

'You take off the stalk here,' she said, 'and spread the back with lime. Then you lay on some betel and fold it into four.' She opened her mouth and pushed in the green envelope. I copied exactly and began to chew slowly: it was bitter and hard and I wanted to finish it quickly. Too quickly, it seemed, for she made me chew another so slowly that the saliva swelled in my mouth.

Betel is said to be good for digestion but it helps more to reduce the pain of hunger: it acts as a slight soporific and relaxes the stomach muscles. None of the other women had stained gums: they had no money with which to buy it and did not dare ask the Manager. He had to think of the family's status: red teeth were the village emblem of old women and poor people.

Bhadramma called to her daughter, and they sat together on the edge of the field, Thayee leaning against her mother's lap, Bhadramma combing her daughter's hair with her fingers. She parted the hair in the centre and with a sudden intake of breath pulled out a louse. She squashed it between her nails.

'You need to clean your hair,' she said.

'How do we have the time?' asked Thayee, picking a handful of

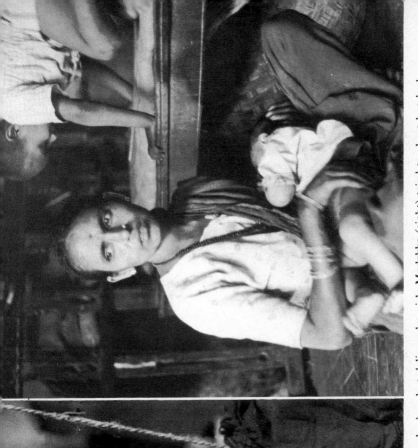

Daughters-in-law of the house: Susheelamma (left) wanted a boy but delivered a girl; Madakka (right) tried to abort but had a son

Jayamma: three sons delivered within three years, but each dead within a day

soil and running it through her fingers. She bent her head forward so that her mother could look for more.

'You should find the time,' said Bhadramma.

Thayee shrugged. 'The old lady . . .' Nothing more needed to be said.

Bhadramma sighed, then smiled at me. Wasn't life full of work? But her daughter's life wasn't bad. At least she had a husband and a family which provided some security, gave her food and clothes, helped her when she was ill. Bhadramma sighed again, not self-consciously to tell me she was suffering, but as some sort of release from emotion. She seemed as though she wished to confide something, yet was struggling to be discreet. I sat quietly and waited, staring at her gently. She brushed away a strand of hair from her eyes. She leant forward to whisper.

'See, it's not the same with my second daughter, the one who's called Jayamma. She has a difficult life. She lost all three of her children, and all of them were sons.'

She stared at me intently to see if I understood the significance of losing so many sons. I understood and nodded.

'She delivered them all at seven months and none of them lived a day. The first was born in my house, it happened very suddenly, and he died the following day. Then within three months – only three months – she was pregnant again. I suppose they wanted to have a child, they were eager to get another. This time she had it at home in her husband's house since mine had been so unlucky. Another boy was born at seven months. It died within three hours.'

She spoke in clipped sentences in a matter-of-fact way as though to restrain her emotion. For myself, I felt great emotion. Bhadramma continued.

'Then she got pregnant again. Must have been only a month or two later. We took her to the doctor but he said he couldn't help. He didn't seem interested. She seemed alright for a while and we thought it might survive, but then at six months – six or seven months – she started to bleed heavily. We thought she was going to die, the pools of blood were this huge.' Bhadramma stretched out her arms in a circle. 'They gave her some injections, she went to the hospital, but when she came out it started all over again. Once she went to the temple – it's more than five miles – and then the bleeding stopped. All the way there and all the way back she didn't have any bleeding. Not in the temple, not on the road, only when she got back. She bled for five days. Then the baby came out. It lived for two hours. It was quite well grown: they were all well grown.'

Bhadramma choked on her words and wiped the tears from her cheek. All animation had left her face, her voice was deep and distressed.

I nearly cried for Jayamma's misfortune, not in any benevolent sense but as one human being for another. I was also moved, even disturbed, by Bhadramma's trust in recounting the story to me, and I touched her arm in assurance. But there was worse. Jayamma and her husband, Kalle Gowda, were very poor; they frequently had no food and the land they owned was barren. He made her work very hard, he treated her very harshly, and whenever anyone tried to help, he got angry and told them to go away. Sometimes he beat her also – he had no father and no brothers to restrain him. And now he was threatening to marry again and get some living children. Where could Jayamma go? What could she do?

Bhadramma questioned me and questioned me about what she could do for her daughter. Didn't I have a solution? What could be wrong with her daughter? Surely I knew of something. But each time I made a suggestion – doctors, pills, rest – she said it had all been done.

'There's only one thing left,' she said, 'and that's to make a proper pilgrimage to one of the holy centres. God is the only one who can help us now.'

I vowed that if I could help, I would. Perhaps God would help me too.

It was growing late: Thayee said she would take us back to the road so we could reach Krishnapatna before nightfall. She herself had to go home to start the evening meal while the others finished the work. We walked in single file along dusty tracks as the sky was fading into a paler blue. Thick clouds hung over the eastern horizon, their lowermost edges slashed into strands by red from the setting sun. A solitary cloud muffled the peaks above Pig Valley so that grey rock became grey vapour and chasms of cloud covered thick faces of forest.

'Isn't it beautiful?' I said.

'It might rain,' said Thayee. 'We must hurry. You mustn't get wet.'

We crossed her sister Jayamma's lands where millet had recently been planted and sorghum was six feet high.

'It's very neat,' I said.

'It's thin,' she answered. 'It needs rain.'

'And flowers, look, they grow chrysanthemums,' I exclaimed. The brown earth was splashed with white and yellow.

'They're nearly over,' said Thayee. 'They're hard work. Last night my sister and mother stayed up all night, tying them into a chain. They walked to Krishnapatna at three o'clock in the morning. They had a basket each – it must have weighed nearly as much as a plough.'

She bent and picked some flowers for us.

'Take, take,' she said. 'Which do you want, red or white?'

'Red.'

She handed me a yellow one. 'It's nice for you.' She took a grip from her hair and clipped it roughly into mine. She laughed, her full lips widening – she looked like her mother though her nose was flatter and her face more plump. She held herself erect but without the flamboyance of Bhadramma: she was still young and obedient, submissive to those above her. Only the length of her stride and the slight lift in her shoulders hinted determination.

It was the first time Vara and I were alone with one of the women, and it seemed an obvious chance to ask some intimate questions, about herself, about her husband, even about any tensions within the family. But I could think only about Jayamma. *Why* should her husband treat her so badly?

"It's partly her fault," said Thayee. Her voice had an edge of annoyance. "She's not sympathetic. When he comes in from the fields, she doesn't think, 'Oh he's tired from all his work, let him say what he pleases.' She doesn't keep quiet, she keeps on answering back. Her husband might be quarrelsome but *she's* very noisy, arguing and quarrelling. See, they don't realise they're bringing it on themselves. *She* should realise. Everything depends on us women. Would it be possible if I started talking like that? Wouldn't my husband get angry? If she was quiet like us, why would there be any fights? Tell me."

"But you have children."

She seemed surprised, and thought for a moment. "He wants children. Both of them want children."

"And if *you* had no children, would your husband be angry?"

"Oh no," she answered hastily, "he's not like Jayamma's husband. His mind is different. If I didn't have children, my Gowda would say, 'Poor thing, what can she do, God didn't give us children.' He wouldn't feel bad." She stopped to consider her fate. "Maybe I'm lucky, maybe the gods are kind. My sister feels, 'Oh why did it happen like this to me, what have I done?' Her husband feels the same. Perhaps they blame each other."

The next day Bhadramma, my female interpreter Vara, and I went to find Jayamma. Her house was in a narrow lane adjoining the street of the joint family: it was squashed between two houses, humble and insignificant, its walls bulging and crumbling. We had to bend through the open door and once inside it was so dark that we had to stand for a moment to gain our balance and sight: there were no windows or skylights, only the spearheads of sunbeams filtering through the roofholes. To the right of the door was a small mud trough which served as a washing area.

We picked our way through the dung, taking care not to trip on the rough ground kicked up by cattle hooves. At the far end of the room was a small sitting area, partitioned from the livestock by a low mud wall. Bhadramma pulled down a mat and told us to feel at home. There was not enough room for the three of us so she squeezed herself next to the grinding stone.

"Do they have many cattle?" I asked.

"None," said Bhadramma. "Just two cows."

"For milking?"

"They've no cattle for milk. Quite often they fetch it from my house. Nothing. They have nothing."

The sitting area was neat, for the walls and floor had been smoothly coated with dried dung; a clothes line hung along one wall holding their total wardrobe of a few saris and shirts. On another wall were two pictures of gods, a cracked mirror, and one family photograph, above a stool supporting a black tin trunk. That was all.

Bhadramma was quieter today, answering questions briefly.

She was anxious to get to the fields to water her young pumpkins. She had no help from her family; nor from her sons-in-law.

Jayamma entered the doorway, a silhouette against the light carrying two brass pots.

"Oh, you've come," she said. "*Namaskara*, welcome."

She laughed with pleasure and walked towards us, a small girl in a patched sari. She held the pots on her hips, projecting her stomach forward, a stomach which was pregnant.

"Oh, you're pregnant!" I said involuntarily.

"Yes," she said happily.

"You carry such heavy pots when you're pregnant?"

"We peasants can't be delicate," said Bhadramma.

"So you've come to a poor person's house," said Jayamma, bending to put the pots on the ground and grunting at the weight.

"Who's poor, who's rich?" said Vara. "Come and sit with us."

"I was here till a moment ago," said Jayamma. "I just went to get some water."

"And then we came."

"Yes, you came, so now I shan't go to the fields." She laughed again, carefree. She looked even more like her mother than Thayee – a face which had suffering concealed in its youth and a pain mixed into its beauty. For she was beautiful with her eyes set wide apart in a vulnerable, sensitive head. A brightness, an awareness pervaded her presence, and yet she was only twenty.

"Come, sit with us," we said again.

But she walked into the kitchen.

"What can I prepare for you?" she called shyly.

"We don't want anything," we called. "We've had coffee in Bhadramma's house."

"But I must prepare something," she said.

"What can she do for you if you come to her house?" said Bhadramma. "Can she give you a cup of coffee? She hasn't eaten herself today. Yesterday they came to our house to eat. And the day before."

"I'll prepare some sesame seeds," said Jayamma. And she continued stubbornly till the seeds were sorted and roasted. She tipped them onto some brown paper, sprinkling them with local sugar – a common enough commodity but so rare to her that she kept it locked in her black trunk. She refused to eat any seeds herself and made some more for Bhadramma when we tried to offer her ours. Then she sat down beside us.

I liked Jayamma at once. She was so friendly and kind, not in the least suspicious, and not at all self-pitying. She was quite matter of fact, even about her beating.

"Sometimes my husband speaks to me, says something nice, but that's hardly ever. He never really talks to me. And if something's not right or I answer back, sometimes if I just talk, he goes mad and beats me. He beats and beats and beats me. I don't know what to do. What can I do? About a month ago he beat me so badly that I couldn't get up for eight days." She lifted the sleeve of her blouse. A dark bruise ran down her forearm; she touched it lightly with her fingers. "Look, here, you can see the marks all over." She lifted her blouse also. "He grabbed the nearest stick and beat me and beat me. At that moment, he wouldn't have cared if I'd died. Nobody came near him – he'd have turned and beaten them also."

"But why, why does he do it?" I asked. "Doesn't he have sympathy?"

She laughed ruefully. "He's like that by nature. He suddenly loses his temper. If I'm ill for a day he gets furious. It's often like that. And now, now that I'm pregnant, I can't get up at all in the morning, I feel giddy and tired. I'm not sick or anything, I just can't get up."

Bhadramma took her hand. "See how far the fields are from here, they must be two miles. She has to come all the way from there at lunch, do the house, and then go back."

Jayamma smiled at her mother, a hopeless, happy smile, a smile of loneliness. But there was no one she could turn to since she belonged to her husband.

"Who can I talk to?" she said. "I've only myself to talk to."

Bhadramma looked hurt. She knew that Jayamma did not confide her problems. But as a mother, she knew the pain she was suffering and tried to help where she could.

"You'd better go now, child," she said, "it's time to go to the fields. Your husband will be angry."

Jayamma nodded but did not move. We sat in silence, letting the words and images sink into us.

"What would you say if I asked to take you to see a doctor?" I said. "A special doctor in Bangalore?"

Jayamma shrugged. "What do I lose and what do I gain?"

"Would you come with me?"

"I'll go anywhere with anyone."

We all laughed.

"But your husband, would he mind?"

She shrugged. "How do I know?" Then she laughed innocently. "Ayor! What I say never goes."

"Do you think he'd listen to *her*?" said Bhadramma.

"I've no objection," said Jayamma, quietly. "My brother did a lot. But since my husband beat me, he says he can't do any more."

Her face saddened, the corners of her mouth pulling inwards.

"We thought he was a good man," said Bhadramma, angrily. "He'd have stayed good if his lot had been better. See, in my father's house, they insisted she marry a poor man. My father, yes, it was my father. He'd been poor himself, but then he grew strong. He thought the same would happen. He thought if she married a poor man, he'd have to work harder. Poor child, she goes on having babies and goes on losing them – how will she ever get strong? Where will she get her strength from? At least she's got some strength because we brought her up so well. Anyone else would be dead by now."

I felt gloomy, and our voices had sunk to dreariness. Vara and I sat with our chins on our knees, our arms hunched round our legs. Bhadramma chewed her betel dejectedly, and Jayamma was nearly crying.

"Sitting there doing nothing?" said a female voice from the doorway. We all sat up: it was Thayee.

"Oh come in, have some sesame," said Vara. "We've kept it specially for you."

Thayee burst into laughter.

"So you knew I'd be coming did you? In that case, you must tell me what my future is," she said. She sat down with us, leaning against her mother: the three of them together – mother and two daughters – were beautiful. Fine boned, bright, and proud. They looked so similar, so positive, and yet gentle. And I felt very much part of them: it was the first time I had felt completely at ease.

"Why are you smiling, why are you smiling?" cried Thayee.

"You're all very beautiful."

They laughed with pleasure, unused to such a compliment, yet enjoying it for each other.

We talked and teased and joked. Thayee had taken some milk from Bhadramma's house and was self-righteously indignant when we solemnly declared her a thief.

"Why should I steal it? I'm not the sort to steal," she said. "Now my sister Jayamma – she might take it, but they said I could have this milk."

"Did you bring curry too?" asked Bhadramma.

"Yes, I brought some curry."

Bhadramma shrieked with laughter. "And you say you don't steal. Have I given permission?"

Thayee was angry at being caught out, but then she began to laugh. Her real name was Nachuri, for Thayee was only a nickname.

"Nachuri?" I asked.

"It's the family goddess," said Thayee. "It's the goddess near Krishnapatna. They called me by that name. He . . . when we got married . . . he said . . . he . . . 'I don't like this name' . . . he called me Thayee."

"Who?"

She blushed.

"He. My Gowda." She giggled shyly. "Husband. He said the name wasn't nice and so he called me Thayee."

"Thayee, Thayee," mocked Bhadramma and Jayamma. Their laughter rose and died again as they saw her embarrassment.

"Well, wouldn't you be shy to call someone Nachuri?" she said defensively. It was a rare name for a villager and difficult to pronounce.

"But you don't use your husband's name?"

"No, why should we? If we want to call them from far away we send one of the children. If they're close by, we just say, 'Come; come here; go.' " She mimicked herself boldly calling her husband. "We never call their names – it's ill luck, it shortens the person's life – not even when we're alone. *He* calls me by my name – 'Come Thayee, take it.' " Again she mimicked boldly, this time her husband's voice. "But can *we* call them by their names? No, we can't."

I felt a sudden dismay at calling the men by their names: I must have insulted them.

"No one feels bad," reassured Bhadramma. "See, we can call other men by their names – it's only our own husband's names we don't use."

"And your husband calls you Jayamma?" I asked.

"Mm," they all said in unison.

"If he calls me," added Jayamma.

The mention of her husband made us more sober. Jayamma stared down at her lap.

"He talks of another wife," she said.

"Just because he's said that, does it mean he's married already?" exploded Thayee. "Will we let him marry again? Oh ho, does he think it's so easy? Let him see, we won't let him do it so easily. But it's bad. Wouldn't you feel bad? If he brings another wife into his house while my sister's still there, won't I feel bad?" She was talking loudly, her long chin pushed forward.

"Let anyone say what they want," said Bhadramma rationally. "We'll see what happens this time, we'll even wait for the one after that. Even if this one doesn't survive, at least the next one might. That's what we all feel. But he wants to get another wife straight away. He says, 'There've been three children already but all three died. What guarantee is there that the next one will survive? It might always go on like this.' "

"He's right, there's no guarantee," said Thayee. "See, he might have affection for his wife but even then it's no use if there aren't any children. All the others . . . see, all of us have children. At least if there are children, maybe he might . . ."

Jayamma had been sitting listlessly while her sister and mother talked; but she stood up as though eager to hear nothing more.

"Work," she said. "Who'll do all the work?"

She pulled some of her clothes from the line and rolled them into a bundle; in one of the shirts she put a handful of sand.

"What's that?" I asked.

"*Cholu, cholu.*"

I looked with curiosity.

"It's very hot to taste," said Thayee.

"It's delicious," said Jayamma. "Hey, why don't you try some?" And she gave me some in her hand.

"With pleasure," I said and moved my hand to my mouth.

"No, no" they all screamed, "it's used for washing clothes."

"Lovely," I said, pretending to munch. "I think I'll have some more."

Suddenly the laughter stopped. A bent figure stood in the doorway, peering towards our noise. It was the old lady, come to see where we were.

"Hello, Ajji," I greeted her. "Are you well?"

"Well? What? Well? Oh yes, I'm well," she said without enthusiasm. "Your lunch?" she asked abruptly.

"Oh we've eaten," I said lightly.

"Where? Here?" There was a harsh note of jealousy.

"Oh no. We've been sitting here and there. We'll come to your house now. We're going to take some photos."

"We've got work to do," said the old lady sourly. "Lots of work. It never stops for us. I've had to leave it all, I came to find you. My eldest son has come. S.M. Bhadre Gowda. Come. Come and see him."

5 Respect for God and S.M.B.

S.M. Bhadre Gowda was the saviour of the family: it was he who had kept the family together, it was he who had lifted the family from the depths of poverty to a reasonably prosperous level. And all because of his childhood: he'd been sent away to his uncle's house to get an education – his uncle was a teacher who'd made him work very hard and treated him very harshly.

But why had the old man sent him to school? Nobody knew, not even the old man, except to say that plenty of sons remained to help work in the fields. And of course it had turned out well. S.M. Bhadre Gowda had passed his secondary school exams, then found a job in Sundrapura in Government service in the Agricultural Cooperative Society. That was twenty years ago and now he was chief accountant, having worked his way up from the bottom. Since then, the family had begun to improve: he came to the village each weekend to advise on agricultural problems, on methods of farming, on the behaviour and work of the women. All the family feared him: he presented an impressive image, a man of standing, a man of wisdom who wouldn't neglect his own family. He himself felt the family should move up in society.

"According to our Hindu religion," he told me, "people should come and visit us, they should come from the neighbouring villages and say, 'Not bad, this family is good. This son has made all the improvements. He made them all cooperate and develop the land.' "

Yes, everyone knew him as S.M. Bhadre Gowda. His brothers in the village were plain Gowda, but he carried the initials S.M. – 'S' for his uncle's name, Sannappa; 'M' for his father's name, Manje Gowda. He held all the management now, it had been passed on by his father. He did everything: income, expenditure, and any important loans.

In his position, explained S.M.B., he could arrange for government loans: people had come to respect him, they knew him to be trustworthy. Take the well, for example. He'd known the right

73

person to approach for a loan with the Land Development Bank. And he'd managed to get electricity for his pumpset. It had cost money of course – five hundred rupees for presents and coffee and certain items, but look at the green of the crops, think of the cash they'd get. Even when fertiliser had been short, and issued only on quota, he'd managed to get a lorryload transported to the village.

"According to my opinion," he said, "what I say is that if there are dams and a proper supply of water throughout the year, then there's no trouble. In that respect, agriculture is more important than a job. But now, in such seasons when there's no rain, then there might be difficulties. Then it's better to have a government job, one can adjust and carry on."

His legs were frail and delicate for the weight of his body: he was broad-shouldered and full-chested, and his stomach revealed indiscreetly his softer life in the town. Not that he was idle, no, not at all, but his work was different. Didn't his face show the pressures he suffered, the mental strain, the responsibilities? Didn't the whole family look up to him for help, so how could he sleep easily? His cheeks were sunken and tired, his forehead was lightly lined.

The main worry was all the debts incurred in the last four years especially to build the well. The digging and laying of stones had cost more than ten thousand rupees, with forty labourers working for more than a year. And then the cost of the pumpset and installing electricity had brought the total to well over twenty thousand.

S.M.B. seemed optimistic, he had the facts at his fingertips. There were debts of twenty-two thousand; but the sale of sugar-cane guaranteed an annual income of nearly ten thousand. Wouldn't that pay off the debts soon? With his advice and his control the family would manage easily. The joint family was strong.

"We might build another house, we might dig another well, we could buy more land – we can do all these things if we stay united. Now, because we're in the joint family I have the leisure to come here and explain things. If a family is single, a man can't even talk to whoever comes, he has to lock up his house and go to work. But if you're all in one family, someone will drive the cattle out;

if one woman is ill, then the work is adjusted. And if anyone comes, we can sit down and talk while the others work in the fields. We can come and go whenever we like."

The question of debts puzzled me. Even with cash from the sugar-cane, didn't the family have other expenditure and interest on the loans? Twenty-two thousand rupees was a huge sum for one Indian rural family to owe when the average daily wage was only three rupees. It meant twenty years of daily work for one man provided he spent nothing and provided there was no interest.

S.M.B. was frank and efficient: he showed me the deeds of land, the notes of debt and explained the rates of interest on private and government loans.

LOANS (approx.): taken from deeds and information given by S.M.B. and Nanjeswamy		
	Rs	
Pre 1970	2,400	Private loans, various village sources, 18% p.a.
1970	10,000	Primary Land Development Bank. For well and machinery, 6% p.a. on well; 8% p.a. for pump set
1971/2	8,000	Private loans, various village sources, 18% p.a.
1973	1,600	Taluk Office, for purchase of ploughing oxen, 10% p.a.
	22,000	
GRANTS		
1972	3,000	Government Relief Grant, for famine relief – spent on food

It was more difficult with annual accounts of income and expenditure: S.M.B. said his records were in town, since he only dealt with larger items, but he could give a broad outline; Manager Nanjeswamy showed some receipts but never a running total; the rest of the family kept no record and only a few remembered or knew the cost of items. But the real difficulty was sifting the information, for it varied with the informer: if a man did not know, he still provided an answer; if he knew, his answer was influenced by the presence of others and what they would think of his answer; or simply he could not remember. It wasn't much use asking the women for they only had half information since no one kept them informed and they knew it wasn't their place to know.

No answer was ever complete, and our vocabulary often differed.

'Number of children' meant 'number of sons'; 'labour' meant those employed sporadically, not the man I had met who cleared the water channels, nor the orphan who helped look after the cattle, nor the widow who helped to clean the harvested grain. Even with such an important and obvious item as cattle, nothing was straightforward in trying to establish how many the family had.

"We've got about two buffaloes," said Manager Nanjeswamy.

"About?" I queried.

"Another one died. We've just bought one."

"So that makes three?"

"No, two."

"And calves?"

"They're in calf."

"Both?"

"One."

He forgot to mention the two calves already born.

"And cattle?" I asked. "How many cattle?"

"Er, yes," said Nanjeswamy counting. "Six."

"And you use those for ploughing?"

"Two pairs and one pair. There's a pair of milking cows also."

"So four pairs then?"

"No, they're not working cows."

"So two pairs of working cows?"

"No, we've three pairs. Two pairs of oxen. One pair of cows. Then there are the buffaloes and milking cows."

The old man's total differed: four bullocks, five cows, three calves, two buffaloes, ten sheep, two dogs, six chickens, and one cat. Observation provided another answer, but observation was misleading – the dogs and chickens in the house were not always the family's; and not all the cattle were kept in the house at night.

The household account was surprisingly large, with heavy outgoings for food, clothes, and extra labour. Some of the items seemed luxurious such as extra meat and private medical bills, but the family was moving up and so were their expectations. The large bill for food was particularly inexplicable when the family was supposed to be self-sufficient.

There seemed so many contradictions in the figures that I questioned and watched and cross-checked for more than a week. No one agreed the price of anything, whether a kilo of sugar or

ANNUAL BUDGET 1973/74 (approx.): Information given by S.M.B. & Nanjeswamy

CASH INCOME	Rs

	Rs
Sugar-cane (after cost of fertiliser, hire of lorry for transportation, etc. from nearly 3 acres)*	12,300
Various vegetables, inc. pumpkins, aubergines, and onions	600
Various fruits, inc. coconuts, bananas, and mangoes	150
Groundnuts: half acre, dry land, affected by drought	150
Hire of bullock cart, @ Rs.15 to Rs.25 per day, inc. driver	250
Miscellaneous: eggs, curds, milk	50
Maize (excess) and millet (excess)	800
TOTAL	**14,300**

* A second crop from the same plants harvested a further Rs. 4000 in November 1974

CASH EXPENDITURE

(1) *Lands*	
Electricity for pump, approx. Rs. 80 per month	960
Labourers for transplanting paddy and ragi; sowing seed; cultivation of young paddy; planting and harvesting sugar-cane; weeding, harvesting; winnowing and threshing crops	1200
Full-time labourer @ Rs. 90 per month	1080
Seeds purchased for planting	500
Cattle	1500
Tools to buy and repair; ploughs, rakes, leveller	500
Manures, fertilisers (excluding sugar-cane)	500
(2) *Household* (for daily use and festivals)	
Provisions, sugar, coffee, salt, spices, ghee, oil, meat (mutton & chicken)	7000
Sorghum (shortage) and other extra grain	400
Pulses and other shortages from land products	500
Stores, inc. kerosene, oil for lamps, soap, toothpowder, washing powder, joss-sticks, *kunkuma*, hair oil	650
Hardware, inc. clay pots, tumblers, metal plates	250
(3) *Family members*	
Medicine and private medical bills	1000
Clothing: 2 saris and 2 blouses for each woman; 2 shirts, 2 knickers, 2 vests, 2 towels for each man; 2/3 sets of clothes for each child	2000
Blankets, jerseys	400
Miscellaneous	200
TOTAL	**18,640**

NOT INCLUDED IN CASH ANALYSIS:

Rice, millet, maize, vegetables, fruit, chillis and other produce grown on the land
Labour of the family
Seeds from own plants
Millet and rice fed to labourers, and for services of haircutting, carpenter, etc.

twenty joss-sticks. I suppose it depended on where they had bought it and their abilities to bargain. There seemed no way of achieving an accurate picture unless I stayed for a year and noted each item daily. Questions and answers were not sufficient. But still I had to ask questions, for the family rarely offered inform-ation voluntarily unless I prompted some chord; and in order to gain some truth, I had to know the possible answer before I could phrase a question. In the end I gave up, for I realised that the implications of the figures, however approximate, were more important than a definitive breakdown. Whether it was twenty or twenty-five thousand, the family was badly in debt and was overspending annually by several thousand rupees. The chances of paying off loans were small unless the family cut down con-sumption and increased its productivity on the land. Nobody seemed clear whether the sugar-cane income was used to pay back the loans. Nobody seemed to know; nobody seemed to ask.

But they did know that if the family stayed together there was more chance to grow more crops, earn more money, and pay back some of the loans. If only they could irrigate ten acres of sugar-cane, soon they would clear the debts. And if they divided, then each son would have nearly four thousand rupees of debt, with only five acres of land. Why should they want to separate? And yet there was talk of division. The old man had mentioned it once – he said it would make his sons work harder, but he would not elaborate further. Nanjeswamy admitted it might be true, but refused to talk on the subject. Only S.M.B. seemed happy to discuss it.

We were sitting in the house, drinking coffee and watching the women work. It was Tuesday, the day of worship in the temple which overlooked the village from its boulder-strewn landscape. The priest had come to the house to collect the family's offerings – he knew their support was secure since the god in the temple was also their family god. So much depended on patronage; a rich benefactor from a town had paid for repairs to the temple but now he was growing old, and his sons were less generous. Manje Gowda's family did not do much: they always gave rice but never cash or labour for the building.

Few of the family went to the temple, but today S.M.B. had the time and inclination. He had no work in the fields, he'd done

Free labour in the fields: the family chop up sugar-cane for replanting. Manager Nanjeswamy oversees (back left); the old man sits with the grandchildren (centre, facing, with turban); Thayee and Lakshmi stay in the background, watched by the old lady

The old lady's two sons in the village: Manager Nanjeswamy (left); Rame Gowda (right) spreads a herbal paste on his son's sores

his inspection on Sunday, and had only stayed on to make sure I was properly cared for. The women needed such supervision, they were lazy and quarrelled too much.

"Our Indians ladies, they have to adjust to each other," he said in clipped English. "It's difficult. Among gents it's possible, but with ladies . . ."

He drew out a packet of cigarettes from the pocket of his shirt, a freshly pressed white shirt of homespun cotton, the symbol of simplicity, the sign of conscious equality. He offered me one but not Vara, and when I refused, he slid his delicate fingers into the packet and slipped one out – his hands were pale and well-manicured, with a thick gold ring on the middle finger.

"Women's trouble," he said, bending his head to catch the flame with his cigarette. "They talk to their husbands and tell them to divide. It's all because of the womens." He spoke in his own tongue now, injecting the occasional English word in an effort to impress. 'Womens' were always a problem.

He nodded his head confidentially and smiled in apology that he should talk disparagingly of members of my sex. Still, *I* would understand, I was educated, just as he was educated. We understood these matters.

"The womens don't move about much – only among local peoples. These villagers don't know much. But the gents, they've been to the cities and seen joint families so they know we must stay together and make improvements. The men – they want the family to stay together."

The day was hot but we felt relaxed as we made our way to the temple. His daughter came with us, a girl of fourteen who went to a convent school. She wore a scarlet blouse with puffed sleeves and frilly neck, and a long skirt in white and scarlet checks. The village children seemed to accept her clothes as part of the privilege of those living in town.

We carried our offerings on plates: coconut, bananas, flowers, some buttermilk, ghee and curds, and half a dozen scented sticks. A breeze idly flapped our clothes and dried the sweat from our foreheads, but it brought no refreshing scent, for it was dry with dust and heavy from lack of rain. The air seemed barren, burdening the land with its sterile weight, suffocating us with a mask. Yet I felt excited, challenged by the desolation and unproductive

79

contours, and elated by the colour, the wide expanse of sky, a plain unmoving blue which stretched through the heavens in an arc above me. My head was dizzy from heat and space, my lungs sucked scentless air; and there below the sky were big grey boulders starkly resembling burial cairns and small square fields prized out of precious land.

But soon my feelings faded. It was not the sort of land where the soul is softened and words grow lyrical: it is too hard for humans, an unremitting soil where you live on what it gives and have no choice. Stones, rocks, boulders, bushes – these are accessories to a landscape which has witnessed the struggle of men to survive; it dominates those who live, destroying and nourishing them in past time. Present time. And future time. Who knows what these villagers' forefathers suffered, except it be the same that some suffer today. Who cares what they suffered when the rains have failed, the crops are thin, and thousands of rupees are owing. There is no room for paternal sentiment for the soil takes care of both the living and the dead.

Yes, if the family were to divide, life would be much harder.

"None of them could give their children education, or do anything else," explained S.M.B. "They'd have to cultivate their pieces of land with all the children they had. They couldn't afford labourers, they'd have to do everything on their own, there'd be much more responsibility for each one. And possibly even hardship."

"So why do they talk of division? Surely the women don't have that much power?"

He agreed that the women couldn't do much, but then he began to prevaricate. "See, you can't measure what's in a person's mind. One might feel it should happen; the rest might want to stay together. But it will happen only when everyone feels it should. Now if one fellow wants it and the rest don't allow it, it won't happen. I don't know. Maybe some of them wish it. Who knows what ideas they have. So far no one has asked for partition. There's no chance of it happening soon because there are all the loans. And there's still the marriage of my youngest brother. But after two or three years, who knows what everyone will feel?"

We reached a small stone tank tucked out of view beneath a bank: the water was high, the surface unsullied. S.M.B. walked down the steps and washed himself for worship: he splashed his face, washed his mouth, and spat out the phlegm on the stones.

When he retired, the women moved to the water and hitched up their skirts to their knees. His wife had been walking behind us, respectfully silent while her husband expounded. She was wiry and sparrow-like, with a face of pert prettiness now over-scored with pockmarks; she wore no make-up, no extra jewels, and only a cotton sari splashed in orange and white. The family had said she preferred to stay in the town and only came when specifically called for a festival; they said she was very aloof and didn't help much with the family. She didn't seem haughty as she helped me to wash my face, but perhaps the sari itself, so different from the plain ones of the women, was sufficient expression of her separateness from the village.

We climbed the rocky bank and emerged at the top through a solitary gateway: a hundred yards on was the temple. It seemed monolithic, a massive block of stone rising above the dry earth in emptiness and neglect – the steps to the temple were cracked and sunken, the doors were closed and locked, heavy wooden doors set back from hunks of granite. The building was unadorned except for the small grey *gopuram* where carved figures had been worn by wind and rain.

No others had come to worship, for the family was the only one in the village to have Bhadreswami as its household god. Once, in the place of Palahalli, there had been a village called Pura. Long ago. Its people used to worship Bhadreswami, but one day sacrilege was committed against the god because of some pollution and the whole village was destroyed. The people scattered to other places and only the ancestors of Manje Gowda remained. Now the old man and his family came to the temple alone, though others came from far away in the month of Shivaratri.

S.M.B. was annoyed that the priest had not arrived, so he took off his sandals and sat near the base of the steps. He smoothed back his hair, adjusted his shirt, lit a cigarette, elegantly blew out the smoke in a long thin stream. He ordered his wife back to the tank to fetch water in case he should suddenly want it. We could see the family lands stretched out below: the small white pump-house with its electric line running back to the road; the square plots of green surrounding the deep well; the brown uneven ground which awaited rain for planting.

"Yes, if the family divides," he mused, "we'll have to divide the land. Each brother will get his share. We'll bring all the respected villagers and let them decide what the share should be. We'll make an equal distribution. Irrigated land, so much; dry land, so much. No one will suffer injustice."

He spoke persuasively, never raising his voice with emotion; but his eyes never looked at mine. His fingers stroked his knees – lithe fingers, delicately soft, uncracked by hard labour. Even his feet were the same: long, tender, slender. Only a hint of threat underlined his words, a threat to his brothers that if the family divided they were the ones who would suffer. For he was the one with influence, he was the one who could handle money, and work things to suit himself.

Through the solitary gateway came the old man tapping his way with his stick, his back bent, his toothless mouth chewing words. He did not look towards us until he was right in front of us when he raised his hands to his forehead in exaggerated greeting. He did not acknowledge his son, and S.M.B. said nothing.

"Times are growing hard," said the old man, leaning towards us. "The rains are like this, the crops are like that, the rains don't come and the crops don't grow. There are too many difficulties."

He looked hard at S.M.B. as though challenging him to solve them, then picked up his stick and climbed the steps of the temple.

"My father *used* to manage things," said S.M.B. "Then he said, 'Hereafter you look after all the business, you're the one who does it all.' But even now he gives advice. He says, 'You should follow this path, you should do that.'" There was a note of contempt in his voice.

"So who is the head of the family?" I asked. "You, or your father?"

"He's the eldest," said S.M.B. "I come next. But he's illiterate, and all the others in the family, they're all illiterate. Because I'm educated, they all say, 'Let's consult our brother.' Even the old man."

The old man had settled on the top step and was searching his pockets for a *bidi*. He brushed away the flies which were buzzing round his eyes, but when they persisted he dropped his hand in a tired manner.

"There are so many children now," he said. "Grandchildren and great-grandchildren. They don't work, but don't we have to bring them all up? Won't the parents quarrel?"

"Educated people know it's better to keep the families small," said S.M.B. loftily. "One or two is enough. I give this advice to everyone. If they listen, well and good, otherwise they'll suffer. If man doesn't eat properly, he'll find things difficult. But if he can earn a salary, if he's educated like me, it's alright. Then he can give his children medicine, he can give them horlicks, etcetera."

"Horlicks?" queried the old man.

"Horlicks," said S.M.B. "These people know what I mean."

A bell was ringing through the temple, and Sanskrit mantras echoed the chant of the priest who moved round the inner sanctum, round the idol of Bhadreswami, an incarnation of Shiva. It was dark inside and the flickering light from two small oil lamps shadowed the walls with muted images. The god was barely visible, a blackened statue in a black womb. The chant was constant and repetitious.

"Whatever sins have been committed during this or other
    lives,
Whatever sins have been committed, we must walk round
    the god,
We must walk round the god, and all such sins are
    destroyed.
I am a sinner, my soul is sinful; I am a sinner, I am a
    sinner,
O Lord Saviour, take mercy on those who approach you.
Take pity and save me, O Vishnu, O Vishnu,
I have no other refuge, I have no other refuge,
O King of the World, save me then with mercy."

That the priest appealed to Vishnu in a Shiva temple, that he could not remember his lines, was immaterial to the family since they could not understand Sanskrit. They sat on a stone bench at the entrance to the sanctum: S.M.B. was cleaning his nails with a twig while his wife replaited her hair and fastened some flowers at the nape; the old man imitated tunelessly the priest's chanting.

The temple was damp and cave-like with its low roof supported by close-set lines of granite pilasters: there was not the refinement of arches and domes, for this was a temple which came from the earth and gave itself back to the earth, existing for gods not men. Perhaps the ritual and atmosphere touched the family's subconscious, but it had little to do with their daily lives: it belonged more to gods and priests and knowledge which lay beyond them.

"The religious texts are with the Brahmins," the old man had said. "The Brahmins bathe, they chant, they worship, they're God's people. But can we be like that? Do we have such things? See, there are some people in our caste who have started to do these things. My eldest son, S.M.B., he takes a bath every day. But what does caste matter? Everyone's the same, the same blood flows through each body. One should just worship God so that everything's alright, then we'll get salvation."

The priest drew down a white curtain in front of the god to hide it while he washed the image with milk, ghee, curds, and coconut water as offering and purification. He also presented food, saying, "Oh God, eat this rice, Oh God, eat this coconut," ringing a bell as he did so. Then he pulled aside the curtain: pink flowers caparisoned the dark stone statue of Bhadreswami, single petals vividly simple against ornate carving. Flames burned, softening the shadows to one complete image, warm and glowing as though caught by the evening sun. The priest swayed beside it, encircling the god with smoke from a wick of camphor. He had washed the god, fed the god, dressed the god in private, and now was the time to show the god and give him light to see.

None of the family knew anything about Bhadreswami, except that he was their household god and somehow belonged to Shiva. The true story was complex, for Bhadreswami had been created to destroy the king Dakshabrahma. This king was both father-in-law and enemy to the God Shiva, who had married his daughter. The king spurned this daughter, until distraught she threw herself into sacrificial fire. Then Shiva swore to destroy the king and from the sweat of his rage came Bhadreswami, who was ordered to fulfil his duty. So Bhadreswami destroyed Dakshabrahma. It was only after the execution that Shiva repented and restored the king to life by replacing his head with that of a ram. Bhadreswami continued to live.

S.M.B. entered and walked round the idol; but the women stayed behind, forbidden to cross the threshold because of any contamination they might have after child-birth or during their monthly periods. Finally, the priest emerged to distribute offerings to the devotees: he was a nervous, wiry man with tense movements and taut legs. Three parallel lines striped his forehead as a sign of allegiance to Shiva, and a red silk cloth hung from his waist to protect him from defilement.

The family gathered round as he held out the flaming camphor: they passed their hands through the smoke and touched their eyelids reverently; they cupped their hands to receive some coconut water dropped from a silver spoon; they drank it noisily, then wiped their palms on the crown of their heads so as not to waste any moisture; they placed small coins on the plate as offering to God. Then the priest brought the *prasada* – rice and grated coconut conglutinated with buttermilk. He distributed it on banana leaves, taking care not to touch anyone's outstretched hands.

"These villagers," the priest said later, "they have faith in God, but they come to God only when they have troubles. They don't have the deep faith which people in cities have. They come and ask advice. So we say, 'Saturn or Jupiter is unfavourable towards you, you will have to placate them.' And so they make their offerings. These villagers – do you know how they treat their women? They make them work like animals. 'Didn't we give a dowry of twenty-five rupees?' they say. She may be breast-feeding her child, she may be pregnant, but she still has to gather fuel. She must gather fuel, work the fields, and then cook at home. Otherwise the husband takes a stick to her. O Rama! The well-being of the whole world depends on the woman. She is the fire. If she becomes angry and takes the devil's form, however mild her husband is, everything is ruined. However poor a family may be, if the woman is good, it's alright. Man is there because of women."

Manager Nanjeswamy was waiting for us as we left the temple. His face was solemn and discreet as he folded his hands to his eldest brother and bowed towards the temple.

Respect for God and S.M.B.

"Ah, Nanjeswamy," said S.M.B. He introduced me to him as though we had never met. "If there's any business here," he explained, "such as giving or taking cash, he knows a bit about it. He also works on the land but he's built up contact with people. Relationship with officers."

Nanjeswamy stood some distance from his brother, his eyes downcast: he did not acknowledge us nor show any familiarity, and I suddenly realised that my relationship with the men was part of the structural hierarchy which determined their authority. I could not be friends with them, for they were male and I was female, yet my approval was important – I was the means of increased status since I was a Westerner who must be rich because I had flown to India. And yet I was only a woman. Should I be given respect?

S.M.B. escorted me back to the village, ensuring I understood the role of Nanjeswamy.

"See, he's only my deputy here, he's the in-charge manager. We've entrusted these things to him because he can do it in a *civilised* manner. Hindu traditions of our country. And when I come once a week, I ask him what he's been doing – hiring of labourers, profit and loss, what he's made from the land."

When I looked round to find the old man, S.M.B. seemed annoyed: he shrugged and strode on ahead. I dropped back and accompanied the old man as he was struggling down some steep steps.

"You fold your hands and pray to God and ask Him to do good," he repeated over and over again. "You break a coconut, you light some camphor, and then you burn some scented sticks. You say, 'God, oh God,' and fold your hands. See, God is kind, but we also work very hard."

I felt comfortable in his company, for he presented no threat or aggression; but then I suppose he was classified more with the women as one who made no decisions and who did no heavy work. Suddenly his frail body swayed precariously as he stumbled on one of the steps. I tried to hold his arm but he drew himself up, gaining his balance immediately. He leant heavily on his bamboo stick. "No, no, go on," he said, "I've got a stick. Carry on, carry on. What's life now, what's there for me to do?"

Nanjeswamy lagged behind his eldest brother until he was

walking beside us. He wanted the chance to restore his image of independence.

"My brother isn't an ignorant shepherd to leave everything to me just like that," he whispered. "He knows I'm not a person who tells lies. See, at the right time I'll say, 'So much has got to be spent,' and then it'll happen that way. See, my family trusts me, even though I handle so much money." He swaggered a little and rocked his head. "Yes, even without thinking, I can spend money."

He lifted his voice so that S.M.B. could hear. "It's all the result of his efforts. He does everything. He and his wife could have been rich and happy. If he'd gone away on his own, nobody would have known which village Manje Gowda's house was in. We'd have been begging on the streets."

"Hard work, that's what we have to do," repeated the old man. "We can't escape our fate. Mother Earth says, 'Work hard, and I'll give you food in return.' She tells us to work, so we have to work."

Nanjeswamy whispered again. "The way my father keeps talking, he goes on and on, I can't stand it sometimes."

"Old men have to talk."

"My father lived like a prince when he was a boy. He was the only son."

"That's why he asks for things. You should give him what he wants."

"Oh my eldest brother, he keeps him happy. My father's always going to his house in the town, he's always asking for things."

"Poor thing, as long as he's alive . . ."

"Oh let him live! Let him advise his children as long as he's alive. After that . . ."

"You'll have control of the family? And what if the family divides?"

"He says that, he just says it. It doesn't mean much. He wants to divide us all before he dies. He thinks we'd get further, he thinks we'd work harder. But don't we work hard? Just because he sits at home a lot, he thinks we don't work. This morning I said, 'Go to the fields yourself. At least there should be someone on the land. Why do you want to sit at home nagging? Go and graze a cow. Then at least you'll be useful.' " He laughed. "Aren't we giving the old man good advice? But all he can say is that we're spending too much money. What does he expect with such a large family? I think it's a bad idea – why should we need to separate? We help each other, we make a good team, and each does the work for which he's best suited. We make a good team."

Back in the house, there was a sudden burst of activity. S.M.B. wanted his lunch, but lunch wasn't ready yet, for the women were behind in their duties: they had spent much of the morning tying bows in the children's hair in honour of S.M.B. The old lady was furious, but she didn't shout or curse, not in front of her eldest son and all the family from town; besides, *she* had been out in the village, trying to borrow some milk to make coffee for everyone.

Two of the women were grinding together near the front door, swinging the heavy stone with lithesome ease; near the bedroom door, Susheelamma was seated on the floor, legs apart, pounding some spices in a dip in the floor with a huge stone pestle which she worked with both hands; Thayee was in the kitchen cooking the food, while the children ran backwards and forwards, carrying extra chillis for Susheelamma, extra baskets for the grinders, and fetching sticks from the verandah for the kitchen fire. The old lady swept the floor, up and down, up and down, ensuring everyone kept to their work.

S.M.B. sat on the bench and surveyed it all without comment. His wife was in the store room checking supplies and giving out food for the cooking; his daughter was grating a coconut and telling her younger cousins what jobs they could do to help; his four sons were playing a game outside.

S.M.B. insisted we sit and talk with him: he wanted to express his opinions on Mother India, the importance of education, and the necessity of a joint family. But while he talked, the village family continued their work, and as they worked, they talked, a constant hum in the background. By talking I don't mean conversing or communicating, but isolated monotones interspersed with orders from one to the other. I shall include a transcript to illustrate this.

"How did you buy the beans?" asks the old lady of no one.

"It seems they were two rupees. Two rupees. There's nobody down near the fields. There's nobody. That's why we have to go to Krishnapatna." She pauses for a moment. "Have they put firewood to heat the water last night? See, you haven't done it at all." She turns to a child. "Has your mother gone to the fields?"

The child doesn't answer.

"Has she gone to the fields?" She turns to another child. "Go and pick those things up. Those sticks. At least put those things under the pot for firewood. Susheela, eh, Susheela, you come and wash your face, wash your hands. Haven't the chickens been cleaned out? I wonder if they've been cleaned out."

Thayee calls to her daughter for more firewood.

"Fetch me some water," calls Susheelamma at the same time.

"I've no wish for groundnuts," says one of the women grinding. "I don't eat them. Those whose crop of groundnuts has been plentiful don't have the people to eat them."

The old lady's second son, Rame Gowda, enters the house with a plough on his shoulder.

"Why are you so late?" he asks, referring to the food.

"Come in," says the old lady. "Did they give you hot water?" She calls a child. "Hey child, fetch some hot water."

A trader comes to the door. The children run to greet him.

"The tomato man! The tomato man!"

S.M.B.'s daughter buys three tomatoes.

"She hasn't taken it at all," the old lady starts to grumble about something else. "If we talk to her, she starts quarrelling. She'll take it and give it when she wants. What is it to us? Why should we talk? They're not going to be here. You see, all the other children go. Her children don't go. That's justice. They won't even go to school. They're spoilt. He just gets them ready and gets them ready to take them, but doesn't take them. It's as though their bones were broken, they can't do it themselves. Let them not be broken." She suddenly turns on a child. "Hey you, gather these things, all of them." But then she changes her mind. "Hey, what are you doing? Leave them where they are. Let them be like that."

"We've been washing the clothes continuously," says one of

the women grinding. "We've washed and washed, rinsed and rinsed, and put them out for drying there. I soaked them and washed them a little."

"I can't keep anything within her reach," says the other. "Ghee, that's all she wants. Nothing else, not buttermilk, curds, fruits. However ripe the fruit is, she won't eat it. Only ghee. If she sees it, she won't leave it, she'll just gobble it up. So yesterday I told him while serving food, 'Alright, bring up those who are going to work for you. Send her away somewhere.' "

"Now we have to go to the millet field, and take the manure there," says the old lady to her second son. "We'll put the manure there."

"Yes, the manure should be put there," he answers. "That's what I feel. Today we'll put the manure. We'll spread the manure over everything, starting on the upper side."

"Well, take all the equipment you need for spreading it," says the old lady.

"Spreading manure is your work," he answers sharply. "We had planned to cut the sugar-cane. Where had you all gone?"

"We'll do it tomorrow, cutting sugar-cane," answers the old lady. "We can do it tomorrow. You still haven't started planting the sugar-cane."

"We'll do it," he says, walking towards the large vessel to take some hot water. "They haven't heated water at all," he says angrily.

"See, they haven't heated it at all," says the old lady apologetically.

The old lady calls the children to eat and takes them into the kitchen. I can hear her cursing as they start to eat. "Shut up, you, just cover yourself and keep quiet. Haven't you learnt to behave properly, haven't you fallen in a good place? This *rotti* will be for tomorrow. You can use it for tomorrow. Saroji, did you keep it there? Thayee, you take it. Why keep it? If coffee has been prepared, then give it to everyone."

Three days later, Vara (my interpreter) and I arrived by bus in the main square of Sundrapura as the guests of S.M.B.: the loudspeaker blared, buzzed, cackled its music over the roar of the buses; outside the cinema were posters of ravishing women, their lips scarlet, their hair raven, their breasts seductively rounded. Ice-cream, plastic combs, dusty tangerines, batteries, torches, watches, were all laid out on rickety stalls to entice the passer-by. A crippled man manoeuvred himself on a miniature mobile platform; a girl of ten or so, with a baby slung round her hip, swung her bottom provocatively, her hand out, her eyes pleading: hunger had made her an actress.

Much was the same as the village, the bargaining, the shouting, the cursing; even the bullock carts lumbered through with creaking wheels and cracking whips, while many wore village clothes. Certainly some were more sophisticated in their nylon shirts, drain-pipe trousers, and black pointed shoes, and there was a tension which only the town can give. For the soil was missing, the open earth, the fresh wind, and the produce which nature gives. Everything has to be bought in town, everything needs cash.

"We don't send any provisions from the village to the town," the old lady had said. "What we grow is just enough for us, so my son manages with what he earns. It's difficult for them, they've got so many expenses. They're five, six, seven, eight, nine people. They have to feed guests, they have to buy everything – they only have about three hundred rupees a month."

Away from the main square in a quiet open street was the Agricultural Cooperative Society, a two-storey building with a deep curving balcony.

'Come up, come up,' said S.M.B., leaning over the edge. 'You'll find the stairs on the right.'

He led us into his office and pulled up two chairs, calling the bearer for coffee. He sat behind his desk, a neat desk void of papers and strategically placed beneath the fan. Yes, he was the accountant, a very responsible job. He'd been there twenty years, he might be another twenty.

'Gentleman age for retirement,' he said, and opened the cupboard beside him. He pulled out a metal cash box, unlocked it carefully, and picked up a bundle of notes. He waved them at us, counted them carelessly to a thousand rupees, then locked them away, and called again for the coffee.

After we had drunk it, he showed us round the building: into the conference room with its easy chairs and long table; into the director's office where charts and calendars covered the walls; into the juniors' room.

'A friend from England,' he called. 'I'm taking the afternoon off. Indian hospitality.'

He thrust some papers in a black plastic briefcase, brushed down his shirt for ash, and clipped four pens to his breast-pocket. The watchman stood to attention as we walked the length of the passage, but S.M.B. ignored him. We crossed the market square, bought some grapes and oranges, then entered a small restaurant. He ordered some coffee and *dose,* then broke a match and scraped his teeth. One was chipped and another was capped with gold: they were crooked and turning grey at the gums.

It seemed logical to talk of material status and S.M.B. was happy to expound his success.

"From '56 onwards, I saved money each year: I took some to the village after I'd paid my expenses." He pointed to the food. "Come on, eat up, eat up." He shovelled some of the *dose* into his mouth. "But expenses are very high now and I can't send anything to the village since all my family is here. With only three fifty salary . . ."

'Three hundred and fifty?'

'Net proceedings,' he said hastily. 'Monies deducted each month for rent, insurance, and other things. Gross earnings are four hundred and fifty.'

'After eighteen years of service?'

'Four hundred and seventy-five.'

'I thought it was nearer six hundred?'

'Four hundred and seventy-five,' he said firmly.

We returned for lunch to his house, a concrete cube in a government compound not far from a cool river which despite the drought was full because of a dam higher up. We went through a wicket-gate past a line of dahlias and entered a darkened room. A pink and orange curtain flapped in the doorway, for the open windows transmitted a gentle breeze. S.M.B. unfolded two metal chairs and placed them beside a pile of wood on which were humped two bulging sacks.

He saw my questioning look.

'They send the wood from the village,' he remarked casually.

'But I thought . . .'

'Together with main provisions – rice, millet, sorghum. They bring it by cart whenever we say we need it.'

It was a contradiction. The village family said nothing was sent to the town. Perhaps such items were basic necessities that no one bothered to mention; perhaps on the other hand nobody wanted to make the eldest brother seem greedy in receiving both free food without labour and a monthly salary.

S.M.B. played with a pair of dark glasses and turned on the radio; he wound up the clock and filled a fountain pen with ink. Then he fetched a white shawl and wrapped it round my shoulders: it was made of soft wool embroidered with Kashmiri paisley. He stood back and admired me.

'Mrs. Gandhi, our very good Indian lady,' he said, and bowed. Then he dressed me as President Ford and Mr. Mao.

S.M.B. gave respect and value to politics. He read the papers, followed the party movements, and voted in every election – not just for central government, but for state government, local government, Taluk Board, and panchayat. He himself had been elected as director of the Cooperative Society in a village near Palahalli – unanimously elected. His brothers voted also but he told them how to vote: weren't they illiterate, how could they know what to do? The women voted also, according to his advice. The Congress Party. That was the party. They'd ruled for thirty years.

His wife served lunch, a special feast ordered by S.M.B. It was a luxury after village food, with *puri*, sweets mixed with cashew nuts, lime pickle, slices of mango, vegetable curry, a warm drink of ground rice, coconut and jaggery, several dishes of rice, and finally milk sprinkled with white sugar mixed in plain rice. She did not eat with us but smiled happily as we praised her delicious cooking. Her daughter ran in and out, and when we had finished our meal she was instructed by S.M.B. to read us some of her lessons. She recited the passage in a clear unfaltering voice.

'Very good,' he said, and giving her some grapes told her to take her meal in the kitchen with her mother and her four younger brothers.

He turned to us.

"What can a girl do?" he asked. "With you, it's alright, but for people like us, it's different. For us, if there are girls, they can't do any ploughing, and now when we want to get them married, we have to give two or three thousand rupees to catch a good boy. If we don't give that much, we won't get a proper boy."

The real problem, however, was his youngest brother, Chikke Gowda. Twenty-eight and still not married and no secure job either. He lived here with them while trying to find employment, but what did he really do about it? Did he listen to S.M.B.? Not at all. He'd got a very good job as a bus conductor, earning a regular salary, but that had been only temporary, and now he was back sitting idle. It wasn't as if he were ignorant, either, for he'd got up to university standard, and how many people had that? Well, they'd marry him very shortly, it was only a question of finishing off the arrangements. His wife had found a girl, a cousin, whose parents would give a good dowry. Perhaps that would help him to settle.

While S.M.B. had his afternoon sleep, his wife Eramma showed us round the house. She led us into the adjoining room where the gods had their corner and the clothes were piled on wooden racks. More sacks of paddy and millet from the village, packets, books, and lamps were heaped on recessed shelves; a wooden bed with mosquito net stood in front of the windows. And opposite was the bathroom with its running water, unlimited, no need to walk to a well. Even an outside lavatory. It was all very plain and simple but it represented the beginnings of the possibility of security against poverty and famine. Could anyone blame S.M.B. or Nanjeswamy for wanting to gain some status, to fight their way out of the mire which holds so many people? I couldn't blame them, but I felt sad that the family was left behind in innocent awe and that city mores were envied.

Yet Eramma missed the village, she missed the bustle and work, and being with other women. Here she had little to do except cook and care for the children, and attend to the needs of her husband. She knew her responsibilities, to be obedient, patient, and willing; to bear children, to work hard; and by respecting her husband, to love him. At least those were the qualities her husband himself outlined.

She was lonely. And because she was lonely and because she had lived in a town, she accepted me much more easily. She saw the chance of friendship and offered me one of her saris. She wanted to make me an Indian woman. She wrapped it round me and folded the pleats in front. No, the sari was too short – at least my legs were too long; the pink was nice but I didn't suit it; why were my hips so large?

As I wanted to buy a sari, we walked to the shops in the centre of town. Eramma never shopped for herself, but she knew what I ought to have, a brown silk sari woven with golden thread. It was too expensive, so she found me a garish pink one. But I wanted only a village sari, preferably emerald green. She was worried. Why should I want that, what was I going to do with it? I found one which was similar to Thayee's.

'Not good,' said Eramma, feeling the material. 'And the colour doesn't suit you.'

'It's fine,' I said, and paid for it.

For two rupees I had a blouse made with long sleeves and baggy bodice and buttons down the front. Eramma wanted me to have a town blouse with short sleeves, tight bodice, and buttons down the back. When we returned to her house, she made me try it on. She taught me the village style of a sari, knotted on the hip without a petticoat, but she was obviously embarrassed.

'It's not pretty,' she said. 'Why didn't you buy a proper sari? You don't look nice at all.'

6 Daily Tasks

Vara and I walked down from Krishnapatna at twelve o'clock in the morning. We stood at the top of the cliff staring into the valley and along to Palahalli: the wind stridulated against the wires which carried electric current to outlying houses beside us. White clouds came over the hill, like surf, adorning a blue sky.

We climbed down the steps, huge flat slabs with edges which were rounded by the thousands who had trod them. A woman was climbing upwards driving a cow before her: its hooves clinked on the stone as it staggered and slid on the polished surface. Opposite us, on the other side of the valley, were laminae of pink rock echoing back the sounds of the holy town; to the right, below, was a sacred pond where waterlilies soaked their rounded leaves and pointed their flowers to heaven, rosy blooms on a silent surface. When we reached the valley floor the path turned south towards the village. The land lost its eminence, it sank to a flat plain which sauntered across the horizon in a blue haze of scrub and trees and the occasional outcrop of rock. In the middle, as though without purpose, was Palahalli's cluster of roofs – self-contained, isolated, remote from the temple town, a village like any other of the hundreds of thousands in India when superficially considered, but one with its own identity when approached more closely. It is strange how groups, or structures, or activities, are so often analysed and categorised without regard to the individual as though separate characteristics have no value except to prove a general pattern.

Far to our left a boy ran over the landscape, nimbly jumping from rock to rock and twisting between spiky shrubs. 'Awah, awah,' he called, his voice thrusting out against the wind. He climbed a knoll and stood beneath a thorn tree, cupping his hands to his mouth. 'The sheep must water now.' Another figure stood up, four hundred yards away. He called idly down wind, 'Grazing now, grazing.' The first boy shouted again, 'The old man says we must bring them to water.' The answer shot back, 'Let mud fall into his mouth.' The two boys argued four hundred yards apart with a strong wind blowing. It made me realise why the family always spoke so loudly, even when they were whispering, for vocal chords had strengthened with constant communication across the fields and over others speaking.

A posse of women approached on the open road, silently walking beneath their bundles of sticks and baskets. Although their saris were tattered and faded, they carried them with an elegance and casualness which belied any self-consciousness. As they came close, I could see them staring at me with uncertainty, wondering where I had come from. My pale skin, the village sari . . . they shrieked with delight as suddenly they recognised me.

'Now you're a proper woman.'

'Now you're a village woman.'

But they soon found the safety pin holding my skirt in place and the lack of proper jewelry: they made me feel inadequate, particularly one woman. She was magnificent in her bold peacock sari with a turquoise and gold border; her hair was combed in a soft full bun, her eyes darkened with *kadige,* and though her face was scarred from small-pox, her skin seemed fresh, her mouth alive. I wished I looked like her.

The land now was scored with the marks of man, the fringe of cultivation where a villager walks two miles before he can start work, where drought and sandy soil wilt his crops and crush his hopes. Closer to the village the land was tattooed with greater effort: a pool of water, a terrace against erosion, fences of scrub to keep out wild boars. And paths everywhere, like ants' tracks in a land of pebbles. On the edge of each field was a cracked clay pot which was meant to distract the evil eye from the beauty of the crop – the ripe tomatoes, the full-blown pumpkins, and the millet whose heads were turning black.

The village itself, located at the pivot, was the centrifugal force from which energy emanated. We could hear its noise half a mile away: the barking of dogs, the squalling of children, the banging of axes, and shouting of men. It swirled to the sky like dust sucked up in a whirlwind and dispersed in a thousand directions, a vibrant, diminishing sound.

Daily Tasks

As we entered the family house, the old lady noticed my sari. She made me walk and sit and stand. 'Why did you get such a short one?' she asked, her stiff fingers fiddling with the folds of the skirt to make them hang more neatly. 'And why is your blouse blue? You can't wear blue with green.'

The blue matched perfectly the blue of the sari's border but she would not accept it: only red or orange would do, or some such hot colour. There were definite village rules of dress – not set rules but practice brought by custom and conformance. Change was always slow. Some of the younger women wore brown now instead of the village green, and some had tiny checks in their saris – but only a few and only for special occasions.

Thayee was happy I'd bought a sari so similar to hers and even called me 'sister' in a moment of affection – we hadn't met for several days for she'd gone to look after Bhadramma's house while her mother and sister were on pilgrimage. I was hurt they had gone without telling me, for I somehow assumed we were friends, and that friendship meant we would share news and talk of any activities. But they had gone and now they were back, and I wanted to see them as soon as possible.

We sat for an hour until Thayee signalled that the old lady had gone to a neighbour's. We hurried out of the house and slipped into an alley. Thayee looked back anxiously and laughed with relief that no one followed. The hood of her sari fell from her head but she left it draped on her shoulders: strands of hair flapped round her face so she brushed them back with her fingers; and when they came loose again she did not bother to tidy them. She seemed carefree, discarding unconsciously the restrictions engendered by living with so many people. She was normally frightened of their anger and their cruel taunts of idleness: she did her best, she went on working, whether she could or she couldn't. What else did they want? Her mouth set in a hard line and her face changed from bright daring to determined resistance.

We walked out of the village beneath a draping palm. The street was narrow and empty except for some chickens which pecked at the dust, but the noise of the houses drifted through, of cooking and grinding and cursing. Thayee moved slowly, falling heavily on each heel: she was breathless from her pregnancy. Suddenly she grasped my arm; she retched violently, water swelling into her eyes. We sat down for a rest on a bank at the edge of the village.

Her last bleeding had been five months ago, and though she'd been very ill, her husband had done nothing. She'd taken herself secretly to the hospital in Krishnapatna, but nothing they'd done had helped much. She felt so ill in the mornings that sometimes she couldn't get up. And then how the old lady screamed! If she wanted to rest, she wouldn't eat – only those who worked had food.

"Anyway, whatever I eat, it doesn't digest, and my thighs ache, and there's throbbing. Even now the doctor says, 'Thayee, it's weakness, you'll have to take some tonic and two or three injections.' But how can I go regularly? I manage once a week but I can't go more often. My husband's giving me money now – he had to borrow it from my mother, since *they* won't give me expenses."

"You mean Nanjeswamy?"

She snorted slightly and pursed her lips in disdain.

We resumed a tiny path which wound through lumpy soil: no one had tried to plant it, no one had tried to revive it with water from the village well – wells gave water to humans who must live to work the land, and the land must be succoured by rain. After only a minute, we reached the adjacent village. It seemed a sister to Palahalli: similar size, similar layout, predominantly Vokkaliga caste. The houses were familiar with their shadowed verandahs and red mud walls, their fibrous roofs and shuttered windows. To strangers, both were known as Palahalli, but to those who lived in the second village it was known as the Place of the Friday Market, a name which had come from ancient times since the market no longer functioned.

Thayee had spent her childhood there in her mother's house until she had married her uncle. She herself had been nine; he had been much older. At first he'd refused to accept her, saying she was much too young. But then when the ceremony came, he had to accede to the old man's wishes. Thayee moved into the family house on her nuptials three years later.

"And now he looks after you well?"

She grimaced.

"He doesn't notice anything. Even when I'm lying down, he

99

never asks anything. It's only when he sees the children hanging
round that he wants to know when I'm going to feed them.
Otherwise he doesn't talk. He just goes away. In a big house, it's
no use telling anyone anything."

"So what do you do when you're ill?"

"When it gets really bad, I just go away. I don't talk to anyone,
I just go to my mother's house and lie down there. She looks after
me till I'm better."

"But can't you talk with your husband?"

"We don't do all that. What's there to talk about?"

"I talk with my husband, I tell him everything."

"If we talk among so many people, what would they say?"

"But at night?"

"That's only once in a while."

On the edge of the village was a small hut whose thatched roof
was pitted with holes and whose door was sagging precariously.
An old woman lived there alone, without friends or relatives: her
husband had died of typhoid and her son had been killed in an
accident. She played the *tambura* and sang holy songs in return
for a little food. The village made sure she survived and accepted
her crazed state – she thought the English were ruling still and
insisted she'd seen the king in Mysore who had commented on
her beauty and the pinkness of her skin. Now her skin was dark,
her worries had turned it black.

Thayee understood the problems of a woman living alone. With
a joint family, there was security and food, the work of the women
could be shared, and if any of them were confined to bed, the
others took over the duties. She didn't want to separate from the
family, even with her husband: who would do the cooking when a
woman had her periods; who could pour water when a woman
took a bath?

"Your husband can pour the water."

Thayee laughed. "No, no, we don't do that." Then she became
curious. "Do you do it?" she asked.

"My husband does it without asking."

Thayee was embarrassed. "We can't have it that way. Only the
women do it for each other. See, when my confinement comes . . ."

"Do you want it to be a boy?"

"We'll see. Let it be born."

100

"What will you do if it's a girl again?"

"What can we do? See, in these villages we bring up many children. We'll see. We'll see after this one is born. But if it's a girl then we'll wait for another."

"Till a boy is born?"

"Yes. Won't those who have boys mock us?"

"And if you have five girls, what will you do?"

"I won't have five girls, my mother has only three."

"Suppose you have six or seven . . ."

"No, no. My mother has three girls and four boys. Anyway, she belongs to an older generation when they had that many. Will we have that many? Will we keep quiet till then? The minute we have a son, I'll have the operation. The sons work and feed us. The girls go away to another house. A son is nice for anything."

"Even when he marries and you don't get on with his wife."

She laughed wryly. "That's a day's story."

Thayee's mother, Bhadramma, sat in her house against a pillar combing her tousled hair; she was relaxed, happy, full of the recent journey to Dharmasthala with Jayamma. They had gone to the god for help to prevent another miscarriage, and it seemed they were promised help. In her excitement, Bhadramma had ignored her chores: chaff dusted the floor, blankets had been tossed to one side instead of neatly folded and put away; even the vessels were unwashed, and plates from the evening meal were scattered about the room. It was a small room, and square, wrapped in red plaster which glowed in the dusky light. Open beams and a central pillar were carved with delicate flowers from pale, grainy wood; the cattle were kept in a separate room so the place seemed calm and intimate when compared with the bleaker grandeur of Manje Gowda's house.

Not everyone in the village could afford to make such a journey – it was nine hours by bus on a road which wound through the mountains and through forest so thick that those who travelled it were frightened. But then not everyone had the need to travel so far.

Bhadramma's eyes were full of wonder at the things she had seen and experienced. She wanted to tell everyone the story of her journey; she'd already told it several times to her family the night before. First they'd been given food free by the temple priests. Free! Not just a bit of this and that but rice three times in a single meal and several types of curry. Then there were all the queues, she'd never seen such queues, so many people were there. A queue for fruits and coconuts; a queue for holy water, to take a vow, even to do the puja. And there were tickets given for everything. You paid money and then you got your ticket. Even to see the priest. He'd said that Jayamma's future was good. And he said it in such a definite way. 'Because of her sin she has trouble with childbirth, it affects her womb. There's nothing else. If she takes a vow to do a puja, everything will be alright.' And so they had done a puja. It had cost nearly thirty or forty rupees.

Bhadramma was flushed with the success of her trip. She felt a sense of relief and assurance. The gods would help her at last, would help Jayamma have her child now. Indeed so involved was she with her tale and the power of its achievement that she scarcely noticed those who slipped in to listen: three neighbours, two children, Vara and I. Almost mechanically she undid some dirty packets which held the precious tokens of her journey: red *kunkuma* to be spread on each of our foreheads; wilted flowers from the puja; two oranges which she peeled and distributed; some crumbled sweets; and some white puffed rice which was stale. There was also a bottle of holy water which she passed with care for us to drink from. Once there had been four bottles, but two had smashed and the children had finished the third.

We started to eat ritualistically, silently chewing our food, aware of a special event. When Bhadramma ate, we ate; when she stopped to reflect, we stopped. But most of the time she was talking, repeating the stories and exclaiming about the food. Five of the family had gone: Bhadramma, her husband, her eldest son, her daughter-in-law, and Jayamma. They'd all left clothes to dry in the open, and no one had taken a thing. Not a thing. There were no thefts there. Not even a pebble or piece of mud was stolen by any pilgrim. And nobody locked their shops. It was a very holy place. Even the weather had been auspicious.

"Everytime we looked out at Dharmasthala, the rain was pounding down, ayor, tam a tam a tam. Pouring down. The houses were green with moss." She picked at the mud on her feet. "Look at my feet! We stamped through the mud all the time."

"Didn't you go to the holy river?" asked one of the women listening. She had been to Dharmasthala once herself to ask the god for a child, but all she had got was a daughter.

' Oh yes, we bathed there," said Bhadramma. ' Nowhere else. It's two miles from the town, isn't that so?"

"Why two miles? It's nearly three."

"Three miles then, more or less."

"Didn't you see the god there?" demanded the woman, again, impatiently.

"We went up and saw everything," said Bhadramma. "But those stairs to the temple . . ."

"What did you see?" called Thayee.

"Didn't they carry the god in a procession?" asked the woman.

"No, nothing like that," said Bhadramma.

"But they do it. When *we* were there . . ."

"By the time we finished our dinner . . ."

"You didn't go into the temple again?"

"No, we couldn't do that again."

"So what else did you see? You went to Dharmasthala, didn't you?" the woman asked relentlessly.

Bhadramma's face drooped and she pressed out her lips in annoyance.

"Oh, I didn't feel like seeing anything. My daughter-in-law hadn't wanted to come. She'd made such a fuss. And then she started to sulk. She wouldn't talk to anyone. She even started crying. I began to wonder why on earth I'd brought her there at all. She was the same with everyone, even her own husband. Not talking at all. We didn't feel like going anywhere. We'd paid our respect to the god. That was enough."

She wiped a tear from her eye, the armful of bangles jangling. There was disappointment in her voice and a feeling of anti-climax: her expectations had been so great, and the excitement had mounted and mounted. Why should that one person have spoilt it all so quickly? Bhadramma's voice grew defiant. *She* wouldn't let it spoil things. There were better things to remember, even after that. On the journey home, they had stopped at the sea for an hour. The sea. She had never seen it before.

"It throws out waves as tall as a coconut tree," she whispered with breathless intensity. "It comes all the way up to meet you

103

and then it goes all the way back again. And how many waves!
On and on. When it comes up, and you bend down to touch it,
it's no longer there, it's slipped back again."

"It pulls you away," said the same woman, a touch of fear in
her voice. "It pulls you with it when it retreats."

"Oh even if it sucks you away, it throws you back again," said
Bhadramma casually. "It throws up shells as well. Yes, I went in.
I went up to here, right up to my waist." She licked her lips as
though they were wet with salty water.

Any catharsis derived from Bhadramma's pilgrimage was quickly
dispelled by the harsh reality of daily demands and the need to
cope with the problems which had come in her five day absence.
Up on the hill where her lands were, beyond the temple and
beyond the rocks, a fine drizzle had started. But Bhadramma was
contemptuous: drizzle did nothing for parched earth.

"Until the land is soft enough, moist enough, I won't plant,"
she declared. "Let anyone say what they like. There's no humidity
in the soil. There's not a drop of water in the ground."

She and her eldest son had recently dug a well fifteen feet down
but it had barely reached water. Her husband was down there
now, his feet in mud, his hands scooping the puddle of water into
cracked clay pots.

Bhadramma rammed her basket into the mound of dung nearby
and piled it up with the help of a metal spade. Fat sluggish
maggots the size of giant prawns heaved into white balls at the
sudden exposure to light. She picked them out by hand and tossed
them aside; then bracing herself and with a sudden intake of
breath she grasped the basket and swung it upwards, levering it
onto her head, rocking under the weight. She carried it to the
pumpkin field, set it down, and patted some manure round the
stem of each plant.

Her husband waited by the well with a pot in each hand, his
mouth open, his eyes vacant, his face half smiling. When
Bhadramma called, he hurried towards her, spilling much of the
water, his legs trembling on the uneven ground. He emptied the
pots round the plants, splashing and wasting unnecessarily, and
when Bhadramma asked for more he turned and ambled back to
the well.

She sat down to wait, watching her husband with sorrow.

"When we got married, he used to look after things. Now he can't work, his body is tired."

She did not resent his inability; she treated him gently with kind respect and tried to maintain his regard for himself by letting him work and contribute. But it meant she carried the burden of work in the fields, while at home she was still a wife with domestic duties.

"I won't give up," she said. "I have to look after the family, even if nobody helps me. I'll fight for it alone."

She sang quietly to herself:

> "When you're in sorrow,
> There'll be no one to help you;
> When you go, you go alone in death."

She ran her fingers over the ground and touched her eyelids; she held out a handful of dry soil.

"As long as there's strength in our hands we must work hard and eat the food we're given. I've complete faith in Mother Earth and I'm not dependent on anything else, not on money, nor jobs, nor food. I never think, Oh so and so is living well while we are being destroyed. We must *work* on our land, we must cook the fruits on our stove, we must put the food in our mouths. I've no wish for what others have. I've complete faith in my land, no faith in anything else."

The memory of Dharmasthala must have dimmed.

"And god? Doesn't god help you?" I asked.

"When it's time to think of god you should think of god. Can you leave god completely? When I have leisure, I worship god."

Soon she started to work again, and I helped by piling the dung in the basket. Bhadramma saw my distaste of the maggots so picked one up to throw at me. I dodged and ran away; she chased me, but I tripped and fell. Immediately she was at my side, helping me up, brushing my clothes with concern. One of my bangles had smashed and cut my wrist slightly, so she forbade me to help any more. I insisted, and we filled another basket. This time she asked me to share the weight in lifting it onto her head. "One, two, three." We bent and pulled up the basket. It was so

105

heavy that I tottered helplessly, the basket tilting towards me and tipping the dung down my front. Bhadramma took over and ducked her head under the base, propelling the basket upwards in an effort to get it straight; but it overbalanced and she staggered several yards before it plummetted to the ground, splattering the dung over the ground, wasting her precious manure which she'd carried for months each day a mile or two from the house, or collected arduously from roadways. But Bhadramma wasn't angry: she laughed boisterously and squeezed my arms and shoulders to feel the lack of muscle.

Her second son arrived, a skinny boy of fourteen who looked like a nine-year-old with skeletal legs and bony buttocks; but he attacked the work with ferocity, determined to show he could manage. Mother and son worked in harmony: they did not speak and rarely looked at each other except to nod in encouragement. They knew each other's movements and they knew their own capacity.

For Jayamma, the journey to Dharmasthala was merely routine, another attempt to provide an answer for something which couldn't be answered. She wasn't impressed by the priest's commendation, but she did not deny the hope which the journey had brought her mother. Let her make a vow, let her do a puja, no harm would come. She herself wasn't optimistic: nothing had worked before so why should it work this time? And yet she wasn't depressed. She even seemed cheerful. She always seemed cheerful, and the brightness of her nature humbled me. Whenever I passed her fields on the way down from Krishnapatna, she would run to the road laughing and call for me to stop, to spend some time with her. And she always had something to give – some sesame seeds, a piece of bread, a red tomato, or some water to wash out my mouth. She was uninhibited also: she would hold my hand without embarrassment, she talked as though we were sisters, and seemed to hold no suspicion. I think she understood the warmth I felt for her, and the possibility of friendship.

Today she was working hard in the fields to catch up with all that had been left undone while she had been away. Her husband would never have done it for her – he never did anything if he thought it was her responsibility. She understood his reasoning and did not blame him. If he did her work, people would mock loudly. Why should he hear such things because of her? If she didn't do a little, how could he do it all? Besides, it wasn't the same when a woman walked the fields and gave the earth her work. Then the crops would grow.

Her husband Kalle Gowda was there now, filling the pots in a nearby pool, heaving them up a rock face with nimble ease. His whole appearance was boyish: a spring in his walk; a quick grin; a tartan scarf wrapped round his hair with dashing style. He was not handsome, for his face was too Neanderthal with its wide cheekbones and low forehead running into a flattened nose, but he had a charm and assurance which belied any brutality. Only his limbs were a sign of strength, powerful limbs, bulging with tendons and not to be challenged lightly.

He was courteous, almost obsequious, as he showed us the flowers he had grown. He was proud of his work. Correction. He was not proud, what had he to be proud of? He was only a poor peasant. The drizzle started again, so he led us towards a small thatched hut which he'd built on stilts as a shelter. It was skilfully constructed with leaves intertwined like brickwork and slender struts bent into arches. The exterior was thatched neatly, declivitous sides for the rain. Vara and I scrambled in, but he remained outside.

He should have gone on pilgrimage, for a dual petition to god was bound to have more effect, particularly at Dharmasthala. It was said that husband and wife should always go there together. But somebody had to stay behind to look after the cattle. Since all his in-laws wanted to go and since he had no other relatives, he was the one who stayed. He was used to working alone.

He was four when his father had died, so he'd gone to live with his sister and her husband five miles away, all walking infrequently to Palahalli to work the inherited land. He carried the plough, there and back, there and back, with hardly a helping hand. Then at nine, he returned to the village, to the crumbling house where his mother lived. By now he had learnt to plough, so he worked the land alone. In his first year he managed to grow more than three *palla* of millet which enabled his mother to secure a loan. They bought a goat. The goat had kids, and the numbers grew. They repaired the house and sold some goats and bought a cow for a hundred rupees. They fed it and fattened it and sold it for two hundred rupees. They bought a buffalo, and sold it for two hundred and fifty rupees. They bought another buffalo, this time with a calf. It had only just given birth. Then the buffalo grew thin and weak, and gradually so did the calf. In the end both were sold, for only thirty rupees, though they'd cost two hundred and sixty. And so the cycle started again, month after month, year after year, sometimes gaining, sometimes losing, but never really winning.

Kalle Gowda didn't seem to mind, at least he expressed no feeling of bitterness or anger: buffaloes died and children died, and so one tried again. It was impossible to tell what he really thought for he evaded all our questions. God, medicine, pilgrimage, yes, all of them were good, no, Jayamma wasn't to blame, they'd just have to pray for a son, yes, women should perform their duties, just as men had duties also.

We heard a soft cough, and Jayamma stepped in front of the hideout.

'It's raining,' she said.

'It's only drizzling,' said Kalle Gowda.

'I can't work when it rains.'

'You don't have to stop.'

They glared at each other before Jayamma hung her head.

'You can climb up here with us,' I said.

Kalle Gowda nodded.

'You can climb up there with them,' he said.

She skirted round him and we pulled her up. She smiled, nervously, her lips drawn back over her gums as though it were sore to use them: they were pastel pink in colour, the healthless white of anaemia scored over bloodless skin.

Her husband lit a *bidi* and stared out across his lands. Jayamma stayed silent, gazing across to the opposite wall. She seemed without positive thought, without stress or worry, but a sadness expressed itself unconsciously in the dejected angle of her head and the passive position of hands. She knew that pleas to god, and pilgrimage, were superfluous at this stage.

I can't remember how it happened, but I was invited to stay at the family house. They wanted to save me the walk each day from

Krishnapatna, and perhaps I had dropped a hint that walking
was very tiring. Not that I would live off them, for we'd made an
arrangement which would amply cover any material outlay. So
that morning I had brought with me a blouse and skirt, two pairs
of pants, my toothbrush, soap, and hairbrush, and a box of vitamin
tablets. Vara brought a towel, a mat and sheet to sleep on, and
several changes of sari.

Having spent the day with Bhadramma and Jayamma, we
returned to the village as dusk was falling, a slash of red in the
distant sky: the cattle and sheep were moving homeward, driven
by boys with switches while the men shouted orders and carried
the ploughs on their shoulders. The women hastened between,
like shadows, their bodies bent forward, to balance the loads on
their heads. None of them talked except to exchange an occasional
comment on the lack of rain or the work they had managed to do.
Gossip was not for the road: it was more a leisure pursuit for the
men while drinking coffee in the local hotel or for the women while
working at home.

The motion died as each branched into a house. An ox slipped
as it climbed a step and was beaten across its back; some goats
jumped with alarm as they were pushed through a narrow doorway;
the doors closed one by one as we passed along the street. At last
we reached the family house, feeling it was home; but when we
entered, nobody bothered to greet us. The old lady was coating a
wall with dung and pretended not to see us; Manager Nanjeswamy
was smoking on the bench: he nodded cursorily, then folded his
arms on his knees and closed his eyes in deep thought.

What had we done? Were they regretting their invitation and
once more were filled with suspicion? Or was the old lady angry
that we'd enticed Thayee away from her duties?

"We went to see Jayamma," I explained. "To lose children
like that . . ."

"None of *my* daughters-in-law has anything like that," the old
lady said tetchily. "Do we know what she got from Lord Shiva?
It's her fate, and what is there for us to do?"

"But your granddaughter – don't you feel sad?"

"Huh, wouldn't anyone feel sad?"

We sat unobtrusively in one corner unnoticed even by children.
Thayee's two daughters were snatching a stick from each other in

measured, leisurely movements, allowing the sense of possession to develop before sudden loss. They wore identical baggy dresses with dropped waists and long skirts of printed cotton. The youngest chattered aimlessly, injecting tuneless cries at high-pitched intervals.

Manager Nanjeswamy crossed to the gods' corner. He smeared white lines on his forehead and lighting a scented stick he raised it above his head and bowed three times; he pivoted slowly, calling the names of the gods, Lakshmi, Krishna, Murugendra – their pictures were tilted forward, crammed into frames with garlands and thrones and peacocks, a garish profusion of detail to seduce and entrance the senses. There were three pictures of Lakshmi, the goddess of wealth and prosperity, whose curvaceous figure rose from a lotus to confirm a beneficent image. This was the corner of hope, of urgent prayer, and her favour was sought above all the gods.

Nanjeswamy's daughter imitated her father, bowing her head reverently and peering round the room to see who was watching. A tall girl of six with aggressively broad shoulders and stocky, shapely legs, she wore a pale blue dress of translucent nylon tinselled with silver thread, flounced into a tutu. She stood with legs apart watching Thayee's daughters, but when they did not acknowledge her, she turned away and jerked her hips from side to side. She arched her back and pointed a toe, flicking her skirt upwards to show her naked bottom. When they still ignored her, she grabbed their stick and ran away. The youngest screamed and tears poured down her face, till Thayee came out of the kitchen and without identifying the culprit slapped her eldest daughter. She too began to cry, and Nanjeswamy's daughter looked on with satisfaction.

Apart from Thayee, there were four granddaughters in the household, aged between three and six. They played together sometimes but they rarely played with the boys – a different sex and different age. The youngest of the family was curled up on a wooden chair, staring miserably at the girls. His head was wrapped in a white shroud to protect his ear from the draughts: it had discharged pus for more than a year, but vows and gods and medicine had done nothing to ease the pain. He called softly for his mother, then louder, straining his voice to combat the screams of the girls. But no one came, and he leant his head on his arm.

The old lady wiped away his tears and led him across to the big brass pot whose water was heating for washing. She snapped the twigs and pushed them into the flames beneath.

"Blow then, child, make the flames high," she said.

The boy tried, swelling his cheeks with effort, then popping them in a feeble puff.

'Look, look,' he cried, 'flame, flame, flame.'

But the old lady grew impatient and pushed him to one side. She blew strongly herself, coughing at the smoke, and hitting her chest in pain.

One by one the women returned from the fields carrying fodder and fuel. They entered the house silently, greeting no one and unacknowledged. Immediately they started their duties, grinding, husking, sweeping, moving about like servants.

The men came in, bringing the ploughs and oxen. They washed and fed the cattle, then took it in turns to wash themselves, calling their wives for water. Pot in hand, each woman stood with respect till the husband motioned her forward: she poured it over his arms and legs, controlling the flow through cupped hand to a thin, thrifty stream. She kept her head covered, her eyes lowered, and did not speak a word. Nor did her husband speak. And yet there was an intimacy in their actions, a shared rhythm, a knowledge of each other's way.

"I brought some greens in," called the old lady to everyone and no one.

"Where's the buffalo?" asked Nanjeswamy, eyeing the line of cattle.

"Other house," said one of the step-brothers curtly.

"Shouldn't we fetch it here?"

No one answered.

"There's a sickle to sharpen."

"That can be done tomorrow."

It was dark in the house, but no one lit any lamps: each worked by touch and from years of rhythmic experience. Thayee squatted against the storeroom door, holding a basket against her chin to sort the grit from the millet – she was no longer duty cook. Lakshmi, the youngest wife, husked paddy; and Madakka, the eldest wife of the house, was in the kitchen cooking. Vara and I sat with the younger children in a huddle against the wall, for the old lady had pushed them out of the way. They knew I was good for a game so they crawled up my back, bounced on my knees, tried to climb onto my head; they pulled my hair and pinched my arms without realising how much they hurt. They had learnt rough ways, for the family treated them roughly.

'How can we treat them softly?' said the women. 'They wouldn't survive their lives.'

The women worked to prepare the evening meal, but one by one the men sat down. The old man climbed onto his cot at the far end of the room and wrapped himself in a blanket; his two sons by his second wife hunched themselves on the floor below, silently staring over their knees. Manager Nanjeswamy started his monologue. He talked of the fields, he talked of the cattle, he talked of the work he had done that day. He asked questions of others but filled in the answers. He shouted, whispered, laughed, in glittering histrionics, and lit a lamp beside him to highlight his face. His eyes dilated, flickered, snapped with excitement at his own importance. He did not seek an audience, nor did his family seek him.

Susheelamma, his wife, was grinding alone, the weight of the stone showing itself in her beads of sweat. I crossed the room to help her: Nanjeswamy told me to sit down: I disobeyed. She smiled and showed me how to sit, each leg in a flattened arrowhead either side of the stone; we grasped the winding stick, our right hands touching, and started to swing the stone round. Our bodies moved like windscreen wipers to and fro in parallel strokes from a fixed base. Soon I gasped for breath: I found it heavy and painful, and my hand began to burn. I changed hands, pushing the stone with a grunt.

'You mustn't do any more,' said the old man, leaning over the edge of his cot.

'No, no, I must go on,' I answered stubbornly.

But Susheelamma herself told me sharply to stop – I was wasting the flour on my sari, and she could manage better alone.

At last Nanjeswamy called us to supper as honorary guests to eat with him: his hospitality had overcome his displeasure. We had millet balls, curry, pulses, boiled rice, and buttermilk. The old lady poured liquid ghee on our rice.

'Do you like our food now?' she asked.

'Yes', I said, for its freshness and simplicity made me long to eat it. The old lady sensed I spoke the truth, for she offered me more millet – peasants' food, as she saw it – and I willingly accepted.

When we had finished, we moved away so that others could take their turn: the men came in order of seniority to eat and the old man was called as an afterthought. They did not have ghee or buttermilk and quickly resumed their former places to sit in silence and brood. Although we all sat close together, there was a feeling of privacy about each person as if his territory were defined by a circle drawn tightly round his body. One or two might talk, but few took in the words. Each seemed to isolate himself, to guard against involvement and the cross-currents of any repressed tension.

At eleven o'clock the old lady said we should go to bed. She ordered the women to clean the floor and to lay out two rush mats in the corner beneath the gods. She fetched some blankets, a small oil lamp, and filled a mug of water. Thayee took me outside and we crouched in a gap between the houses – the family's only lavatory except for the fields where they normally went so as not to waste good manure. The family had definite habits of hygiene, keeping water for different purposes in separate pots stored away from each other. Such pots were never interchanged.

We did not undress, nor brush our teeth, nor even wash our faces, but lay down on the hard floor. Vara fell asleep quickly, but I watched quietly. The cattle were restless, shifting their bodies and snorting, munching their fodder and urinating. Rame Gowda, the eldest son of the house, was stroking them gently, feeling the breadth of their backs, gliding his fingers over the glossy hair, talking privately to calm them.

The children were dragged by the women from their mats in the bedroom, shaken, slapped, and fed. They cried, rejected the food, were beaten, and gulped it down tearfully. Then they stumbled back to the room and sobbed loudly into sleep. But Thayee's youngest daughter would not go to sleep: she was lifted and jogged roughly. The child bawled more. Thayee put her down. She asked to be lifted again. Thayee did so. The child yelled to lie down. Tired, Thayee slapped and slapped her across

113

the back. The rest of the children woke and began to cry as well; they quietened only when Thayee left and there was no hope of comfort.

Two of the men went off to the fields for the night to guard against thieves and wild pigs; the rest fell asleep and the old man snored gently on his cot. The women at last were free to eat so they settled down in the kitchen. I stood up and crept inside. They were startled, and wondered anxiously what I wanted; but I slid to the floor in companionship. The room was divided in two by a tall mud partition: the inner darker area was for cooking where the women could not be seen; the larger ante-room was used for preparation and for feeding a few of the family more intimately. A light flickered high on a shelf: the walls were bare and softly brown in the pale light. The house was silent, for the women were too exhausted to talk. They sat listlessly against a wall, shovelling food into their mouths: Susheelamma and Thayee shared a plate; the others ate separately while the youngest served. They ate the remains of the supper and scraped the pots to ensure every bit was taken. Sometimes they glanced at me and smiled uncertainly.

They went to bed after midnight, filing into the bedroom. They tucked themselves onto separate mats with their children, and buried their heads and bodies beneath a thick blanket. The village was calm.

I lay down again. The old lady walked stealthily up to me and without saying a word folded the blanket under my toes and covered my head gently. Then she lay down beside me.

'Sleep, daughter,' she said.

7 *Village Tactics*

At four o'clock in the morning, the old lady grunted and sat up. "Lakshmi," she whispered, squeezing her eyes to try and see in the dark. "Lakshmi?"

She got up and shuffled across the room, her arms limp and her hair matted; she went to the bedroom and shook the youngest wife gently, then more and more strongly. Lakshmi moaned and tried to roll over; the old lady tugged her hair till she stood up and moved unsteadily out to grind the day's millet.

At five o'clock Thayee got up to help, stirred by the cock's shrill cry as it strutted along the washing area piercing the easy stillness; at five-thirty Madakka, the eldest wife of the house, started to grind as well. The sound of the whirling stones was like water over rocks, not the splashing of a cataract but a soft mellifluous flow which never ceased and never swelled. Once it was daylight, the children got up one by one, rubbing their eyes and calling for help with their ribbons and buttons: their clothes were crushed by the blankets and their hair was tousled. When their fathers came in from their night in the fields, the children brought them water and watched them rub their teeth with pink powder. Manager Nanjeswamy was apparently still asleep in the second house – "How can you ask the Goddess of Sleep to come and go at a certain time?"

Susheelamma got up last to sweep and wash the steps outside: it was cool and the air was clear of dust and heat. She drew a *rangoli* pattern in parallel lines of powdered chalk, trailing it from her palm between thumb and forefingers – she did it most mornings in front of the house to bring the family good fortune: she knew a number of patterns, and as the daughter of the patel, the titular head of the village, she carried a special status. Then she entered the house and started to milk the buffaloes, squeezing the udders gently above a brass pot and stroking the animal's stomach to ease any nervousness.

In the kitchen Madakka was preparing the morning coffee; she

filled some glasses and carried them out to the men who squatted
on their haunches and cupped their hands round the hot con-
tainers; when they had finished they picked up their ploughs and
tools and led the cattle out of the house. The old man hobbled
behind, calling back over his shoulder for food to be brought to
the fields as soon as it was ready.

Thayee and Lakshmi began to sweep up the dung; they tucked
their hems into their waists to leave their calves bare. Working
from opposite ends, they swept the ground in arcs, moving
forward step by step. Lakshmi was pretty, her body silkily strong,
but her eyes seemed vacant and a touch of haughtiness flickered
across whenever she looked at her work. Her movements were
slow as if hindered by some drug. She kept her nose to her
shoulder to keep out the sour fumes and crinkled her face with
revulsion. She seemed relieved when I suggested we fetch some
water, so we walked together to the edge of the village. Other
women were at the tank, so we took our turn in the queue. The
water was very low and would probably last only a few more
weeks: a village well nearby provided an alternative source but
no one liked to drink its water, they said it tasted salty and so
used it for washing only.

Lakshmi laughingly showed me how to hold the pot against my
hip with my arm snaked round its neck. I was unable to hold it
steady, and the water splashed down my skirt. 'I'll take it on my
head,' I said.

'It's difficult,' she warned, as she curled a piece of cloth into a
small cushion, placed it on my head, and balanced the pot on top
for me to grip. I was staggered by the weight and started to walk
unsteadily, pain splintering down my neck into my rounded
shoulders, water slopping over the brim to dribble through my
hair. Lakshmi levered her own pot onto her head, bent down with
her back straight, as though crouching on a tightrope, and hugged
two more to her hips. She walked home with supple grace, her
bare feet moulding themselves to the earth, her body gliding
erect, head still, held high, like a dancer in slow motion. She must
have been carrying sixty pounds in weight.

We went into the kitchen and half-filled a storage vessel. I sat
down for a rest. My head had started to ache from carrying such a
weight. Madakka smiled and gave me a cup of coffee. Then she

leant over some hot ashes and placed on top an iron plate; she tossed in some flattened dough, turning it like a pancake. It was dark in the kitchen, but she knew where everything lived and hardly moved from her place: she stretched to the left for some twigs to quicken the flames; she dipped her hand in a pot to the right to moisten the bread as it cooked. Behind her were stacked the cooking pots, black clay and aluminium; in one corner was a flat stone slab with a drain running out of the house.

Her youngest son came in. She caressed his painful ear, then furtively gave him some *rotti* covered with ghee and hot pumpkin. He stood against her crouched body to eat, smiling at her occasionally from black button eyes. But when the other children came in to eat, she pulled it from him and hid it beneath a cloth. To the other children she gave only half a *rotti* each with a small dollop of chutney made that morning from chillis, turmeric, onion, garlic, tamarind, and cummin, all ground into a paste with a little water and salt. She smiled at me uncertainly as though asking me not to tell.

'*Rotti!*' ordered an angry voice from the other side of the wall. It was Manager Nanjeswamy.

Madakka hurried out and served him in conspicuous silence: she never spoke to him now, not since the time eighteen months before when she'd refused to rewash his clean plate and he'd thrown it at her face. It was easy enough not to talk to men, but it was harder with one of the women when you lived with them in the same room for most of the hours of the day: Madakka had not spoken to Thayee for more than two years. They'd had a row when Thayee refused to work in the rain, ignoring the orders of Madakka's husband. So Madakka had taken umbrage and remained hostile ever since. What did Thayee care? Let her mouth burn. She would maintain the silence.

Suddenly we heard a commotion outside in the street. We ran to the door to see four women shouting together, their arms gesticulating.

'Twenty-eight?'

'Twenty-nine.'

'Can't be.'

'It is.'

'How many rupees is that?'

'How can I calculate?'

'It must be more than a hundred rupees.'

Everyone gasped hysterically.

'Whose chickens were they?'

'Malle Gowda's, Bore Gowda's, Ninge Gowda's . . .'

'All dead?'

'All dead.'

'They'll kill her.'

'That shaved widow . . .'

'Eating the ragi . . .'

'. . . put poison . . .'

'Ayor, Rama! The gods will curse.'

'The men will curse.'

'That prostitute . . .'

'My husband hit *me* because I'd let the chickens out.'

'Thirty, you say?'

'Thirty-one.'

The words were lost in dismayed screams. Never before had such disaster hit the village. Four, five, six, seven, the whole village had lost a chicken that morning through poison put down by a woman called Devakka to protect her ripe millet.

A man ran into the house asking for Manje Gowda, then sped off to the fields. The women gathered quickly – neighbours, relatives, passers-by – to hear the news and pass it on. Those who were less welcome stood at the door and listened, those on good terms walked in freely. The commotion reached a climax, and suddenly, quietly, died. Hadn't Devakka spread poison only to keep off the wild birds? Hadn't she told everyone to guard their own chickens? Everyone? Yes, everyone: she'd visited every house only the day before. So whose fault was it? Could anything be done about it?

The old lady repeated the story over and over again as she walked to and from the storeroom measuring food for the midday meal. She had an air of self-pity, for she'd removed her blouse to be washed, and one breast hung outside her torn sari – a sagging breast gathered into a shrivelled nipple. She displayed it almost defiantly as though to prove her poverty and her selflessness in suffering. There were no men around to be attracted or repelled, or simply to tell her to make herself decent. No younger woman would have dared show such nakedness.

Village Tactics

One of the village women was standing against a pillar, watching the old lady.

'Our millet's all finished.'

The old lady paid no attention.

'We've nothing to eat today,' said the woman, 'we're buying some tomorrow.'

'Do you think we have so much ourselves, cousin?' retorted the old lady.

'We only need a seer,' said the woman.

The old lady walked to the storeroom. She crossed in the dark to the far corner and lifted the lid off a clay pot; she filled a metal measure and brushing the top of extra grain handed it to the woman.

Much of the wealth of the house was stored in that one room. Black clay pots were stacked in diminishing size like tiered minarets. The base of one sealed the neck below so that insects and grubs could not hatch within and destroy the grain and provisions: millet, maize, sorghum, dried chillis, dried pulses, and spices. The paddy was kept in a cylindrical wicker container sealed to the floor with dung. Rope baskets hung from the beams for pots of curds and ghee; dried onions and garlic were tossed on the planks of the roof. The single tiny windows had been shuttered against curiosity, but the soft curves of the metal pots caught touches of sun through the roof, turning brass to gold and tin to silver. The family trunk stood behind the door on a small wobbly stool: it contained the deeds of land, the notes of debt, and petty cash for the household, and was firmly locked with double padlocks for which only Manager Nanjeswamy and S.M.B. had keys.

Everything in the storeroom was shared by the joint family: it had been gathered over the years from the dowries of incoming daughters-in-law, or from purchases at market whenever money allowed. The door was always locked and the key hung round the old lady's neck. But when Eramma came from the town, she was given the key to look after, since she was the wife of a big man in town.

"For everything it's Eramma, Eramma", said Susheelamma with bitterness. "The old lady calls her and gives her the keys to the rooms and the boxes, she gives her everything. But does she ever give them to me, even though I'm the wife of the manager? She never lets us do anything, she never gives us responsibility."

The old lady put more trust in her grandchildren, and used them to do small jobs. She called the eldest now, a lanky boy of fourteen with a sulky mouth and swaggering manner who sat on the old man's cot idly throwing pebbles. He mimicked her voice, shrinking the tone and raising the level. The old lady called him again. He started to whistle insolently, so she grabbed a stick and tried to strike him. He ducked, jumped off the bed, and ran to the storeroom: he pulled himself up on the door and swung onto the beams, shifting baskets and pots like a thief.

The old lady peered up. 'Not that, not that,' she cried. 'Take care. Don't throw things about.'

He found the bunch of onions and hurled them down on top of her. She brandished her stick.

'Alright, you can come down now,' she threatened.

The boy ran backwards and forwards across the planks, then suddenly jumped to the floor: as he was gaining his balance, the old lady thwacked him across the shoulders. The boy swerved and grabbed her by the arm, almost toppling her over.

She screamed and cursed and tried to strike him again. They tussled in the doorway until the boy thrust her away and ran out of the house, laughing and waving his hand; the old lady chuckled at his power.

The neighbour was still watching.

'I'll bring the grain tomorrow,' she said.

'The container comes back today, cousin,' said the old lady. 'And the millet's repaid tomorrow.'

She never demanded extra in repayment for she lent mainly to relatives, and though she could write nothing down she always knew what was owing. Sometimes she lent to the poorest of the village: a deserted wife who was paralysed, a widow without a family, the potter. In these cases she never expected repayment, nor reminded them of her charity.

Two hours later, the village elders gathered under the neem tree* to discuss the death of so many chickens and to decide the necessary punishment. There was Susheelamma's father, the patel,

---

* The neem is planted with the peepul tree in many Indian villages. When both are fully grown they are 'married' with a wedding ceremony, and the site used as an auspicious place.

whose official position as the titular head of the village gave him the right to judge; there was Manje Gowda, whose family's wealth and power made him a favoured leader; there were two others who had prospered and bought land. Each received support in the village according to kinship or power: there were one hundred and eighty-three inhabitants, all of whom, apart from the potter, belonged to the same caste. Many of these were related, and this gave unity and some security, and also a spirit of independence since few were destitute and only three families were landless. None were tenants under a landlord.

Officially the elders had no status, for the village was represented in government terms by a group panchayat which covered five villages: Palahalli's one member had been unanimously elected, a respected man whose father had been honourable, and more important, was related to the patel. This panchayat met once a month to deal with complaints and quarrels, but most of the villagers preferred to keep their quarrels contained within their own village, to be settled by the elders.

"Yes, these villagers quarrel over anything," said the patel lethargically chewing tobacco. "They can't keep quiet. About the field, cattle, this, that. What else would they fight for here? How can they fight just like that? There must be some reason. One man's cow goes into another's field, and for that they fight, that's all. Tell me what else they'd fight for here?"

Chickens were always a problem, they ran from house to house and were difficult to control; they picked at any grain and laid their eggs in different places. That was the trouble, Devakka's fields weren't so far from the village, but was that her fault? Of course it was, she should have stayed in the fields to keep away the birds instead of putting down poison. But she'd told everyone, they should have taken care. Weren't there nine birds dead? Well then . . . the elders argued and argued while others joined the discussion: Manager Nanjeswamy, the patel's cousin, a man whose son had education. Kalle Gowda, Jayamma's husband, hovered on the edge, unsure of the support he would get.

Only the old man stayed silent, watching, listening, unobtrusive, until he felt it was time to speak. The others fell silent as he gave his judgement. He felt no punishment should be given. The people who lost their chickens had suffered a shock and would now protect them better; Devakka would be punished by the anger of the village.

The arguments lingered on, but no one could think of a better solution. Finally, the patel pronounced the decision along the lines of the old man's argument, and everyone dispersed. The patel stayed on, since he'd found a cool position beneath the trees, and he ordered a young boy to bring him coffee from the local hotel. He was a hefty man, well-preserved, with a shock of ice grey hair, and a shirt which was stained with sweat and the droppings of food – a neglected man, neglectful of himself: his yellow fingers shook as he lit his *bidi*, and his eyes were slightly bloodshot.

The patel's family was seeing hard times, now that the government had removed the monopoly of power the patel used to hold in a village. Once they had seen glory and prosperity, owning hundreds of acres of land – some even said thousands. But fate had been against them and had wiped out most of the family. The patel's eldest brother had died six months after marriage; his second brother had died from smallpox with his wife and only son; his youngest brother and wife had died soon after. His father had died when he was only one; his uncle had died after one year as patel. He himself had only a single son. It was destined that way.

His wife – Susheelamma's mother – could remember the early days. She was a proud woman, like a madonna, for there was grace and softness coupled with strength and a touch of masculinity.

"We used to cook in huge cauldrons," she recalled. "We'd kill a lamb whenever there was planting, or when they were harvesting, and feed all the labourers. It was a big household. The mother, brothers, all lived here. Then everything happened. One by one, they all went, all of them died.

"When the patel's house died, another house improved. Manje Gowda's house. I'd seen them in a grass hut, why, it must be forty years ago. Mosquitoes and flies would come in droves to their house. You had to bend your head to enter, the door was so tiny. Under our own eyes, their children grew up, got educated. Slowly Lakshmi grew. Their luck was also good. They became clever and hardworking; they built a new house. Things were cheap then: it's only possible when times are cheap.

"They built their second house on our land. They claimed the land. They persuaded the patel to be on their side: they bribed

him and got his signature. They also bought up some forest land –
they managed it all very cleverly. But *we* don't do all this, we
don't use such devious ways. I've never done any injustice, our
family has never ruined anyone or snatched other people's
property."

The patel himself was uncommunicative and answered my
questions with a surly 'Yes' or a nod. He seemed a sad figure,
arrogant, but sad. He had seen his house decay, he had seen
another rise, and nothing could change his fate. Loss of power
and position was harder to bear than death. The crows were
eating his millet. Soon the coolies themselves would be asking him
to work for them. In his grandfather's house, people used to work
just for a ball of millet, four, five, six labourers. Now all he got was
fifty rupees a year for collecting the village taxes on land and
remitting them to a central source. Sometimes if an officer came,
he'd give him a tender coconut, or a lemon, flowers, something
like that – he didn't give him a meal or anything. But still, he had
his pride, and his land: he wasn't quite sure how much, since
most of it was uncultivated and belonged to some of his cousins.*
And he still had a bit of influence, he still gave people advice, for
he was an upright man who never went on the wrong path, who'd
never done any harm. People respected his words when he told
them about good behaviour.

It was true that none of the villagers criticised him: he was free
to enter their houses whenever he had the inclination. They were
well aware of the land he held and his strong connections with the
household of Manje Gowda. The patel and Manager Nanjeswamy
– father-in-law and son-in-law – were friendly, and who would be
foolish enough to contradict such a combination? By tradition and
custom, the patel was a man to respect, to fear, and never to cross,
for he held the reins of power. Or so it had been in the past, and
change is slow when alternatives are few.

It took the patel's wife to tell us the truth about him, for she
had no respect for her husband, and had nothing to lose by telling

---

* Some of the villagers claimed the patel's family owned more than a hundred
acres. The old man said: "They used to be very big in the village. They're
very well to do." The old lady also said: "They're a very old family. They've
lived well." They were both proud at having the patel's daughter, Susheelamma, as part of their family now.

us. Her husband had kept a mistress, a woman in the village whose own husband had been lame. She was dead now, sent to the grave by the justice of God.

"She enticed people to her," said Susheelamma's mother. "She'd make evil charms. Oh, if I start talking about all that, it's a long story. That evil woman was always spending her time wishing, 'Let that husband be mine, let so and so be mine.' She wasn't even good-looking. She couldn't equal my left foot! When I came from my father's house wearing a beautiful sari, with my hair combed, and wearing flowers and jewels, everyone used to stare. They said, 'See how people stare, it'll bring her evil.' And hasn't it happened? But that woman was just artful, she knew all the tricks.

"I never went in for such vices. See, whatever I was forty years ago, I'm still the same. It's the same heart God gave me, a constant heart. See, I can't play about like other people. Only Mother Earth knows all that. This isn't the time for good people. It's only for people who are loose and unfaithful. See, it's a time for such things. You'll believe whatever I say, whether truth or a lie, but the Mother Earth, the moon, the sun, and the sky, they know I speak the truth."

The patel had had other women and played around with prostitutes, so after the birth of Susheelamma, his wife walked out. But since she had nowhere to go – her parents could not look after her because of the shame it brought – she returned to the patel to live in a separate part of the house. She had survived famine and loneliness in order to bring up the two children.

"They also suffered a lot," she said. "They used to feel very bad. But what could they do if they felt bad? What could they do? If he was beating me, they'd stand there helplessly watching. What could they do? And on the day of my daughter's wedding, I shed so many tears. Instead of having me at the front at my daughter's wedding, he did the ceremony without me. My only daughter. They took me away from the marriage. My daughter stood on the marriage platform and said, 'Why does my father make my mother suffer like this?' "

According to the patel's wife, there were some in the village who disapproved of the patel's activities, but there were others who did the same, and there were also people who said, 'Oh, he's the patel, we need him for all the cases.'

124

"What can they do other than keep quiet? He's the patel, and they need him, you see."

It was difficult for me as a woman to speak to the patel about his affair, just as it was difficult for me to get to know any of the men in the village. I had no access to their fields, nor to the local hotel where they gathered to exchange their news. It was only a room with a bench and a radio, where coffee was ready throughout the day, but women were rarely seen there. Even the exchange of glances was sufficient cause for gossip in the claustrophobic atmosphere of the village, and I took care never to be too free in greeting a man in the street. Nor did the men approach me, probably because I was female, and probably because of my link with the family which meant I was bespoken. The family had moved up in the village scale and was no longer so accessible.

In contrast the women and children of the village came out of their houses and answered my smiles and greetings. There were days when I didn't see them, either because I was in the fields, or because the doors of their houses were closed and locked; but sometimes I stopped to talk. I learnt nothing of their private lives, only of generalities, for they were as suspicious and guarded as the family had been originally; yet it was easy to predict something of their lives now that I knew the family – the work in the fields, the work in the house, the tensions of living together with poverty always so close, the lack of privacy, the endless monologues, the repetition of daily tasks. It must always have been like that, generation after generation, with only slight variations according to limited factors: the number of children, the will to work, the quantity of land. Sometimes life was better, sometimes it was worse, and sometimes there were changes which came from outside forces, not from personal choice. Certainly famine, death, disease, altered each man's chances, but at least he knew to some extent the boundaries of his life, and so could work within them. He also knew where his children would be, and their children, and their children: the land and the village were part of that life, both supporting a man's existence and restricting it very severely. In the future, it might be just as predictable; or the pull of the town might shatter its equilibrium.

It took me several weeks to visit every household, to calculate the number of people in each, the amount of land belonging to each, and the kinship ties if any with the household of Manje Gowda. Those with the most land were mainly related to the patel.

Most of the households had problems: either there were no sons, or there was no land; in one family, a son was deaf and dumb; in another, the woman had lost four of her five children; and Jayamma had of course lost all three sons. There were ten widows, four of whom lived alone in poverty; one paralysed woman whose husband had disappeared so that she mainly depended on charity in order to survive; and one wife who'd been left with her three children while her husband went off to another house to live with his children by an earlier marriage.

The men had an easier time – four widowers had remarried and the fifth was finding a young bride. But they did have the stress of debts and keeping the family alive: only two households were in credit and the debts of the rest varied from four or five hundred rupees to four or five thousand rupees. Manje Gowda's household was much the heaviest in debt, and even if it divided each brother would owe nearly four thousand rupees.

A prominent feature of village life was the stone of justice, a granite pillar three feet high sunk into the ground near the temple. The elders said it brought truth and put men on the right path. They said it had been used only once in the last few years, when a man was tied to the stone for stealing some fruit from a grove. After three or four hours he confessed, and as punishment he was left for another two hours to receive the derisory comments of any who passed by. Such shame had stopped him from stealing again.

There was another occasion when the stone of justice was used, but the village tried to conceal the story, presumably because of its indication of moral laxity. I learnt it from Kalle Gowda, Jayamma's husband, who wanted to prove he was part of political power in the village and so had authority to tell me. A man and woman ran off together, the man from Palahalli, the woman from a neighbouring village. Both were separately married. They took with them some money and her jewels, but soon everything was spent. They started to quarrel and he left her. He made his way back to Palahalli, and she returned to her village. A week later, a huge council gathered to bring the couple to justice. People came in their hundreds from all the surrounding villages. They ques-

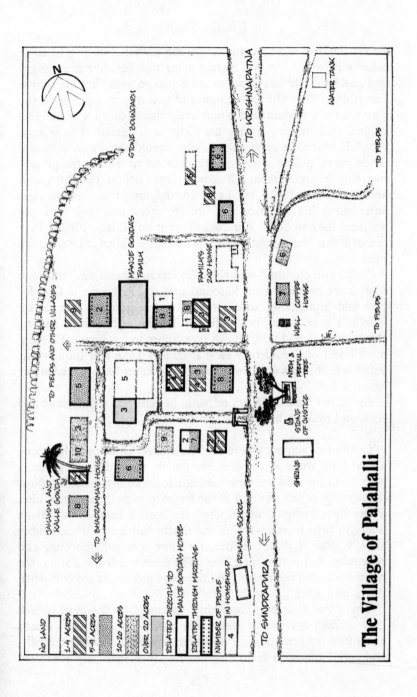

The Village of Palahalli

Legend:
- NO LAND
- 1–4 ACRES
- 5–9 ACRES
- 10–20 ACRES
- OVER 20 ACRES
- RELATED DIRECTLY TO MANJE GONDA'S HOUSE
- RELATED THROUGH MARRIAGE
- NUMBER OF PEOPLE IN HOUSEHOLD: 4

PRIMARY SCHOOL

TO SUNDRAPURA

TO BHADRAMMA'S HOUSE

JAKAMMA AND KALLE GONDA

TO FIELDS AND OTHER VILLAGES

STONE BOUNDARY

MANJE GONDA'S FAMILY

FAMILY'S 2ND HOUSE

COFFEE HOUSE

WELL

NEEM & PEEPUL TREE

STONE OF JUSTICE

SHRINE

WATER TANK

TO KRISHNAPATNA

TO FIELDS

N

tioned the man and they questioned the woman, but he refused to acknowledge her. He said he had never met her. She grew angry and said he'd told lots of lies to get her to go with him. He denied everything. Then she took a rope and tied him to the pillar – she was a strong woman and could even throw down a man. The council said he must marry her. The man agreed. The woman refused. Everyone grew angry. Why should she be so difficult? Then three people tried to catch her to tie her to the pillar – but she brought them all down. One fell in the ditch and another nearly broke his head. In the end, four or five men surrounded her and tied her up. He faced one way, and she another, back to back. The council went on all day. Finally they decided that she should go and live with her father. She went the next day.

"After two months," said Kalle Gowda in conclusion, "someone must have persuaded the husband, and the fool went to Gowda-gere and brought his wife home. If it was someone like us, we wouldn't have called her 'wife', or looked at her face. Earlier, that simpleton had said, 'If she ever comes to my house, I'll hang myself and die.' And now look at it, he's gone and brought his wife back. If it was someone like us, we'd never have looked at her again as wife."

As for the man she'd run off with, he returned to his home and wife, and took up his normal life.

Communal activity was rare in the village. Once there had been a boar hunt when all the men had joined, but a dog was gored, a man wounded, and the meat inadequate for so many people. Now only groups of ten went off to the forest to hunt. Sometimes, also, a few men gathered and recited the stories they knew, taking hours in turn to tell what all the others had heard several times already. But it didn't matter, for time was unimportant, and reiteration was part of their lives. The more one heard a story, the more one could remember, and the more one could enjoy it when it was said again.

There was also the village kitty, managed by the patel, which gave a small amount to every man on his wedding day. Funds were none too generous, for donations were gathered haphazardly, and relied more on fortuitous circumstance than any organised plan. One man was forced to present a fortune with a fine of fifty rupees because he'd stolen a chicken belonging to the patel. He killed it, plucked it, and made it into curry. The whole village sat in judgement, declared him guilty, and made him sell his only sheep in order to raise the money. Five rupees went to the patel to replace his chicken; forty-five went into the village kitty; and everyone ate the curry except the poor culprit.

On the whole, the affairs of the village were remote from the joint family, engrossed as they were in their daily routine, and the maintenance of their status. Sociability was also limited: they ate in others' homes only at times of a feast or a ceremony. Visits without reason or invitation were unusual and unwelcome except from relations and neighbours. Who could afford to feed more than his own family?

Manager Nanjeswamy, of course, had more contact with people. He hired the labour, he arranged their wages, and made sure he knew what was going on in the village. He also had some friends, though friendship for him was full of self-interest: a man with a dog whose pup he was hoping to have, and a rich man's son eight miles away whom once he had helped in a brawl. He wasn't much interested in others. He stopped to talk if someone said hello, but what did one get by going to others' houses, what was the point?

The rest of the men in the family had no time to make friends. They had to be in the fields and preferred to be there working with Mother Earth than to sit on a bench drinking coffee. There was the religious drama, when two of the brothers and Nanjeswamy and some of the men from the village rehearsed for more than a fortnight part of the *Ramayana*. They all had to learn their roles, to hire the costumes and lights, and then on the night itself to perform in front of the village. It was good, they all got on together, and some of the villagers gave them presents and asked them to do it again. They offered to put on a performance for me if I paid them a thousand rupees.

The women's experience of friendship was mainly confined to each other: any intimacy developed in youth with girls from their own village was severed by marriage, and relationships thereafter were ones of respect and obedience, to in-laws, husband, cousins. Only mother and daughter had some possibility of friendship, but theirs was a minor partnership in the hierarchy of roles, and the joint family itself prevented too much involvement. Likewise, contact with village women was brief, restricted to chatter when passing by: few had the chance to visit each other's houses whatever their wish might have been.

To the women I presented an enigma, I fitted no previous pattern. "Somehow we've grown used to you," was all they could articulate. They had shown concern and curiosity, but once the restraint of hospitality had given way to familiarity, their moods included me: not that they cursed or were rude, but they were silently unresponsive particularly when they were jealous. Only Jayamma and Bhadramma were always welcoming, always smiling, demonstratively affectionate.

I was becoming part of the women, and yet not part: I had the option to leave, I could choose not to work, I had time to listen. They knew I was separate, nothing to do with their caste or any other caste, but because I was outside their rules of behaviour, it seemed to make it easier for them to talk to me.

Such limited means of friendship was easy for me to understand; but caste was something I found difficult to assess, partly because it was totally outside my experience, and partly because it did not greatly impinge on the family. The old man said that the same blood flowed through everyone, and I think he probably felt it. The others just shrugged and said that caste had always existed, but things were changing in towns, people were mixing more. Certainly the family showed no special deference to Vara, who came from a higher caste. Rather the family was sympathetic with and sometimes annoyed at her problems of adapting: she needed a bath every day, she nearly fainted at the sight of meat and refused to watch people eat it, and she cooked her own food on a separate stove. They were aware of *her* discomfort, but did not attribute it to *their* caste.

They knew they were peasants, for society had termed them so; and though it is my conjecture, I think they felt they weren't worth much because no one had told them otherwise. At least in the village the family had some importance, and in town S.M.B. had pride in his own position. But as he gained more status he was likely to support the structure of caste in order to protect his power while trying to move up in the scale. He already emulated some customs of higher castes, insisting on a dowry for his daughter, bathing every day, and talking of village peasants as though they were different people.

In the village, contact with other castes was brief and usually based on labour. The carpenter made their ploughs and carved the beams for their new house from the banyan tree which had fallen the year of the storms; the weavers lived in a village eight miles away and made the wool of the family's sheep into coarse white rugs; the dhobi washed polluted clothes; the priest received supplication; the blacksmith, the midwife, the teacher were used. Beggars and officials passed through the village infrequently.

The barber provided the most regular service to the family: he had come to the house today to shave Nanjeswamy. A small man in shabby clothes who walked with pigeon toes, he laid out his equipment on the floor just inside the front door: a cracked mirror, a worn blade, a stone for sharpening, and half an old coconut shell filled with water. He wiped his client's chin, brushed it with soap, and started to scrape gingerly. When he had done one side, Nanjeswamy felt it.

'That's no good,' he said. 'Do you call that smooth?'

'It's the best I can do,' said the barber mournfully, staring at the chin without interest – the hangdog look of a man who can never improve.

'It's the best he can do,' mocked Nanjeswamy. 'Then I'll have to go up to Krishnapatna and get it properly done.'

The barber nodded sorrowfully, but his eyes suddenly brightened. 'They charge seventy-five *paise* there. And with me you pay only twenty.'

'Twenty and some grain,' said Nanjeswamy. 'Or seventy-five and a good shave.' He rubbed his chin again. 'They've got proper tools there – scissors, blades, a chair, even a long mirror.'

The barber looked at his tools. 'If you paid me more,' he said wistfully, 'I could buy better things.'

'How can I pay you more if you shave me so badly?' retorted Nanjeswamy.

'How can I shave you well if you pay me so badly that I can't buy tools to shave you well?'

He laughed from wry awareness at the hopeless cycle of life: to cry or protest was futile, one could not alter fate. The only compensation that I could see was the lack of caste distinction between the family and the barber: if he had shaved a Brahmin or other high castes, they would have considered themselves polluted and immediately taken a bath.

By spending time with the women, confined to the house or the fields in an endless cycle of similar jobs, I perhaps was receiving a partial view of the village activities. Not that I particularly wanted to join the broader arena of men's activities, their politics and manoeuvres, but I was worried at such a gap. However, I was lucky enough one evening to witness a village function where only men attended.

As it was getting dark, I walked out of the house alone in order to get some peace and a little solitude. The constant noise of the children and the suppressed tensions of so many people within a confined area were beginning to get me down. It was dark; along the street some lamps burned where women worked in the cool of their verandahs. I walked towards the edge of the village, thinking I would head out to the fields. Then I heard the drum. It beat slowly, and stopped. There was silence for almost two minutes. Then it started again.

A procession approached in the distance, straddling along the road. About twenty men, some with lamps, talked in subdued tones. In front was the drummer. Every thirty yards, he stopped to light a pile of leaves to heat the skin of his drum: when it was taut again, he started the rhythm once more and the procession moved on. At the centre were two goats and a sheep, dragged on a tight rein: they reared and kicked with fear, spilling some of the flowers which were tucked into their collars. When the procession reached the stone of justice, they were tied to it securely.

More men arrived, including the washerman from the next village. Without any preparation or ceremony, he slit the animals' throats efficiently and drained out the blood. The bodies twitched for a moment.

Some of the men went into the shrine nearby to plead with god for rain – the reason for the sacrifice. They offered flowers and scented sticks and told their god the price they had paid for the animals. And finally they asked for rain. Why were the rains so bad these days, always late and always meagre? This was the age of Kali, an unjust time when none but the evil prospered.

The washerman carried the animals' bodies through the stone gateway, past the well to the forecourt of the patel's house, and laid them on some planking. The village men gathered round, cramming themselves onto two balconies which overlooked the forecourt. About forty men were there, at least one from every household: the old men sat in the front squatting against the pillars, the younger men stood at the back leaning against the walls. I was the only woman and they questioned my presence when I slipped in from the alley to take a seat in the shadows away from the rest of the crowd. After that they forgot me.

The men were excited by the sacrifice. The flickering light of the lamps, the shadowy figures, and the restricted enclosure of space dramatised the effect. It made me think of a play from the Middle Ages with a travelling group performing outside to a village – the planking was the stage, the men were the audience, expectant but noisy, and only the actors were needed.

A man stepped into the centre: he picked up one of the bodies, and wrapping some rope round its forelegs, strung it up to a beam which protruded into the forecourt. He tried to string up a second, but failed for lack of room. He called for help. No one came forward. He called again. Two boys were pushed from the crowd. He made them stand ten feet apart and balance a plough on their shoulders. To this he tied the goat and sheep.

Another man entered the pool of light, clutching a large knife. He slit the first goat's stomach and pulled out all the entrails. The audience murmured with pleasure. The man began to skin, carefully slitting the hide from the fat, anxious not to spoil, anxious not to waste. Then he cut up the carcase and threw the joints on the planking.

The spectators told him to cut up the next goat. The man turned angrily to face them.

"You bastards," he yelled. "You stand about like bridegrooms. How can I manage alone? Can these boys with the plough stand around here all night?"

But no one came to help. They were much more interested in relaxation after a hard day's work. What was the point of sweating your back off when others were there to do it. A man worked for himself, not for the whole village. And what was relaxation? A good smoke, a good argument, and giving plenty of orders.

Eventually some older boys of the village were called from their houses to chop up the meat into cubes at the direction of the audience. They worked on the guts, the liver, the legs. Some of it was so tough that they had to use hatchets: soon their hands and wrists were bright red and the planks ran with streams of blood. All the time they called for help: they wanted an axe; they needed water; they needed another lamp. All who watched repeated the orders like an echo; others went off to piss to avoid being called to work.

A dog ran onto the planking and snatched at some of the meat; everyone howled with rage till it was kicked off the stage.

The boys worked on, cutting the meat into cubes, tossing it into piles, starting again on the next piece, slice, cut, slice, cut. They worked with concentration, ignoring the endless orders. But the onlookers grew restless: they wanted it all done faster. They wanted their meat at once, why was it taking so long? Some of the men lost their temper and started to shout at each other, their faces livid with anger: two men bore into each other and had to be pulled apart.

Jayamma's husband, Kalle Gowda, sauntered into the light. He ordered a boy to fetch him an axe, then started to splinter the bones. The dull thud of his work seemed to quieten the men.

Suddenly the drummer staggered into the light reeling from side to side, peering at all the faces. He lurched towards the meat but a roar of anger from the crowd made him back away. He stood swaying uncertainly – a pitiful man in a torn vest with blood-shot eyes and a yellow stain down his pants. He asked for money as payment.

"What money?" roared the crowd, finding once more a target for its aggression. "How can you ask for money . . . you didn't do your job . . . you only had one drum . . . why not another . . ."

They resented paying him money for he had only half-done his job: he was meant to have gone round the village the day before to announce the time of the sacrifice. But he'd done it only that afternoon, *and* he'd announced it wrong – he'd said it was going to be tomorrow.

"So now you must go round the houses telling everyone it's today," they mocked. "You must tell all the men to hurry and bring their coconuts or else they'll miss the procession."

The drummer hung his head. "I did the usual thing. If there's some slight mistake . . ."

But still he insisted on payment. Again there were howls of rage and a prolonged debate as to whether he deserved any money. Finally he was paid his two rupees, and everyone jeered as he left. It wasn't his inefficiency they minded so much as his drunken stupor: they as a caste were teetotal and condemned anyone who drank.

It was getting late and some of the men joined the boys to help cut up the meat. At ten o'clock the trader came to divide the meat into equal shares. He had come from a village several miles away because of his skill, for if there was any disparity, the men would complain for a month. His fee was a little meat plus two of the animals' heads. The third would be given to one of the widows.

The trader divided in turn the legs and shoulders and kidneys which all had been cut in a hundred cubes. He counted out thirty places, and slapped down the pieces one by one on the planking, making them stick together in gradually swelling mounds. The audience watched him keenly to make sure no cheating was done.

The trader decided to show his skill: he took to flicking the meat through the air to land on the appropriate pile rather than stretching out to place it down himself. The mounds quickly became untidy so he stopped to knead them like dough into balls, swinging backwards and forwards on his haunches, and gripping a *bidi* between his teeth.

Two hours passed. The trader continued to divide the lumps of fat and flesh and offal, on and on, his skinny fingers opening and shutting like claws. The men were silent now, nodding off in the dim light, borrowing *bidis* and snuff. The thought of eating the meat that evening had probably gone from their minds: it would have to be cooked tomorrow. Red meat was a rare luxury – some could afford a chicken every now and then, but who could afford mutton except for weddings and deaths?

The trader started to weigh each pile, balancing it on his scales against a special stone, adding or subtracting tiny pieces of meat. The men began to rouse themselves, and when the piles were all weighed up, they came forward one by one. Some used a basket to hold the meat, some the flaps of their shirt, while others just held out their hands and clutched the pile to their bodies. It wasn't a vast amount.

Village Tactics

Each paid eight rupees to an elder, then slipped away in the
dark. Two women crept up in the shadows, silently waiting their
turn: another called down the street for her husband to come and
eat – he cursed her to go back home.

Slowly the courtyard emptied till only a few were left to wash
down the planks and tools and turn off the kerosene lamps. The
scene of sharing among village men was over.

8　The Virtuous Wife

A wife had been chosen for Chikke Gowda, the youngest son in the family, and preparations were nearly complete. Invitations were printed in English and Kannarese – quavering pink over-printed with midnight blue.

Smt. & Sri. Manje Gowda of Palahalli
request the pleasure of your company with family and
friends on the occasion of the marriage of their son
Chi. Ry.* N. Chikkegowda
with
Chi. Sow.* M.S. Bhagyamma
(daughter of Sidde Gowda, brother of Anke Gowda, Teacher)
on Thursday the 29th at Brides Residence
10.30–11.30　　　　　　　　　Please avoid presentation
With best compliments from relatives and friends

On the eve of his wedding, Chikke Gowda came to the family house in Palahalli. He was bathed and massaged with oil, then dressed in a new white lungi which hung to his feet from his waist. He stood in one corner beneath the pictures of gods while his family and cousins and some of the village women sprinkled his head with rice in order to give good fortune. I did the same, touching his knees, his waist, his shoulders, before emptying a handful of rice to slide down his sweating face.

At three o'clock that morning, Eramma from the town, the wife of S.M.B., woke me for a ceremony. Five women, all cousins of the old lady, stood in an arc round a pounding hole which was filled to the brim with paddy; like sentinels they each held a husking pole – rich, red wood, polished from years of handling, with a brass disc at the base to husk the paddy more powerfully. Eramma circled the poles with smoke from a burning joss-stick,

* Abbreviations of Sanskrit appellations used for auspicious reference.

137

tied small garlands round their girths, and blessed them with *kunkuma* and turmeric while calling the names of gods. Then she cracked a coconut on the floor with one sharp thrust and poured the juice down the poles. The women started to pound, singing as they worked:

'See the poles for husking paddy, see how smooth they are: a woman can work for hours and never get tired from husking; a woman can work for hours and her hands will never hurt. See the poles for husking paddy, see how smooth they are. The man who made the husking poles knew his work well.'

A horn blared outside: it was S.M.B. who had managed to procure a lorry to carry his guests to the wedding. He strode into the house, shook my hand, and made me sit beside him. He was pleased with the marriage, he'd done his brother well, for the family he'd chosen was prosperous and the bride was his own wife's cousin. He yawned.

'The lorry leaves in half an hour,' he said.

The women woke the children and hastily tried to dress them, combing their hair and fumbling in the dark with buttons and ribbons and sleeves. I was surprised, for they wore nothing special – somehow I had expected a glamorous display of clothing. Even S.M.B. wore only a crisp white lungi and his paisley shawl tossed casually over one shoulder.

The women were strangely uncoordinated, for none had been to bed that night and few the night before in an effort to finish the gifts to be given to the bride. They had not changed themselves yet.

S.M.B. looked at his watch.

'The lorry leaves in ten minutes.'

In panic, the women scraped back their hair, tied some flowers to the nape, changed into their smartest saris which nonetheless were crumpled cotton, and struggled to put on their jewelry: glass and gold in the ears, a thin gold chain round the neck, a silver belt round the waist. In ten minutes they were ready.

I changed quickly into a blue and white cotton sari and hurried out with the women. We left the house in a mess: clothes and baskets were scattered across the floor, a floor which needed sweeping of chaff and dung and twigs. But the old lady was too preoccupied to harass such idle neglect, for she was trying to coax the youngest wife to change and leave the house. Lakshmi was weeping and shouting something about her jewelry, refusing to move, refusing to answer, so that eventually the old lady departed impatiently. Lakshmi and the older son, Rame Gowda, were left behind to look after the house and cattle.

'Hurry,' said the women, taking my arm. We stumbled down the street in the dark and balanced our way up a plank onto the back of the lorry. Men stood on the outside and the women were crammed in the middle. When the lorry started, it lurched forward, throwing us all on the floor. We shrieked, but remained squatting, jostling our elbows to make room around us. It was no use, there was no space, so we just had to suffer: I had a baby on my lap, a head on my shoulder, an elbow on my head, and someone pushing into my back.

The women quietened as the journey lengthened, so we could hear above the engine's clatter the swish of branches against the lorry's cabin. We must have driven for nearly an hour over dusty tracks and potholed ruts, winding through rolling country. It was dawn when we reached a calm, spacious village whose brown mud walls were cooled by the shadow of sunlight. Everyone got down.

'Where are they?' said S.M.B. with a frown. 'Why aren't they here to meet us?' He sent someone off to find the bride's party, then paced up and down clutching a black leather briefcase. The women sank onto some steps and closed their eyes with relief.

At last we heard some music, and through a narrow passage came the band – a trombone, two trumpets, two drums. They played a fanfare in greeting, and the bride's family stepped forward to raise their hands to S.M.B. He bowed in return and heading the procession with the bridegroom, ordered the crowd to follow.

We wound through the village, past the temple, down a lane, over some open land. It was early so no one else was about, but the noise of the band and the cries of the crowd quickly brought some spectators. Finally we entered a narrow street. Half way down was a straggly awning woven from coconut leaves which announced the marriage house. The bridegroom, the old lady, some of the women, and I, were hustled into a dark room where a black bicycle was propped against the wall: its handlebars gleamed with fluorescent paint, and its crossbar and wheels were beribboned with plastic streamers.

'Coffee,' said S.M.B. as he entered the house. 'We all need coffee.'

The bride's father scuttled across the hall and consulted with his cooks. He came back a little shamefaced.

'I'm afraid . . . we didn't realise we should have coffee prepared,' he stammered.

'No coffee?' said S.M.B. loudly. 'You'll have to get us coffee.'

The bride's father hurried out of the house to order some from the coffee house.

S.M.B. sauntered round the hall. The opening in the roof billowed with white cloth; the cattle area at the far end was levelled to hold three mud fireplaces which supported three huge cauldrons. Men were stirring the contents with long wooden poles while others ran backwards and forwards with food and water and spices.

'It's not very smart,' said S.M.B., adjusting a pair of dark glasses. He peered about him. 'I hope there'll be enough room?' The house was larger than his family's in Palahalli. 'We'll take breakfast anyway.' The bride's uncle hurried to tell the cooks.

At 7.30, the bride was led from a room into the main hall. She was a large girl with broad face, stubby nose, and a full determined mouth; she was dressed in a bright red sari made from silk and bordered with gold – worth more than a hundred rupees, so the onlookers calculated. It only needed a silver belt to complete the luxuriant image but that would come later from S.M.B. Now was the time for bangles. She plumped herself down on a small wooden board and hung her head as the bangle seller approached to lay out his wares in a seductive line of bright colours. He picked some up, he put some down, he clinked a handful together, running them through his fingers; he held some against her sari; he artfully showed her the best; and when she selected a dozen, he threaded them over her hand with a deft twist of his palm.

Five women stood up and offered her five pots of water filled from five wells; they offered five coconuts, five lumps of jaggery, and bundles of betel leaves. God was worshipped and called for blessing, and then the argument started

'Where are the five baskets?' shouted a woman from the bride's family.

'Why aren't the coconuts at her feet?' said one from the bride-groom's side.

'There should be five baskets.'

'Move the coconuts over.'

The bride kept her head bent and demurely adjusted her toque which was made from hundreds of flowers; but as the argument lengthened, she impatiently stared about her, then stood up without permission and returned to the bridal room. A bride's duty was to be meek.

The bridegroom was eating breakfast: he wasn't meant to eat breakfast but the old lady said he should in case he grew weak. He didn't demur. Afterwards he put on a pale blue jacket, fitted his gold turban, and making sure the bride was not about stepped outside.

He was escorted through the village beneath an improvised canopy of vivid pink fabric draped over an open umbrella; the band preceded him with fanfares; the guests succeeded him with vessels of flowers and baskets of grain. Near the steps of the temple he received the black bicycle, a nylon shirt, a stainless steel plate, and bicycle clips for his trousers. They worshipped the god and returned with the priest to the house.

S.M.B. was organising the guests: with deference he offered a bench to his work colleagues and clicked his fingers for coffee. More than six hundred people had come and were waiting for the *Muhurtham* to begin. It was past 10.30. S.M.B. delayed: the President of the Cooperative Society had still not arrived – how could they start without him?

The old lady had changed into a new sari so finely woven in green that it floated about her as though she were wearing a party dress; the old man also wore new clothes and sat uncomfortably in a corner.

'Look at him,' said S.M.B. 'Isn't he proud of the clothes I bought?'

He called the bride and her parents into the hall for the presentation of jewelry. He produced his black briefcase and opened it with a flourish. He pulled out a silk sari and paused so that everyone could see it. He pulled out a nylon sari. Pause. Then he took out a thin gold necklace studded with tiny mock rubies and emeralds. He put it round the bride's neck himself, and stepped back to admire it. The bride's parents leant forward. They held the chain in their hands, trying to feel its weight. They frowned, and looked up at S.M.B. They looked back at the gold chain. Undeterred, S.M.B. took from his briefcase a pair of gold earrings set with mock pearls. He dangled them near the bride. Pause. He took out a silver toering. He closed the briefcase firmly.

The parents looked surprised and the bride hung her head in disappointment. Where was the silver belt, and the traditional silver anklets? Where were the four gold bangles which S.M.B. had promised? Before they could protest, S.M.B. ordered the bridegroom into the hall.

Bride and groom were conducted into the washing area beneath the billowing canopy. They faced each other, he turning his head to one side, she hanging her head in confusion. A priest chanted beside them. Male and female relatives enclosed the couple three times with threads, then wove the strands into two thick strings. The bridegroom tied one to the wrist of the bride with a piece of wool and turmeric stick; she did the same to him. Neither looked at each other.

The bride put her chin to her chest and a woman lifted her plait to reveal her empty neck. The bridegroom leant forward to tie the black bead necklace, the sign of a married woman. He fumbled with the knot and blushed as he touched her skin. The priest chanted the marriage vows in Sanskrit, then took their hands and placed them together round a coconut. The bride coyly looked at her husband: he lifted his head arrogantly. The elders from the bride's side poured water over their hands. Then the guests surged forward to throw red rice at the couple. One, two, three pinches straight into their faces. The bridegroom began to shed tears at such indignity, tears and sweat rolling down his cheeks. A friend wiped them away with a handkerchief and fanned his face with leaves.

A corner of his marriage shawl was tied to her sari: he hooked his little finger round hers and they turned in a circle three times before walking towards the door. Outside, they sat on a dais beneath the awning to receive their presents and blessings. Several times she looked at him with pride; he ignored her to talk with his educated friends.

S.M.B. watched the presentations, assessing their value and use. No one knew how much the dowry was that the bride's side was giving – some said four thousand, some said eight, but it was

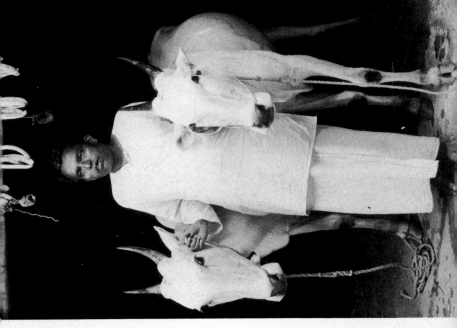

The old lady's two sons from town: S. M. Bhadre Gowda (left); Chikke Gowda on his wedding day (right)

Preparations for the wedding feast in the family house: cooked rice dr
in the baskets

probably nearer three. And the gifts themselves must have added another four hundred in cash.

'Photographs, photographs,' shouted S.M.B. and waved his hand at me. 'Bride and groom. More,' he shouted, 'more.' He pulled me in front of the benches where the high-ranking guests were seated. 'Now honourable guests and gentlemen.'

He did not think to suggest any photographs of the women, not even his own wife. She had retired to the dark of the small room and was weeping into her new silk sari.

'Are you unwell?' I asked when I joined her.

She did not answer.

'Are you unhappy with the bride?'

She said nothing.

'Something to do with the jewelry?'

'They cursed our family,' she cried. And gradually she revealed that the gold necklace presented to the bride really belonged to her, that her husband had borrowed it as only a temporary measure till they bought the bride another one when the price of gold went down.

She heard her husband's voice giving orders outside: she shrank back in the shadows. 'Why does he have to shout?' she asked.

The other women entered and flopped against the wall to try and sleep for a while. But soon they were shifted outside to eat the wedding lunch.

Manager Nanjeswamy, dressed in a new shirt, stood beside the cooks to watch the final touches; and when the food was ready, he organised the lines – men on one side, women on the other – which twisted round the house and onto the verandah. Runners spooned out the rice, the curries, the vegetables, with a quick turn of the ladle while boys sprang in between with salt and mango chutney. There was only water to drink.

S.M.B. provided the chorus.

'What, no sweets?'

'What, no millet?'

'The buttermilk's very thin.'

The bride's aunt was sitting beside me, a fine-boned woman whose sari was caught at the back of her head on steel grey hair scraped back from her face to enhance her prominent cheekbones: a silk sari in tan and turquoise, with a turquoise band round the hem.

'We've done our best,' she whispered. 'We wanted to do it well, we've never done it before.'

The bride was her favourite niece, a niece whom she loved as her daughter, since she had no daughter herself.

'See, we gave four thousand, as well as all the presents. We wanted a good husband, and a good family which had some land. And he's a well-educated boy.'

Processions and ceremonies continued throughout the afternoon as guests slowly drifted away. It was sultry, and those who stayed were lethargic, while the bridal pair were wilting. But they revived a little at a competition which determined who would become most dominant in their life as a married couple. They were seated next to each other in front of two plates half-filled with rice. The bridegroom went first, scooping as much of the rice as he could in three handfuls and dropping it on her plate. Her pile of rice was large now, but unabashed she scooped up her three handfuls and dumped them on his plate, giving him more than he'd given her. He tried again: she passed it back, adding more from her own pile. The third time she won again, so that his plate was three-quarters full and hers only a quarter full. She giggled boldly, and the onlookers moved away with disapproval.

After that, a cloth was hung from a beam, symbolising a cradle, and a stone pestle was placed within to represent a baby. She had to rock the cradle, take the baby into her arms, and hand it to her husband. He stood awkwardly, and she ran to her mother with a flutter of pink silk sari.

It was six o'clock when the bridal pair were ready to leave. They walked down the village street and stopped in front of the temple. The elders were waiting to receive their respects: the old man stood alone, proud, silent, separate. The bridegroom went to him first and touched his feet, then touched his own eyes. The old man laid his hand on his son's head and stared straight ahead. The bride ran from person to person, touching their feet three times – her uncles, her in-laws, her cousins – but she forgot the old man. He stood patiently till someone noticed and pushed the bride towards him. She bent briefly without apology; he touched her head in a tired manner, then turned and shuffled away. She ran to her parents and mournfully touched their feet.

The Virtuous Wife

S.M.B., the old man, the bride and groom climbed into the front of the lorry; the rest of us climbed on the back and waved as we left the village. The bicycle was propped against the tail-board, held steady by two of the grandsons. There had been a row about it: S.M.B. had wanted to leave it behind, for a bicycle was not worth the bother, a scooter was what was needed as part of a proper dowry, but the old lady said it would give too much insult, and in the end she won.

When we reached Palahalli, the bridal pair paused at the stone of justice, paid their respects at the shrine, then walked up the street to the house. The moment we entered, the old lady ordered the women to clean and sweep and prepare the evening meal. She herself took the bride to the storeroom to rest.

The plans for the bride were vague. She would probably spend a few days in Palahalli getting to know her in-laws, then she would move to the town to learn from Eramma the duties of wife, cook, sister-in-law. Nobody knew whether she was destined for work in the fields as the newest daughter-in-law of the old lady, or for life in the town with Eramma. So much depended on the work her husband could find. But she did know that during the next few weeks, she would not talk to her husband unless he spoke to her first, and that at night she would sleep with the women: the nuptials were planned for three months' time, when the marriage would be consummated.

The bride grew bored with resting under the watch of the old lady and without permission she skipped into the ante-room of the kitchen where Thayee and I were grinding chutney. She wanted to show us her jewelry: two rings from a favourite uncle, a gold nose-stud from her father, a beautiful thick gold clip from her mother to hold her hair in place. Yes, her family had spent more than ten thousand rupees on the wedding. It was a lot to spend on a bridegroom. She did not say whether she thought it was worth it. Nor did she show us the jewelry which S.M.B. had presented.

The bride was called Bhagyamma, like one of Thayee's daughters, but this provided no solace. Everything seemed so strange, she said: the house, the people, the names. It was hard being a girl, you were torn from your parents on marriage, not like a man who merely went back to his family. She'd been so

145

happy at home, she'd played with her friends all day, and her family had never scolded. She'd helped a bit in the house, swept a bit and things, but she'd never worked in the fields.

Thayee was unimpressed. 'Whether she worked or not,' she said to the room in general, 'she'll have to help us now.'

Bhagyamma looked surprised. 'Oh I'll help,' she answered. 'I can grate coconut and wash vessels and . . .'

'You'll have to do more than that,' said Thayee.

The bridegroom stood hesitantly at the door, staring at his bride. She noticed him with a start and as he entered to sit beside her, she stood up and rushed from the room.

'She's very shy,' I said.

'She's very simple,' he said.

He invited Vara and me to sit in the hall with him, almost as though to prove that we had a special alliance because of our education. He was careful to use – incorrectly – English words in his speech, and seemed anxious to have our approval. It was only sad that no one else was about: interest in the bridegroom had waned and tiredness had taken over. He wanted to know what we thought of the bride and was surprised when we said we liked her. He said he was disappointed. He had seen her only once before, and marriage had not improved his opinion. She was ignorant and ugly, for she had no education and her skin was very dark. Besides, the family had given no dowry, at least nothing much to speak of. But what could he do? He had to accept what his family had chosen if he was to get their support in the future. A man wasn't helped by society if he married the woman of his own selection. If only his family had chosen a girl with some education.

"See, these village women, they have no thinking capacity," he explained. "You can't leave them to do anything. They need guidance and help from us. And yet if I had a wife from the town, how would she manage? She'd find it difficult in the village. No encouragement."

Chikke Gowda was tall, a head taller than Manager Nanjeswamy, and handsome with his elegant hairstyle and drainpipe trousers which he'd changed for the village shorts.

"There are many superstitions here," he said, "and when I come here, I have to go along with them. If I use my ways here it won't hold. See, if I wear trousers and walk around they'll say,

146

'Oh, he's a stylish fellow, he just keeps loafing about, he can't do any work.' Because of this I do whatever they do."

Not that he liked village work nor was he very competent, I noticed: his legs were too frail, his body lacked muscle, his experience was more theoretical. Even a sack of chaff he could barely lift without spilling. He wanted to work in the city, because of his education – nearly pre-university level, he claimed, although he had failed in English. He liked to show off his English to the family, who had no idea of the meaning. Yes, he wanted a proper job in private enterprise or perhaps a government appointment. He'd been looking for two years but nothing had really come up. 'Unemployment problem. Indian unemployment problem,' he reiterated. Why should he want a janitor's job or some such similar work? He'd wait till he got something better.

"Till then, I'll stay near home, and have two good meals every day. First class meals. I could do what work I can at home."

He felt he should manage the fields, that he was better qualified than his brothers in the village. He could read and write, he could keep accounts of labourers and work: it was like company management. He wanted to grow grapes and sapota and hundreds of coconut trees, but his brothers wouldn't let him. They felt that with his education he shouldn't be working the land.

In many ways, Chikke Gowda was like his eldest brother, S.M.B.: his urban mannerisms, his expectations, his feeling of superiority because of his education. And yet one thing was different: S.M.B. made a contribution to the family's survival through advice and contacts and earning his own salary. But Chikke was only a burden: his potential productivity, whether in town or village, was wasted, and he took from the family without giving. His brothers knew it, and resented it, but tolerated it nonetheless. A family supported its members.

There were more ceremonies in the next few days including visits to relatives and to the temple: not least was the feast given by S.M.B., to honour the bride's family. Hired cooks and servants dressed in khaki uniform came from Sundrapura to prepare the food – no meagre menu, but meat, and millet, and salad, and sweets, and rice, and curries, and very thick buttermilk. The guests were greeted with rose-water sprinkled from chrome holders; they were presented with flowers and betel leaves and tiny packets of betel nut which could have come only from the town; and their hands were smeared with expensive coconut oil to spread on their hair.

S.M.B. commanded the operation: he ordered the sweating men to hurry with baskets of rice; he shouted at his brothers to serve the food at once; he cursed the women, the children, the dogs, for getting in the way; but when it was all over he considered it a triumph. So many big men had come – the lawyer, the banker, and the President of his Society. Yes, the President himself had come this time. His only complaint was of the bride: she answered too quickly, she answered too boldly, the family would need to control her.

When all the guests had left and all the villagers had been fed as they came in off the fields, S.M.B. sat down to eat himself. He chewed the meat and sucked at the bones; he licked his fingers and squashed his rice with curry; he called for more of everything and belched with satisfaction.

Two days later, S.M.B., his wife, the bridegroom, and the bride, left the village for Sundrapura. The house returned to normal and the family resumed its chores. But at least now each person had something new to talk about.

The marriage of Bhagyamma and Chikke Gowda challenged my own beliefs that a man and woman should live in mutual respect while pursuing the role they wish individually, supported by the other. But then I tend to confuse the function of love with marriage, thus limiting both states. For Bhagyamma and Chikke Gowda, love had nothing to do with their partnership – and I'm afraid I forgot to ask what they felt was the purpose of marriage, for I was more intent on discovering their attitudes to each other. Probably for them, marriage was something to which there was no alternative, and so they never questioned it as an institution: it brought children, it brought security, and some kind of welcome conformity, all vital elements when struggling to survive.

In the West, perhaps we have cloaked marriage in a veil of romantic and sexual love, forgetting that status and economics and fulfilling mutual ambitions are just as much a part of it. But at least, if we choose, there is time to love, whether inside or outside

148

marriage. For the family in Palahalli, there was neither time nor energy. For them, 'love' as a word was rare: they 'loved' the land like a mother, they 'liked' certain foods, they 'wanted' material objects. Even feeling itself was rarely expressed in words, except when they got angry. It was true that their emotions jumped about like quick-silver, but it was perhaps the muting of self-expression and the repression of any emotion which induced such chaotic imbalance, rather than the strength of emotion itself.

The word 'love' was used as one of the wifely duties, but it meant more duty and obedience. This, I suppose, could be part of love, but it depends on your definition. If giving, respect, discipline, and patience are other aspects, then the women knew something of love. Or did they? Such qualities were enforced on them, not pursued voluntarily, as part of an ideal. And the qualities were suspect anyway: the giving did not invoke much receiving; the respect was largely indoctrination; the discipline was not self-imposed and certainly not enjoyable. And where there was some responsibility, awareness, and tender caring, however small, it was mainly confined to parent and child.

Of all the wives in the house, Susheelamma had seemed to me the most perfect. She was meek, obedient, passive, she never cursed or lost her temper, she was patient with all the children – I found her a little dull. I don't know how well she worked when she wasn't pregnant, but it probably didn't matter, since she'd married Manager Nanjeswamy. She also had a sexual languor which seemed to attract her husband and, besides, she'd borne him children, and through their marriage allied him to the patel.

Life should have been good for Susheelamma, but something seemed to be stressing her, for she was often surly and uncooperative. We were sitting late one evening in the room where the women slept – just she, Vara, and I. The room was small, seven by fifteen feet, which meant a crush when four women and six children stretched out at night. Vara and I had also moved in to sleep there. It was dark even in daylight, a closed, private place where secrets were kept and men excluded. Not that it had any glamour with its mud walls and bare floor and saris hanging like skeletons from a rope stretched across the roof. Four metal trunks, bolted and locked, held the private possessions of each wife: a comb, a mirror, red *kunkuma* powder, the monthly ration of ghee given out by the old lady, a bangle in glass or plastic, silver anklets, a pair of earrings. Susheelamma had also locked away her silver belt since it no longer fitted her pregnant stomach, a stomach which was swollen like a large balloon draped thinly with khaki material.

Her two children were asleep beside her. She loosened her blouse round her breasts and rubbed the base of her neck as she stretched her shoulders back: she had often been shy with me, but tonight she seemed more at ease.

One more son. If only God would give her a son this time, she needn't have any more. It made her so anaemic, it made her suffer so much, the pain, the tiredness, the work she had to keep doing if only for others' sake. If she got a son, she'd have the operation to stop more children.

"And your Gowda agrees?" I asked.

"Of course he'll agree," she said. "Why shouldn't he? See, in this house they treat the women well."

"But you haven't asked him yet?"

"No, I haven't spoken to him. But if I tell him, 'We don't want any more children,' he'll listen to me. So far we haven't talked about preventing or having more children."

"And he respects your wishes of course?"

"Three children are enough. If we don't have another son, our one son will have everything to himself. He won't have to share anything. We have one son, don't we? That's enough. He says there should be another son. Instead, we'll bring up the girls well. Educate them a little. And get them well married. Oh he'll listen. Aren't we seeing the doctor soon?"

She turned her head to gaze out of the bedroom door, and the light of a small oil lamp flickered across her face. Her pupils were strained to one corner to leave her eyes bulging and white; small beads of sweat clung to the downy hairs clustering her upper lip.

Nanjeswamy stood in the doorway. Susheelamma bent her head. 'Do you have time to talk?' he asked.

She did not answer.

He watched us for a moment, then turned and walked away.

Susheelamma had always had difficult pregnancies. At first, after marriage, she tried to get pregnant, and then she had stopped her periods. But it had not meant a child.

"I became so pale, there was no blood. There was no other sickness, just no blood. My whole body used to become pale all over. Wherever you looked, there wasn't a single drop of blood. Yes, to this day, it's the same. But the children are born quite healthy. 'Only you are so weak,' the doctors say. It must have been a shock, I must have had a fright. There was no other disease."

She went to consult with the doctors, and her husband spent hundreds of rupees. Then she went to the medium. For twelve days she walked to his village, six miles there and six miles back, taking fresh milk every day as offering to the god. The last day she came back, when she was walking home, she started her bleeding right on the way itself. After that, she visited him every week, and then once a month. After six months, she was pregnant, and now she had two children. Now, also, she wished for no more after this was delivered.

Nanjeswamy harnessed the oxen and padded the cart with straw, then rolled out a mat as covering. Susheelamma, Vara, and I climbed up, while he straddled the shaft and flexed his whip across the oxen's back. The cart lurched forward, its wheels crunching the sand, huge wheels taller than a man, rolling us backwards and forwards. We were going to Krishnapatna to see the doctor at last.

'Ayaagh!' shouted Nanjeswamy till the oxen pulled into a trot and the wheels clattered and shuddered; he urged the animals on faster, waving his whip and shouting. We went over a stone and the whole cart bounced: Susheelamma gasped, and clutching my arm dug in her nails deeply.

'Hey, slowly,' I shouted. Nanjeswamy turned round in surprise. 'You must take care,' I told him.

He looked hurt. 'Don't I always take care?' he asked, then turned to look at his wife. 'Eh, Susheela, what god do you worship that you have such a good husband?'

'I worship all the gods,' she said with her head bent.

'And what do you wish for in life?'

'I wish for nothing,' she said.

He laughed with satisfaction. 'It's easier to trace the footprints of a fish in the ocean than it is to know a woman's mind,' he boasted, in the certain knowledge that he knew his wife's mind.

His own mind was far harder to trace with its rising and falling moods, its need to assert, its sulkiness at neglect. It was almost as though he were schizophrenic so swiftly did he change and so eager was he for support of all his actions. He seemed to fear condemnation and tried to avoid any criticism: with a sudden display of generosity he would order a special meal for us, or pick us a fresh coconut. Didn't he treat us with kindness, ensuring we were happy, ensuring we were fed, that his guests were properly cared for? That was the sign of a good man, to offer hospitality.

Nanjeswamy talked continuously as the cart ambled along: he had eased the oxen into a walk, dropped the reins on the crossbar, and swung himself round to face us. But he said nothing new. It was the same old story of how he had made the family grow, how the well was the wonder of the district, how the debts were nothing and would soon be cleared under his able management. Yes, he was the one who could manage, he was the one who was honest. The others had no responsibility, they couldn't be trusted to handle money. What would they do without him?

I felt a sense of frustration that I'd got no further in understanding the men and the problems of division. Their talk was meant to impress and presumably to mislead: I knew Manager Nanjeswamy would never speak openly with me, and I rarely had the chance to speak with the other brothers. They, too, were guarded, unsure of the situation, and since I was only a woman there was no possibility of sharing secrets or confiding in each other. I had questioned and questioned Nanjeswamy, but however I phrased my words or concealed my intention, he was always ready with a skilful circumlocution. Perhaps Tony, my husband, would do better when he came to film in the village: as men they might talk together, just as I had talked with the women.

I felt anxious about Tony's arrival, at the thought of the family confronting a film unit. I wanted to share with him the feelings I had for the family, but professionally there was conflict: I had become so involved with the family that I wanted to write their story, yet I still had specific research to do for the film, on fertility and family planning.

Susheelamma stayed silent throughout the journey though sometimes she moaned with pain at the roughness of the road: she clenched the side of the cart and wedged herself against me.

But I loved the journey, its bumpiness and discomfort, for I had a feeling of freedom to be moving away from the village. Perhaps the men felt it also whenever they took the cart with some goods to sell at market, even as far as Mysore. There was a sense of space and luxury, of time to consider the world, and a mesmerising motion as the oxen pulled and the wheels turned and turned. It was a slow, idle movement, and it took longer to reach Krishnapatna than if we had gone on foot.

Susheelamma smiled with relief when at last we came to the hospital: it was a squat concrete block with its entrance doors open wide to show a patient consulting the doctor, while three others sat nearby. We took our places in the queue, and the doctor nodded curtly. It was a small hospital run on charitable funds subsidised by the government, with one doctor, one nurse midwife, and two helpers, serving a region of ten thousand people. There were five rooms and a total lack of privacy: two wooden cots without linen were used in emergencies till an ambulance could remove the casualty.

'Yes?' said the doctor when it came to our turn.

Nanjeswamy walked forward.

'I've brought my wife. She's very weak.'

He waved Susheelamma towards him: she stood by his chair while he took her pulse and asked her to stick out her tongue.

'Go to the other room,' he said, and called the nurse to take her. 'Anaemia,' he said. 'They all have anaemia.' His face was gaunt with narrow eyes set tightly against his nose.

I sat in the patient's chair.

He raised an eyebrow.

I explained about the film project.

'Would you tell me about the villagers?' I asked. 'What sort of illness they have?'

His answer was very direct.

"Mainly anaemia. Secondly, coughs and colds. Then laryngitis –that's flu. But mainly worms and anaemia. They don't know what they have – they just say they feel weak, they feel very tired, that they're unsteady on their legs. But they only come when it's really bad, when they can't stand the pain. See, these villagers come for three days expecting a miracle cure and if they haven't been cured by then they think the doctor's no good. Suppose they have

153

typhoid, they have to have injections which cost ten rupees. But they want to be cured for only two rupees. Of course they're not cured. How can you cure in a day? And they never spend any money. They say they'll pay and take the medicines, but as they never pay, how can I give the medicines?"

He spoke with bitterness: his annual budget of free medicine was only three thousand rupees and that was enough to last him barely two months.

"For a simple wound I ought to give two anti-tetanus injections and one antibiotic," he explained. "But how many do I have? Twenty ampoules a year. How many injury cases are there? Twelve to twenty a day. Even for a blood test the results take three months, or else a patient must go himself to Mysore or Bangalore; but is that possible for such poor people?"

He stood up and walked into the examining room where Susheelamma was lying; a nurse was also there, so we waited in the adjoining room from where we could hear their voices. There was silence, then a soft moan from Susheelamma.

'Two weeks,' said the doctor. 'Do you have any pains?'

Susheelamma hesitated. 'Feel weak,' she said.

'Yes, yes. Anything else?'

'It's so hard to have children,' she whispered. 'I wanted to stop . . .'

'I'll give you some tonic. I'll give the prescription to your husband. Take it twice each day.'

He walked out of the room without further discussion.

Susheelamma joined us on the bare wooden bed: she leant against my shoulder and tears slowly trickled down her cheek. Then she began to sob. I put my arm round her shoulder.

The midwife came in, for she had sensed Susheelamma's unhappiness: she bent over her trying to comfort, talking of easy deliveries, of healthy babies, saying there was nothing to fear. But the doctor called brusquely, demanding her assistance, and she hurried out to help him.

"I tried to talk to my Gowda about the operation," said Susheel-amma quietly. "But what can I do with so many people about? It's not for me to decide. Everyone else decides these things. And the people in our village are always saying to him, 'Your wife's a tight-bellied woman, she can't bear children easily, she can't work or anything. Look at her, every three or four days she lies down. Just think how strong she'll be if you get her to have that operation! Think what work she'll do after that! Oh yes, that's what she should have.' And so he gets frightened."

And yet Susheelamma did not criticise her husband. How could she? She was fed, clothed, released of worry, given light work in the fields, and if she had any problem, with the children, the house, even the old lady, she could go to her husband with it. It was the men in the family who complained against him constantly.

"They say he doesn't work," she whispered, "that he hangs around and goes from village to village, without working, without taking care of the money. They even say he keeps much of the money himself."

Susheelamma wasn't sure of the truth of such accusations – she played no part in these things. But she did know, and repeated it, that her husband Manager Nanjeswamy was the reason the men spoke of division.

"He causes many fights, and all the brothers are bitter," she said.

But *why* should he have such power? She did not know. Then *why* didn't all the brothers refuse to do what he said? Again, she did not know. And before I could further pursue her startling admission, the nurse interrupted: Manager Nanjeswamy had ordered his wife to rest while Vara and I went to the market with him.

The weekly market in Krishnapatna with its noise and gossip and cosiness attracted hundreds of people from outlying villages: they came to buy, to sell, to gather news and see the world. There were no stalls, only the soft hues and textures of bouldered rock, the faded sari, the grey trunks of trees. It was set on the edge of the town, beyond the municipal boundary – an arena of earth worn bare, its cracked surface submerging with beige beneath a coating of grey. Goods were set out everywhere, the monopoly held by traders of different castes who had come by bus for the day with their spices and trinkets and metal pots. Prices were very high.

Above the market, almost vertically, stood the hill temple, quietly commanding, quietly ignored, part of the Indian landscape. A distant bell and trumpet marked a pilgrim's procession, but the intermittent ringing sank unnoticed in the hubbub of the market, enclosed as it was from space by a ceiling of trees and the bouldered hillside.

Nanjeswamy walked from trader to trader, comparing prices and goods: he carried a new cloth bag striped in brown and orange, an improvement to him on the basket since it cost more and held less and could be slung on a strong shoulder instead of the village head. He bargained hard for every item, insisted on paper wrapping, then tossed it into his bag: turmeric, salt, pepper, cummin.

The market was mainly for men, since they were the ones who went shopping. But the division was not immutable. If a man was weak or short of labour, his wife would go to market, carrying fuel and curds to earn a bit more cash. The village women came barefoot in twos and threes, lithely gliding in similar saris, bearing their heavy baskets. Most were more erect than the men, men who bent their backs in ploughing; and many were taller, perhaps favoured at crucial times of puberty and pregnancy by special foods and rest. They wandered the lines of goods, then squatted to unfold their treasures: an egg, green herbs, a handful of shrivelled onions, unripe tomatoes. They waited for custom, scratching their heads, staring ahead, chewing their betel nut.

Susheelamma never went to the market now, nor did she ask to go.

That evening, Susheelamma turned castor oil seeds over an open fire. The flames lit up her face and wet hair, for she had had a bath while the family was out of the house. Thayee came to help and they piled the roasted beans into the pounding hole. They stood facing each other like statues, left foot forward, right arm holding on high a wooden pole. Thayee let hers drop, slipping it through her fingers. Thud. She pulled it up with her left hand as Susheelamma let hers drop. Trrumm. Thayee slipped hers loose again, bending her body forward, thud. Trrumm, thud, trrumm ... trrumm. Thayee lost her rhythm and waited a turn before slotting her pole in the pounding hole. The beans crunched, cracked, diminished, swelled over the sides as the poles plunged down unremittingly. Susheelamma's foot kept swishing them back in time with the beating motion.

156

The Virtuous Wife

Thayee's eldest daughter peered into the crushed mess and darted her finger between the poles. Both women cursed, and Thayee told her to take the pole herself. The child found it heavy, but begging a slower beat and using both hands she managed to work with Susheelamma; then she missed her cue, and the pole floundered into the beans, scattering them over the floor. She looked at her aunt with fear, in expectation of beating, but she was only motioned to sweep up the beans.

Susheelamma's son screamed suddenly. Nanjeswamy was whipping him across the back with a switch, for the boy had ripped off some buttons in trying to remove his shirt. The boy screamed more, but the whipping did not stop.

Susheelamma turned her head to watch, her eyes staring, her mouth shut. She continued to pound mechanically.

'It's the only way to teach them,' said Nanjeswamy with anger.

Susheelamma did not move.

The old lady sidled out of the kitchen, grabbed the switch from his hand, and threw it away in the cattle area. Nanjeswamy laughed. The boy ran to his mother and buried his face in her skirts. She did not try to comfort him, for she knew her husband was watching; but she did not push him away. She pounded with greater intensity.

Nanjeswamy talked of his wife at a much later stage, but I feel it appropriate to include it here. He himself had decided that Susheelamma should be his bride.

"Do you know how many people wanted to give me their daughter? There were so many who said, 'I'll give you my daughter, I'll give you my daughter.' They even said they would write their property in my name, but I said I didn't want anything. I have my body, I can earn something. They even wanted to adopt me, in one house, but I didn't want it.

"Susheelamma's parents used to live well. They were even better than us. I'm not talking about now. They commanded great respect. And they have a lot of property. My mother said we should get the girl from their family. I said, 'Alright, if you want it, I'll marry her.' And I got married. See, my parents had looked in two or three places but my mind wasn't on them. I said I didn't want those ones at all. If the girl is good-looking, it's nice, the house will also be nice. But if you bring an ugly stupid one, the house will also become ugly and stupid. If you don't desire her, then you start thinking, 'What's the use of a wife?' Then you start going to other women."

Bhadramma, the old man's only daughter

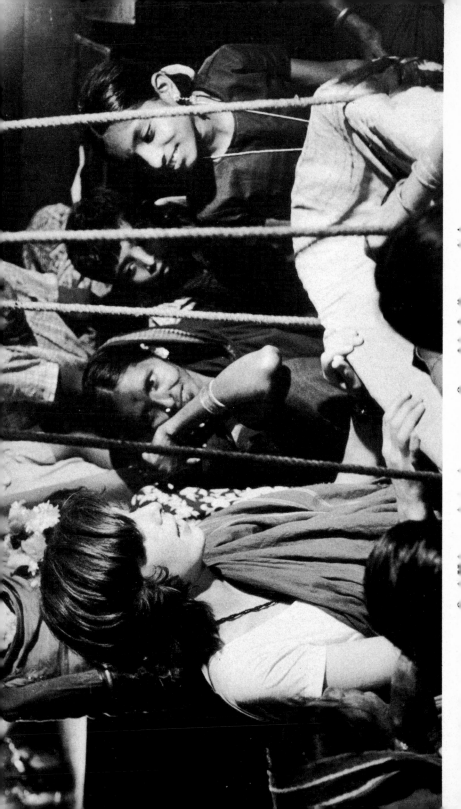

9 *Film Unit*

The film unit arrived. All seven of them – two English, including my husband Tony, one Canadian, one Bengali, a Sikh, and two other Indians. They came with a car and driver, their equipment packed in a long-based Land-Rover: trunks of film and cameras, cases of clothes, tape-recorders, cassettes, a guitar, crates of drink . . . they said they were travelling light, and installed themselves, two to a room, in the Travellers' Bungalows in Krishnapatna. It took all afternoon.

I was thrilled to see Tony, but openly suspicious of what the filming might mean. I felt very torn: I wanted to stay with the family, to demonstrate that they were the most important; and yet the company of the film unit was a seductive alternative – to laugh and talk and eat, to communicate without effort, to understand the nuances of a gesture or grimace without having to question my own responses. I didn't go to the village for two days.

Within that time, Tony read the notes I'd prepared and was talking of what would be good to film. He wanted to see the village and to meet the family so he could find a story. I felt possessive and said the unit should visit in stages, first Tony as director, then three more, and finally all seven. It seemed cumbersome and intrusive, and I frequently made suggestions: not to drive both cars down to the village, not to film the women first, not to change clothes too often, not to give cash as part of the transaction. Nobody listened: the whole unit went down together in two vehicles. But the family was not distressed – Manager Nanjeswamy was even proud of organising the filming of his family. He strutted about arranging this and that; he smoked English cigarettes; he saw himself as a hero. He thought it was for the cinema: he had never heard of television.

'Of course,' he said, 'I can arrange anything.' He ordered the potter to take a tile from the roof to let in light for filming and stood waiting in the shaft of sunlight for the camera to point

159

towards him. The family, the neighbours, the patel, watched warily from the distance while the women continued to work.

'Bring coffee,' he ordered the eldest grandson. 'Enough for all the film people. Susheelamma, eh, Susheelamma, wash out the glasses for our guests.' The camera turned to watch her wash, and Nanjeswamy turned also. 'Why do that? She's only doing her duty – what's there of interest?'

He wanted to look through the camera; he wanted to test the microphones; he insisted that every word which he spoke was played back on the recorder. How much was it, the camera and the equipment? Thirty thousand rupees? That was more than the whole well including the cost of the pumpset. How much was the Land-Rover? Enough for a new tractor? The crew had nice shirts too, with smart cut trousers and heavy boots and big boxes of cigarettes. But who were they? They must have seemed odd to the family. Two had beards and bared their chests while another was tall like a giant; three said they were Indian, but they must have seemed equally foreign, with different language and different religion. Only the male interpreter, a Lingayat, came from a village himself and now had a salaried job, working in a government office in Health and Family Planning. He could speak their language, and was able to tell them everything.

The second day the camera filmed Susheelamma sifting the flour, scrubbing the vessels, milking the cows and buffalo. She did her *rangoli* patterns with powdered chalk on the doorstep but Tony made her move to the street for better light and a wider angle. All the neighbours watched and whispered, and when Jayamma strolled past with curiosity he asked her to nod to Susheelamma; when she giggled, he made her do it again. Manager Nanjeswamy told him not to bother: he said she was only a granddaughter, not living with the family.

The third day, the unit filmed Susheelamma collecting water, sweeping the house, drinking a tumbler of coffee. The old lady was respectfully quiet, keeping the children in control and tying their hair with ribbons. The women never looked up, they never looked at the unit, but they wore identical new orange blouses with quiet satisfaction.

The film unit paid a lot of attention to Jayamma, perhaps because of my interest, but also because of her story and the tragic

160

loss of children. They asked her to draw water in pots from the pool near her fields and to heave them up the rock face while her husband watered the plants. She didn't dare refuse, and he did not object. It was later they learnt that this was the only job she never did when pregnant, as her husband fully recognised its dangers.

The family thought the film was the story of their lives, a story of success, of power and achievement. S.M.B. came from the town for a filming session to instruct and advise his brothers: one cleared the land and levelled it, heaving an iron plate through rough lumpy soil, calling his oxen with tenderness; another lifted water by hand to irrigate the onions; another knocked down a coconut. The old lady scared off the birds by banging a tin with relish, and the old man pointed out in her presence the place of his second wife's grave. The other women continued their duties. Manager Nanjeswamy pressed the pumpset button and watched the water surge into the sugar-cane. Yes, he'd organise some cutting and planting when all the family would help: the film unit must film it so that people in England would know how well they managed their fields.

Yes, he understood, the film was to show a big family: in England they didn't have big families, and the children didn't help their parents when they grew old but left them to die alone. It was better here in India: children learnt to respect their parents. A big family was good. He'd organise the whole family to harvest the groundnuts together: the children could come, the men, the women, the labourers. It wasn't much of a crop since part was lost through drought, but all the family would come, including the pregnant women. He understood the film unit's interest in children; he understood instinctively the major theme of fertility.

He was right. Tony had been asked by Oxfam and the BBC to make a documentary film showing Indian village attitudes to children and contraception. Official reports in Delhi had revealed that, despite the millions spent by Indian and international sources, the government family planning campaigns of the last two decades had failed to reach their high targets. It was nothing peculiar to India, as the World Population Conference in Bucharest quickly showed. But India's vast population of more than six hundred million, coupled with low per capita income, made the problem critical.

We wanted to find out why the campaigns had failed, not from any official point of view, but at the village level. What did a villager feel about children, what affected his decisions – if any – on family size, what pressures and methods made him accept contraception?

There was much controversy in Delhi. Some said that resistance to contraception was natural to rural families and that sterilisation should be enforced in order to solve the problem; others claimed that the family planning message was so urban it bore little relation to the needs and understanding of the rural poor, for whom larger families offered some security; yet others stated that the promotion of contraception in isolation did not much affect fertility levels: contraception should be part of a wider programme of health, education, child care, the emancipation of women, and the improvement of living standards, since people with higher incomes tended towards smaller families.

With Manje Gowda's family, I hadn't reached any conclusions on their feelings towards family planning – there were still major gaps in my information, on sex, contraception, decision-making, and social pressures. Tony therefore decided that in order to examine their attitudes and actions, he would trace their history from the marriage of the old man to the impending birth of Susheelamma's baby. With luck, the women would reveal their thoughts to me, and the men would talk to Tony.

The film unit soon had problems. Manager Nanjeswamy did not understand the technical demands of filming: the repetition of action, the cumbersome equipment, the need for silence from all but those being filmed. He began to grow petulant and to foul arrangements, so that every day when the film unit came to the village, some drama or change of plan meant waiting for several hours. Waiting cost money, on wages, schedules, equipment, and money was tight and precious since half the budget came from a charitable fund. The unit could have manipulated the family, commanding sequences to suit a story, but that wasn't the point of the film: they wanted natural events, for which they would have to wait. At first they waited patiently, but then with increasing impatience. The working conditions didn't help, with the heat and inaccessibility of some of the locations. There was no electric current for lamps, only silver boards for reflecting light whenever they worked inside; and the sound could only be synchronised when the camera was muffled by blankets. It was very unprofessional, and the tension was further heightened by the mixture of nationalities, of technically skilled Western union-men and emotional Indian vegetarians.

Nanjeswamy was constantly asking for gifts for himself and refusing to help with arrangements. One morning he wasn't around and nobody knew where he was; no one was in the fields and the only person at home was his wife, Susheelamma. She was cooking a meal in the kitchen, and the unit decided to film her. Four men crammed themselves into the tiny room with a camera on its tripod and a large directioned microphone.

'Tell her to lean forward over the flames of the fire,' shouted the Sikh cameraman in rapid Hindi. The sun had come out briefly between thick clouds and he wanted to capture the extra light which filtered into the kitchen. He cursed as it disappeared and told her to stoke up the fire. 'Put them on, put them on,' he said, pointing to the sticks, but she could not understand. He leant down and thrust them in himself, almost touching her shoulder. She drew back quickly.

'Lean forward, lean forward,' he shouted.

The Canadian soundman was irritated for how could he record with so much noise? He was in a bad way generally: his equipment was jolted every day to and from the village, and he himself had been ill from Indian food. Instead, he sustained his high-protein diet with jars of peanut butter, hardboiled eggs, an occasional tin of spam. And in the evenings he consoled himself by playing his guitar.

I was also angry. I felt the unit was trespassing in quarters where men didn't go – certainly not strangers. How could they trample about like that, and treat Susheelamma like an object? But Susheelamma seemed unmoved. She was stirring the millet with a fat wooden pole, driving the sticky substance round until it was properly mixed. She stood up to get some water.

'Tell her to sit down,' said the cameraman.

'Shut up,' hissed the soundman.

Someone outside turned on the radio full blast.

'Cut,' said Tony with resignation.

Manager Nanjeswamy entered the kitchen.

'Who said you could film my wife?' he asked.

'You said we could film the sugar-cane planting, so we came at nine o'clock,' said Tony.

'I had to stay in Sundrapura. I had urgent business there.'

'So we filmed the house instead.'

'You can film outside the kitchen.'

'There's nothing to film, there's no one about.'

'You can film the cattle and chickens.'

'And what about the sugar-cane?'

He shrugged. 'You can't do it today. Maybe tomorrow. Come at nine o'clock.'

'And then you'll be somewhere else.'

'Who can say? A manager can't do everything.'

'So what can we film today? What are the family doing?'

'They're busy. Each man is working in separate parts of the land.'

After much discussion, the film unit called it a day; and in order to avoid further confrontation, they stayed away for another day: when they returned to the village, Nanjeswamy was not about. Instead they took Jayamma to the medium.

'Everyone goes so I go too,' was all she could say of his powers. But still she went once a month whenever she was pregnant.

She was thrilled to go by car; it was six or seven miles, a long walk for a pregnant woman under the burning sun. It was a lonely road, winding over the countryside through rocky land and distant villages. Once from the top of a hill we could see a huge lake stretched out before us; the plain beyond was blue, sinking into a haze of swirling, watery mirage. She often walked it alone, for though she could go by bus from one of the neighbouring villages, she never had any money.

The medium's house emblazoned itself in the village with its green and scarlet façade, its ornate pillars and silver door, and groups of people outside. Inside, the crowd murmured expectantly for soon he was to begin. About fifty women were sitting in lines cross-legged, and others pushed in behind to pack the tiny room. The men stood on the opposite side, chatting and smoking, generally less concerned. Up on the stage in front, the medium was completing his ritual prayer: he was half-concealed by a wire cage whose sides were entwined with plastic flowers, spangly mirrors, layers of cowries attached to scarlet ribbon, and silver paper wrapped into weird shapes. This was the home of the god, the inner sanctuary, the place from which miracles moved. The god itself was laden with garlands of flowers, and paper lace wrapped its body in layers.

The medium came out of the cage with an armful of flowers and threw them into the crowd while the women moaned and held out their hands for more; but he forced a gangway between them and beckoned the film unit forward. He bowed and grinned, and made Tony sit in the chair of honour; then he silenced the crowd with a raised arm and placed garlands round each of the film unit's necks. He grinned again, a calculating grin, and told them it would be a great honour for him to be filmed by them. He was a skinny sallow man with rubbery limbs and hair shaved back to the crown of his head to fall to his shoulders in greasy strands; his face was deeply lined, his fingers were bony like claws.

He seemed nervous and glanced at his watch. Still ten minutes to go. He checked the film unit's progress. Yes, they would be ready in time. He turned on the lights – strings of coloured bulbs flashing along the wall – and lit a bunch of burning sticks whose scented smoke wafted over the women. Then he whispered to one particular man: he stared at the unit intently, nodded, craned forward, nodded again, and looked down at his watch. Two o'clock exactly. Time for the trance to begin – from two till five each Friday.

A trumpet started, sounding like a wail: the film unit turned on the spotlights. The medium stood like a weight-lifter with a flat iron bar against his chest – it held eight cups of burning oil whose flickering firebrands rose to his face. He jerked his head forward as though pretending to eat them. The crowd quietened. The cameraman moved closer. The medium plunged the point of the bar deep into his stomach: there was hardly a mark to be seen. The crowd muttered. He began to twirl, swinging the bar round with him into a circle of flame. He stopped, abruptly, handed the bar to a friend, and dropped to the ground in agony, moaning with ecstasy. The trumpet stopped; the god had entered his body.

He lay motionless in foetal position. The crowd moaned in

sympathy and tossed their flowers across the room; some hurried to the platform to lay their garlands across his back until his body was covered. The camera followed their movements. Everyone waited, tense. They waited at least three minutes, but nothing happened, no one spoke. The god seemed silent today. Had he no oracle for those who had come so far?

'There is a woman in blue,' said a deep voice from the medium, his mouth buried in his wrists. The god at last was speaking. 'She has come from that direction.' He lifted one arm and pointed behind him. 'Her name is Ratna.'

The crowd looked round to see if he spoke the truth. Shyly, but with happiness, a woman stood up and pushed her way to the front. The women she passed touched her sari and shouted at her to tell her story, to ask the god for his help. She climbed onto the platform and walked round the flower-covered figure. A drum began to beat.

'I've had four children,' she chanted, caught in the mystical aura. 'One has died, and now I am pregnant again.'

'There will be no trouble for you,' said the medium with the voice of god. 'You must come every month and make your offering here. Then you will have no trouble.'

The woman nodded and continued slowly to circle the body. The cameraman tracked round behind her.

'Will I have many children? The one who died was a boy. There's only one boy left.'

'If a woman is honest and makes offerings to god, then she'll have no trouble. A woman can bear four, five, six sons, and not have any trouble.'

'I have four sons,' called a woman from the crowd. But the others quickly silenced her in case she should disturb the god by speaking out of turn.

The god was silent again and the woman resumed her place. It was silent for nearly ten minutes. The film unit changed their position, swinging the floodlight onto the crowd to film the expectant faces.

The voice of god called out again. The film unit turned back to the stage, trailing their wires and equipment. A light fused, and the cameraman cursed. His assistant was sent to find the fault: he pushed his way through the crowd, stepping over the women and children.

'A woman who's come very far,' the voice of god was calling. 'Her name begins Be . . .'

Two women stood up.

'She wears a green sari.'

The woman came forward.

'I've been married five years,' she said, clasping her hands together. 'See, I've had no children. Please help. What can I do to get one?'

'You will have to wait many years,' came the deep reply. 'But one will come. It will be hard. It is hard for a woman to bear so late, but you must remember god. You must come to make offerings.' There was a pause. 'And your husband will get angry.'

She nodded vigorously. Tears came to her eyes. 'What must I do for him?'

'Tell him the god has decided that when he grows old, the joy of youth will be his through young children.'

Again the god was silent. This time the unit turned to film Jayamma. She was standing near a pillar, her hands clenched together in front of her pregnant stomach. As the light swung over her face, she blinked, but remained impassive. The crowd muttered with hostility, recognising some link between her and those with the cameras. She showed no emotion.

The medium called two more women forward and, after a long pause, he pointed to a man.

'He must come forward.'

The man looked startled, but those around pushed him forward. He stood staring down at the medium.

'Walk round, walk round,' shouted everyone in the crowd.

He walked unsteadily, hesitating over each step.

'Speak,' commanded the voice from the ground.

'I . . . I . . . there's . . .' he began.

'You have some troubles. The god knows. You have to tell the god.'

'It's . . . there aren't any children. See, my wife hasn't borne any children.'

'Where is your wife today?'

'She couldn't come. She argues a lot and won't work. She doesn't do the cooking, she won't draw water.' He seemed relieved to talk.

'And you?'

'Me?'

'When did you last see your wife?'

'I . . . she's not nice.'

'Where is she now?'

The man dropped his head. 'She's gone to her mother's.'

'Did you tell her to go?'

The man nodded. 'How did you know?'

'The gods know everything,' said the voice. 'Men and women live on this earth but they cannot live for ever. Only the gods live on, they see and understand all things.'

'And what should I do?' asked the man.

The medium did not reply.

The man leaned forward. 'Tell me what I should do. I'll do what you tell me to do.'

A long moan came from the mouth of the medium. His body stiffened and he moaned again. The crowd began to mutter – why didn't he answer? He always answered so quickly. What was the matter? With a grunt he rolled over, his legs and arms extending like a spring; the trumpet began to play mournfully. He lay on his back: his eyelids flickered open, then shut instantly, then slowly quaveringly opened again. The trumpet stopped. The god had left his body.

The crowd sat mesmerised till a man called out with contempt, 'It's only three o'clock.' It was the man who had talked with the medium before he had started his trance.

'Three o'clock?' asked someone in the crowd.

'Three.'

'That's only an hour.'

'One hour.'

'It's never been so short.'

'We've come so far.'

'I came fifteen miles.'

'I came twenty.'

Some grew angry, shouting above the others; the man pointed at the film unit.

'There are foreigners among us,' he said.

One man spat. 'It must be because of them,' he said.

'They've brought an evil spirit,' said another.

168

'Who let them in?'

The film unit packed their gear quickly. They sensed an undercurrent of violence.

Jayamma walked out of the house, looking straight ahead, her head held firmly erect, her mouth tightly shut. She looked back to see if we were coming. Some women jostled and abused her; she carried on walking. She stopped outside, surrounded by cursing women: her eyes widened and were bright with tears, but she held them back fiercely.

The film unit moved to the Land-Rover: some men gathered threateningly round. Then the medium's friend came out of the house, and everyone drew back. He approached – his head bent, his hands folded to his chest. He wanted to thank the unit for filming such an event; he hoped that they were happy; he hoped they realised the honour they'd had in recording the voice of god. They would of course wish to give a gift to the god.

The film unit thanked him profusely and said they would give a gift. What sort of thing was required?

Oh nothing much. The holy house was in need of a new roof. The unit could give the money.

For a *roof*?

It wouldn't be more than nine thousand rupees.

The film unit were outraged. They turned to walk to the Land-Rover, but some men hemmed them in.

Perhaps only half a roof, suggested the medium's friend. The film unit finally beat him down to a mere five hundred rupees.

'You're very gracious,' he said, as the money was handed over. And in return, he gave them each a handful of flowers and sprinkled their heads with rosewater. 'The god will welcome your gift. You must return again and listen to the wisdom of the oracles.'

The crowd let us go in peace.

The Sikh cameraman was disgusted, and angrily threw banana skins out of the window as we drove back to the village. Tony, tight-lipped, justified both parties. Kevan, the English Associate Producer, said with a grin that the man had smelt so why should he get any money. I defended the medium. Jayamma had no comment.

And then while writing this book, the argument turned into something else: whether the village people believed in the medium's powers. Tony said they were far too shrewd to be taken in by such play-acting, but I don't think that was the point. However shrewd they might be about the demands of their own lives – the ploughing, the planting, the need for cash – they were still superstitious, accrediting those things which they couldn't understand to God and the unknown spirits. I also sensed that they needed in an unconscious way someone to listen and guide them in things which were unpredictable, such as children and human relationships. The priest was too remote, bound up in his Sanskrit mantras; the medium spoke their language and came from the same sort of background. He was a better representative in supplications to God.

The women had said they believed, in a roundabout way, and regular visits when pregnant were proof of their credulity. The men were more sceptical: they had been about and heard stories of impostors. They also knew that holy men cost money. Even Bhadramma commented wryly, when visited three times in a morning by passing religious beggars, "Everyone says they're from God, or else that they're priests. Everyone says that. It's the same disease every morning."

10 Planning a Family of 26

One of my hardest tasks was trying to understand the family's need for children, conscious or unconscious. I myself had not experienced child-birth, and though I suffered the usual pressures of claims that a woman can have no fulfilment unless she carry a child, I was free to choose either way. A child would be for my pleasure, and my husband's: it had more to do with a wish to experience a natural phenomenon than any overriding necessity for children, and I had no need to prove my fertility.

In India, for hundreds of years, fertility has meant survival, not just of people, but of land, cattle, and plants. Year after year, drought, monsoon, disease, death, famine, have conspired to reduce the villager and his family: many children died, so more children were born to ensure adequate numbers as protection against isolation. Alone, man could do little. For all of her history also, India was underpopulated: man and the land maintained uneasy equilibrium, dependent on the other for productivity and life. In such conditions, a villager treads cautiously, strapping himself to traditional mores and methods. He cannot afford to experiment, he will never take risks, but sticks determinedly to skills which have been proved over centuries. How is he to know that the death rate is falling, the birth rate is rising, and that within twenty years, the population will double? How can he tell that the land will soon be short, the cities overburdened, and the sparse fragile services will be further depleted? And even if he does know, why should he risk his family because of some government programme to promote family planning?

For Manje Gowda's family, even religion meant death and destruction and the passive submission to stronger forces. Whatever was on their foreheads, whatever Shiva dictated, so their fate lay with God and nothing could alter fate. However much they prayed, however much they paid, the fertility of a woman could not be guaranteed.

Though religion was part of their lives they knew little about it: they knew no doctrines, could recite few mantras, and even confused their family gods' identities. The books were with the Brahmins, so how could they have knowledge? Village opinion brought more pressure than priestly orthodox attitudes.* Those without sons were mocked for infertility and for being a dying family; those who had lost their sons were shunned for the ill luck which they carried. The patel's family had lost its power when it had lost its men. And no one helped Jayamma since she had lost three sons. And yet, at the same time, those with too many children were mocked for lack of restraint, for failure to show any wisdom. It was only in the old days that a woman had ten or twelve children. Take Madakka, the oldest daughter-in-law of the house: she was trying to abort her fifth child at four months because of family hostility to yet another baby.

Vara and I found her alone while she was washing clothes. She was a dry wiry woman who did not get on with the others: her tongue was rough, her hands were ready to beat the children, and she came from a very poor family – her mother was widowed and blind, her sister was left by her husband, and only her youngest brother was there to look after the family since her eldest brother had vanished the year of the famine.

"You know, it hurts me so much when I see that the other wives come from a prosperous home," she said. "Whenever they go to their mothers, they can get so many things and so much help. If only my people were well off – it hurts, it hurts."

Inflicting great hardship, she had borrowed fifty rupees from her mother to try and abort the child. She had gone to the doctor in secret for pills and medicine and injections – unaware that drugs brought the risk of deformity. Nothing at all had happened, and now the money was spent. What else could she do? She refused to use the village method of sticks pierced into the uterus, for it carried the stigma of immorality, of illegitimate children. She did

---

* Others have reached the same conclusion: 'The simple truth is that the poor Indians, the villagers, are usually not at all religious in the sense of having a thorough knowledge of Hinduism; nor do they rule their actions by religious precepts if, in their view, these ideas are irrational. They almost never cite religion as an explanation for their daily actions.' – Lasse & Lisa Berg: *Face to Face*, Ramparts Press, Berkeley, California, 1971.

try other remedies, like eating paw-paw, drinking salt water, and taking herbal pills, but still nothing had happened.

"I've too many children," she explained sadly. "People mock me and say, 'Why do you want another child?' Everyone's annoyed, even my husband. *He* doesn't want it. None of the family wants it. Even I don't want it – can my body stand it? But they don't know I went to the doctor, except for my Gowda. He'd know, wouldn't he?"

She was frightened we'd tell the old lady, for then her secret would be gossiped all over the village. She didn't want that. Her husband was different, he was discreet and kind – a serious man devoted to the land who respected and cared for his wife. He told us so later. He liked her for what she was, not in a lustful way but because he admired her capacities as a person, to work hard and do things for herself. They made a good team.

The men of the family were more forthcoming now that they had other men to talk to: they continued their work as normal while the film unit followed them round, and answered questions easily on the size of family they wanted. Bhadre Gowda, Thayee's husband, saw the problem in terms of quality. He was spreading manure near the temple, stamping the ground in preparation for rain, picking out maggots from the baskets.

"What's the use of thousands of worms bred in a bit of cow dung?" he asked. "If there was one decent worm then it would be alright. So it's the same with children. You shouldn't want more children. If you climb a big tree to collect fruit, you'll have to climb far. If you're climbing a small tree, you can stretch out your hand and pluck it. The thing is, in the olden days, things were under control, but once Kali was born, when this evil time started, children started increasing and things weren't so good. Even if you want a large family, who knows what will happen in the future? For example, my father is still alive. Suppose he had died earlier, how would so many of us have been born? Suppose he had died after he had had one or two children?"

Two or three were enough provided they were boys, but given a proportion of daughters, it probably meant four or five – the men had fears of child mortality and the worry that if the family divided they might need extra sons to work in the fields. All were painfully aware of the increased cost of living, and the cash that

was needed for food, for clothes, for the land – even for daughters'
dowries. Although the old man had got six sons and had done well
by them, who could afford such a number now? What they
wanted were boys who could work hard and produce good crops
from the land; and perhaps if they were lucky they might have a
son with education.

S.M.B. of course was not confined by village practicalities: he
had a more global approach in understanding the problem. He
also had more time to talk, as he watched the work of his step-
brothers.

"As time passes," he said, gazing into the camera, "you can't
say that the Indian nation will remain the same. There might not
be room for people even to stand. There mightn't be space to sit
down. There mightn't be land to cultivate. So in my opinion it's
better to keep the family as small as possible. I give this advice to
everybody. If they listen, well and good, otherwise they'll regret
it later. See, I can stop, being an educated man. But because my
brothers are uneducated, they want boys. Boys will in future –
according to Indian custom, somehow according to Indian
custom, if we have sons, they can help with the work. If there are
girls, they can't do any ploughing – they might do housework or
they might tend the cattle. But if there are boys, they can plough
the field. What can a girl do? If there's a son, he'll at least plough
the field – provided he's not educated. Old age parents – the sons
can help."

"So many people are born," said Nanjeswamy lightly, "so
many people die. We should leave someone behind to continue
the family. And if there are two sons, one can study and the other
work in the fields. Even if there are three, they can all work on the
land. They can work and get more land. They can do anything."

Such definite thinking was perhaps politely devised to provide
the film unit with what it wanted to hear. The men knew well
enough that the unit's interpreter came from the Ministry of
Health and Family Planning whose slogan was posted over the
country as 'Two or three are enough'. They also knew that family
planning officials were anxious to prove that the message had
reached the villages, and why should the family contradict? But
over the next few weeks, their comments revealed their attitude
that life was not so concrete, decisions were not clear-cut: family

size depended on land and money, it depended on division, and to some extent the stars. They could not decide now, their life was too uncertain – they'd have to see when the time came, they'd see what they were given.

For all the men, decisions were large and complex: they stressed a man and worried him, nagging at his mind. Wrong decisions could alter a family's life, giving it greater hardship, destroying its precarious balance. Should there be more children? Was it the time to plant? Should they buy some bullocks, or try to dig a well? At least with the land, they had experience and understanding which derived from the work they shared, the long routine, the demands of climate and season, the rule of cattle and ploughing. They knew what had to be done, they knew instinctively the fine adjustments, at least with dry land. But with irrigation, much of the work was new: they no longer knew when to plant, for seasons had little to do with it; they were working different crops whose pattern of growth they still had to learn; they were trying out new techniques. The brothers who worked the land were therefore dependent on Manager Nanjeswamy and S.M.B. for information and guidance. But the Managers felt no need to share decisions or to confide information. Why should they – there were no social pressures, no moral necessities to discuss events with others.

I never really discovered who made the final decision on the number of children each man should have. S.M.B. had some influence, as the respected man from the town, and maybe the old lady exerted some control over her own sons. But as far as I understood it, if a husband wanted more children, then there was nothing to stop him. It was his wife and his child, regardless of pressures and obligations while living within the joint family. I knew for certain, however, that the women had little say in the number of children they bore. And the reasons were perfectly logical, within their terms of reference: children had more to do with economics and practical needs than emotional or physical wishes. Such areas belonged to the men. Even if the women's wishes did filter through, it rarely affected the issue: whatever the husband decided, the wife had to accept. Thayee's husband said so. But apart from Susheelamma and Madakka, who felt they had carried enough, the women's wishes were few: they prayed

175

for sons, as was their duty, and left the rest to God and to the decisions of their husbands. And if a daughter was born, then at least it proved they were fertile.

The wives of the family were unsure of the reproductive process, but they felt that the sex of the child and the numbers conceived had something to do with the pattern of births their mothers had had. They did know that if you stopped your period, it probably meant you were pregnant; and they also believed that a woman could never conceive while still suckling a baby. When I pointed out that both Madakka and Susheelamma had done precisely this, the women shrugged as though I had proved nothing. Their belief overrode any logic.

It was harder to talk about sex: I felt intrusive and they were shy, thus limiting information.

"How often do you unite?" I asked Madakka at the time she spoke of abortion.

She hesitated, embarrassed.

"You needn't be shy," I said. "I do the same with my husband."

"There's no saying," she answered.

"Perhaps once a week, or once a month?"

"It may be for a month," she said.

"You mean you don't unite for a month, or you do it every day?"

"No, we don't do such things in our caste."

"Then?"

"Once a month, fifteen days, twenty days . . ."

"And you use something to stop children?"

"No, no, where would we get such things?"

"Then your husband uses such things?"

"What would he use?"

I couldn't think what else to ask which wouldn't provoke a negative answer, so we sat for a moment in silence.

"Can you refuse your husband?" I asked once more.

"Will he listen if I say no?" she answered. It seemed to have touched a chord. "If I'm not well, he might . . . he'll wait another day. He'll wait a day, even two days, but the third day . . ." She laughed with embarrassment. "If I say I'm not well, and this or that . . . if I have my bleeding, then after eight days, after it's stopped . . ." She refused to use any word for sex.

"Is it a trouble when you unite – perhaps because you're tired?"

"Yes, won't we be tired? But I don't feel bad." She laughed again, with timidity.

Susheelamma did feel bad: she found sex painful and so tiring that the following day she always wanted to rest instead of going to work. If only it happened less, perhaps once in two or three months . . . but it wasn't the custom to leave it so long.

The men were more positive in describing to Tony the demands of sex. For S.M.B., it was duty; for Bhadre Gowda, the husband of Thayee, it was expedience stemming from natural desires.

"When a husband and wife get married," he explained, "it's the normal thing to happen between them. But if a married man stops doing it to his wife, his pants will get dirty. Whether a man wants to have sex with his wife or not, he should do it every fifteen days or so. Yes, that's why we do it, to stop dirtying our pants."

For Manager Nanjeswamy, it was lust, lust which provoked him.

"My wife never calls me," he boasted to Tony in private, "so I have to go and fuck her. I never say stop, I want to go on and on. Some women like it, and want it; others don't and want it to be finished. Susheelamma could call me too, but she doesn't because she's shy. But she never objects when I tell her to come. Didn't you know? It depends on the strength of a man – *I* do it three or four times a night. As you go to your wife, so I go to mine. If they hadn't married me, if I'd been a bachelor, there wouldn't have been this desire. But when I got a wife, when I married Susheel-amma and had the nuptials, I felt 'This is my territory, I can do what I like.' "

The men were indignant at the mention of taking another woman; and they felt insulted by the suggestion of sex in the fields – the room where the women slept was the place where a man took his wife. But love was not a matter of tender caresses and whispered enticements: the women kept on their clothes, the men lay on top. Nor could it be spontaneous, since the bedroom had somehow to be subtly booked in advance so that no one else would go there. And how could a man stay hot when he had to wait an hour or two for his wife to finish her work, when his wife was tired and passive, when they lacked easy familiarity? They could not make any noise, for the house could hear everything: the walls did not reach the ceiling so sounds floated rudely over to a row of children and women conspicuously turned out of their room for the night.

Sex was not that frequent, with so many couples to use the room. In any case, the men were often away, guarding the pump and crops, driving the cart to town, arriving late and tired from the fields. And the old lady watched like a hawk. 'If all of them do it too often,' she said, 'and the women bear more children, what will the family do?' Only Manager Nanjeswamy regularly used the room: idle days and a voluptuous wife gave him stronger desires, once in four days, once in eight days, several times a night. But not when his wife was pregnant, the mind didn't want it.

Children came when they came: if the women were pregnant together, if it happened, it happened, the work would have to adjust. But at least there was some years' space between the children of each mother so that work was not badly affected.

In contrast, Jayamma who lived alone with her husband Kalle Gowda had conceived four times in five years. Her husband was desperate for children, so sex was frequent. Even so, the formality of male and female relationships pervaded their sleeping habits: Jayamma slept alone in the ante-room to the kitchen; her husband slept next door near the cattle area. Each had to call the other if they wished to have sex: Jayamma did sometimes, though usually it was her husband.

The emphasis on pregnancy and fertility increased the friction between the family and film unit. The men resented the constant attention to women, and the intimate questions and filming which disrupted their work in the fields. The film unit had little compunction since a fee had partly been paid: they resented more the endless demands of Nanjeswamy for money, for cloth, and even a watch for himself. S.M.B. made it worse by asking for extra cash to pay for new plastic pipes to carry the water for irrigation. To add to the problem, there was tension within the unit from lack of nutritous food, and from the clash of professional temperaments.

My own sympathies lay with the family and I allied myself with them whenever possible: I still slept in the village sometimes, I still ate with the family, and I spent my time with the women instead of the unit. And yet I was part of the unit whether I liked it or not, as their researcher, their spy, the unpaid member of the team who was helping out her husband. That I had got involved, that I had gone half-Indian, was not part of the job, and not their affair. I also wanted to be with Tony, to share our work, to be together, and yet I felt frequently threatened. Perhaps I was jealous of the attraction caused by the filming, for on reflection although the family resented the intrusion they also liked the attention and used it to their advantage. And I was hurt by the women's sudden regard for Tony – what had he done for them except be a man who did not boss them around? Subtly their attitude had changed. My own role, my own identity as a person was lost: the family now saw me as part of the film unit who could carry requests and demands to Tony – they saw me as only a woman whose husband had come to take over.

The crunch came one day when the unit was filming the whole family as they plucked a harvest of groundnuts. It had gone on all morning, so thinking they must be tired, Vara and I heaved lunch and buckets of water for hundreds of yards to the field; but Tony decided the unit should eat by the well and everyone carried the food down again. I dished it out for the crew. Nobody seemed to help, and when the food ran out for Vara and me, nobody offered us some of theirs. It was stupid, but I stormed off in frustration and burst into tears.

Tony was philosophic, for he recognised my tiredness; I had lost a stone in weight, and was rarely sleeping more than five hours a night. And though I refused to admit it, I did feel very un-healthy. He suggested I go to Bangalore, taking Jayamma with me to see a gynaecologist: it seemed an excellent idea, for I wanted to know whether she had a chance of having a family at all. The unit arranged a car, Jayamma's husband gave permission, and we set off two days later – Bhadramma, Jayamma, and I.

Mother and daughter slept for most of the three hour journey, occasionally waking to drink some water or to look at the passing coconut groves. There were green fields, thick sugar-cane, rich fertile soil watered by state irrigation only twenty miles from their own parched lands, but they seemed uninterested and did not know how to look: they were used to crowded buses which gave no view. I was the wide-eyed tourist who emerged from a distant village with a sense of release and wonder. Life with the family, if not oppressive, was at least pervasive. Jayamma laughed at my exclamations and snuggled against my shoulder.

Neither Bhadramma nor Jayamma had seen Bangalore before, and the trip was fulfilling a dream. Yet all their responses contradicted my expectations. As we sat in the clinic's waiting-room, they were not embarrassed by the stares of the rich sleek women who had come for expensive treatment. Only Bhadramma was shy to ask how the lavatory worked, but she quickly coped once I showed her what to do. I found the gynaecologist thoughtful and efficient in her examination of Jayamma: she could find no cervical incompetence, no venereal syphilis, no urinary disease, so she diagnosed malnutrition and hormone deficiency, prescribing a number of pills. She refused to accept a fee. She would 'take from eagles and give to the birds, it was the least she could do to help'. But Jayamma and Bhadramma found her aloof and arrogant; they were also hurt by her comments on village life – the endless sex a man demanded, the beating, the fights, the ignorance of reproduction. I attributed her remarks to lack of experience and sympathy, since she'd done her training in Edinburgh and came from urban India; but they took it as personal insult.

All of us were disappointed that nothing more concrete was found. We had somehow hoped for a diagnosis which would bring swift remedial action. But now it meant months of waiting and pill-taking with no guarantee at the end that the baby would survive. Jayamma kept asking and asking what the doctor had said, what her words had meant, what the chances were of a safe delivery. She listened intently to the explanations and followed me in to the chemist when I went to buy all her pills – vitamins, iron, calcium, protein, plus several for hormone deficiency and uterine contractions.

I could not decide where we should stay. If we went to an expensive hotel, they might be confused by its lavishness; if we went to a very cheap place, they might be hurt at my lack of consideration. Eventually we stopped at a small hotel and found a room with two beds for twenty-five rupees. Bhadramma was indignant: the price was far too much. I decided we should take it, and they settled in with relief.

Dinner was the happiest part of our trip. We found an eating-house nearby, brightly lit and sparkling with coloured tables. We tried out all sorts of dishes, and they tasted fizzy orangeade for the first time with suspicion; we also laughed and laughed as they tried to eat with spoons, and when Jayamma could not manage, we ate with our fingers instead. Bhadramma had no fear of the town, nor seemed bewildered by its size and the network of streets: when we finished the meal it was raining outside so she told me to take the path in case I should spoil my long skirt which I'd exchanged for the village sari. She walked ahead, upright, disregarding the cars which swept water and mud across her feet, keeping her face bare to confront the oncoming rain. Inside the hotel room she washed herself carefully and told us to go to bed. She insisted that I have a bed to myself, though I was happy to share with Jayamma: she tucked her own blanket over me, ignoring my protestations.

The next morning I woke at seven to find Bhadramma sitting erect on a chair gazing straight ahead. She remained there for an hour, patient and protective, while Jayamma slept on. She turned and smiled at me and told me to go back to sleep.

After breakfast we walked round Bangalore: we saw the massive white Secretariat Building, the gardens, the library, the statues, the stream of people going to work. But they were unimpressed. All they wanted was to go to the market to buy a pot and see a plane in flight.

The market was busy: we pushed our way through the crowd, gazing at the stalls, asking prices, fingering products. I was engulfed by the smell of bodies and urine mixed with the sickly scent of jasmine flowers and burning incense sticks; I lingered over the carved sandalwood, the sacks of spices, the lush fruit, the vivid nylon saris; but Bhadramma strode purposefully to each stall to buy some scarlet *kunkuma*, bananas, and betel leaves. She also considered a plastic basket in turquoise and yellow squares, but turned her back abruptly to avoid the temptation: instead, she bought some flowers for my hair.

It took half an hour to purchase an aluminium pot. Bhadramma bargained hard, moving from stall to stall; but still at the end she was unhappy, for Bangalore's prices were high. She gave the pot to Jayamma, who in turn had bought her mother a sieve. I bought Jayamma two plastic bangles – it was all she would accept – and the plastic basket for Bhadramma.

At the airport, we stood on the roof in the wind, waiting

impatiently to see a plane, but one never came. Jayamma grew faint and squatted on the ground: her eyes widened in sadness, her jaw drooped unconsciously, and her cheeks sunk into her mouth. She was thoughtful, perhaps suddenly aware of a new perspective. Not that she had any choice herself, or could change her life, but she had seen with Tony and me the possibility of a partnership. Her own husband went off with other women, he drank and spent all their money. Once they had lots of sheep but now they were down to nothing. Her third pregnancy had been the worst, she bled so much that she had to change her rags three or four times in an hour. She stayed at home stretched out on the floor, weakening every hour: people wondered whether she would survive. She nearly died, died and was reborn. Everyone died some day. She said if she died today, her husband wouldn't care, he wouldn't ask what happened.

We returned to the village dispirited.

For Kalle Gowda and Jayamma, any mention of family planning was a cruel twist of irony. They needed help to start a family, not constant reminders that two or three were enough; and yet if she'd limited her pregnancies to one every two or three years, the chance of survival for one child might have been greater.

For Manje Gowda's family, action was not so easy once a decision was made to space or stop more children. Their knowledge was very limited. They all knew of the operation, both for men and women, which stopped children finally, because some in the village had had it; most of the men had heard of the sheath and some had heard of the loop; none had heard of the pill, but the pill was not available unless they went forty miles. As to the function of each method and the manner of using contraceptives, all were very hazy, particularly the women. None of them knew which was best apart from Manager Nanjeswamy who spoke of the rubber bag. He denied having ever used it.

S.M.B. knew more of course from living in town where the campaigns were more intense. He had tried the sheath, and even discussed with friends in the office the merits of family planning. It was *his* wife who had first had the operation; it was he who had made the decision.

In the village, gossip and rumour prevailed. They had heard

of a woman who bled badly, and so they distrusted the loop; they were fearful of sterilisation because it was linked with an operation. Operations weakened a man, they believed, like the neighbour who lost his strength because of some stomach surgery. Now he was living on air. So how could the village family – the workers, the people – manage without their men? If anyone had the operation, let it be the women.

But the women also were scared. *They* had heard about Bhadramma's operation, and each had a different version: she had stayed eight days in hospital, she had stayed a month, she had stayed nearly forty days; she couldn't work, she had such pains, she was sick every morning; she had done it in secret, her husband had told her to do it, her husband had also been sterilised. The truth came from Bhadramma, without pain or panic: she had spent two days in hospital and could work as well as before. Bhadre Gowda, her brother, thought she had had the loop.

The men were aware of their own ignorance, and were bitter. "In this jungle village, there's no one who will tell us." Bhadre Gowda thought the word 'method' itself meant some sort of contraceptive; Madakka's husband said he wanted to know, but all the doctors would talk of was sterilisation, sterilisation. It was alright if you knew you had had enough and had filled your quota of sons, like S.M.B.; it was alright for those in town, for they could afford to be weak: they could eat nice foods and plenty of fruits and rest for a while in their house.

The emphasis on operations was partly due to the government programme which encouraged sterilisation.* Sterilisation brought firm statistics and permanent non-reproduction: alternatives were not so viable. The loop gave problems of bleeding, and lasted only a year or two; the cap needed careful fitting; the pill was costly to give out free. Only the sheath and creams were practical, but these found little favour with the villagers who considered them unnatural.

Communication was part of the problem, and the lack of proper services. There was an auxiliary nurse-midwife who lived in the neighbouring village and who was meant to give help and advice,

* During Mrs. Gandhi's emergency rule, this campaign was heightened, to the extent of compulsion sometimes – for government employees and for the state of Maharashtra.

but because of the size of her district, she visited each house once in two months or so and then only spoke to the women.

The men were sceptical of her services. "We never get to meet her, and she won't talk with us about such things. Even if she comes, what does she say? 'Let your wife have the operation'."

The women were less critical, but Susheelamma swore that the midwife had shown them nothing – not a loop, not a sheath, no method of contraception. The midwife swore she had. She was a gentle, sad woman, a Brahmin who had been forced to accept the job because of shortage of money. Her husband worked in Bangalore, and they met once a month at the most. She was lonely in the village, for though she had been there five years the people were still suspicious and were only now beginning to accept her. They still rejected her family planning work.

"When I show them the loop," she said, "they say it looks like a worm. They say, 'How can it stop more children? Why should we have a worm inside us? It might go anywhere in the body'. And when I show them the sheath, they say, 'How can we put that on our husbands?' We have to force them to take the sheaths. They say, 'Oh Madam says we must, so why should we offend her? Let's take it'. Then they throw it away or give it to their children to use as balloons."

She also admitted that sometimes she forced a person to go for sterilisation, but she was in a harsh predicament: if she didn't produce her quota of cases, she said her pay was reduced.

"Even if we ask them twenty times, and get them into the jeep, they still say they don't want to come. Do you think our villagers are so forward as to volunteer? It's better in the cities. People come more easily, they come by themselves. When they have four or five children, the women come by themselves and sign for the operation. But you can't expect it here. The men object to it. Even the neighbours object to it.

"We can do any amount of other work," she added, "such as delivering and vaccination. But even with vaccination they fight us sometimes. They say, 'You're hurting the baby'. Then we show them pictures of children with pox all over their faces. They say, 'Because you get paid, you do all this. You've got no other business'."

For family planning she had no posters and no aids to help her explain the methods. I suspect that if she did, it wouldn't mean much to the villagers who had little experience of printed visual communications. I had had two insights on this with the family. First, although the children could draw, they drew only those things they'd been taught in school – the alphabet, a house, a tree. There was no improvisation, and they could not recognise the same items when I drew them. My tree was a different shape, my house had different windows. My dog, my millet, my well, meant nothing. Secondly, the old man, the old lady, and some of the men and the women could not identify themselves in the large photographs presented by the film unit. The family was used to postcard-size, full portraits in formal pose. The natural photographs confused them, and only after constant reminders of who each person was did they develop some visual system for identification. So how much would family planning posters mean, however simple and direct?

In the end, as they always did in desperation, as they did when they had no alternatives, the family turned to God, and left the decisions to Him. What else was there?

"We say, 'Oh God, stop more. Whether it's boys or girls, we've had enough'. The past is done, but the future will change. Will things be the same as they are today? There is always God Shiva. Let a child be born if it must be born. *We* were all born. Aren't we earning enough food today? Shiva won't let us eat grass, he'll get us food from somewhere even in times of difficulty. He who's brought us into the world will surely keep a handful of rice for us in a corner somewhere."

I don't really have many conclusions about family planning in rural communities: I can speak only about one family and even then it is all too often tentative. The film, also, doesn't draw conclusions – it's more a film about people and the problems of living a hard life. But I suppose I do feel some things, and would like to put them down, without pretending to be a pundit.

I feel that wherever you are in the world, it's hard enough at the best of times to cope with the problem of contraception. In England and Wales alone in 1976, for every 100 births there were 18 registered abortions.* I myself have found no satisfactory

---

* 585,000 births, 101,000 abortions, according to the Family Planning Association.

solution, but change from loop to pill to nothing. Yet I have the privilege of information, endless advice, and the clear decision that Tony and I don't want children now.

I don't believe that family planning in isolation can provide the only answer. A change in standards of living, in decision-making, in the age of marriage, and the emancipation of women will affect family size far more. Nonetheless facilities and information on methods should be widely and openly available, without compulsion, targets, or pressure. I believe that the simplest villager is capable of making his own decisions – provided he knows all the problems – and will use contraception if he wants to. I am sure that many would want to.

At the moment, there is often a polite but uncomprehending gap between those who promote family planning and those who receive it, with virtually no discussion, nor exchange of ideas and information to prompt awareness and possible action. Surely the villager should be more involved in the process? Maybe a monthly meeting would help, where one of the village men or a sympathetic outsider could act as a catalyst with constant questions and new ideas. Participants might come if, say, milk were given free instead of a bundle of sheaths, or if there were some activity to capture their interest. With such discussions, they might work out why they should have family planning, if at all, whether women should help with decisions, whether men should marry when older. At village level, the ideas could spread like wildfire. But would an informed representative be able to sit and watch and listen while others made the decisions – or didn't make the decisions?

It seems to me that the gap in information is crucial. How do you get across that a loop stuck up your uterus is nothing to be frightened of? Or that pills taken every day will stop you having a baby, but that if you miss a day, then you might still get a baby? A whole vocabulary is needed, district by district, village by village, family by family, that is accessible to each person's understanding. I think it should be developed by those who work in the villages.

The trouble is there's no quick or simple solution except for compulsory sterilisation, and that's hardly a human answer. The message *is* slowly getting through; the family average *is* slowly reducing, and the impetus could probably snowball. Perhaps I'm too optimistic in believing that action and courage can produce a practical answer, and in feeling that initiative should be given to 'illiterate' village people, but humans have a strange capacity to cope.

With medicine, the family had experienced its benefits so used it as much as they could. But reality was less helpful. It was partly the same old practical problem, of hospitals far away with limited funds and supplies, so that although the system was meant to be free, the family had to subsidise itself for anything beyond the minimal. They had spent four hundred rupees on the old man when he had fallen sick; their annual budget was nearly a thousand rupees – incredibly high for a peasant family.

Death was not so easy now: of the old man's twenty-one grandchildren, only one had died, so it meant one could risk smaller families. The fact that reduced child mortality increased overall the problem of population did not concern the family: they had the luxury of life, the first time for centuries. They even allowed the nurse-midwife to inject their babies against smallpox: they knew what plague could mean. The old lady remembered an outbreak which had killed the old man's sister.

"It was six months after my marriage," she recalled, in her shrill rasping voice. "When I was only seven. I was at my father's house. The plague was growing and nobody knew. Then in that house down the street . . . the woman called Devakka . . . her father died I believe. And in some other house, and everywhere. After my sister-in-law died, everyone realised. There was an epidemic in Krishnapatna. They brought things from their house and gave all the things to us and we kept them in our house. Because we did that, we got the evil disease. It caught my husband's sister. The disease was spreading inside her and nobody knew. She wouldn't open her eyes, she wouldn't talk. She got it under her armpits. It didn't show outside. I believe they saw it after she was dead. They said so. What did we know? We just cried. After that, we left the village and went away for three months. We lived outside in the fields."

Apart from the expense, the family was often inhibited by the attitude of those who administered medicine. The nurses and doctors were usually busy and sometimes a little superior. Some of the family openly called them thieves. As with family planning, lack of communication seemed one of the major barriers, even with such an important issue as pills. The doctors I met mostly claimed it was pointless giving pills to villagers, for they would not take them regularly according to the prescription. The family claimed they were rarely given instructions; and they could not read directions on a label.

I developed a colouring system for Jayamma's pills so that she'd know when to take them each day: there must have been ten in all. On every bottle, I painted a coloured stripe: green represented early morning when she put on her green sari; yellow was for midday when her yellow chrysanthemums bloomed; and blue was for night when the sky had darkened to blue. Some bottles had all three colours; some had two; and some a single stripe. All were auspicious colours she knew, in paint which could not rub off.

Jayamma's husband, Kalle Gowda, was eager to help, and quickly grasped the principle. We had a trial one morning with Jayamma as we crouched over the bottles in a secluded part of their fields.

"What colour's this?" I asked Jayamma, pointing to the yellow.

She hesitated, then giggled nervously, conscious of her husband's commanding presence. "I . . . don't know. I can't make out."

Her husband tried to answer.

"No, no, let her try," I said "What colour is this?" I asked, holding out another.

"Green," she said promptly

"And this?"

"Blue."

"And when do you take each one?"

Her husband was biting his lip, longing to speak. Jayamma could not answer, so he recited accurately all the colours and timings.

"Now, what do you take at lunchtime?"

Jayamma stared at the bottles, then shyly picked up one with a yellow stripe.

"Aren't there any more?"

Her hand darted in and collected all the bottles with yellow stripes.

"What time of day is it now?"

She looked towards the sun. "Midday."

"So what do you do?"

She fetched a pot of water.

"Give them," she said excitedly, "give me the yellow bottles."

She unscrewed the lids and carefully slid a pill from each. With a quick gulp of water, she swallowed them one by one.

"I can swallow any number," she said gaily. "I can even swallow something as bitter as poison."

"And what will you take this evening?"

She picked out two blue bottles and then seemed confused. Finally she transferred those bottles in the yellow pile which also had blue stripes.

We all laughed and clapped our hands. She seemed relieved and happy.

For once her husband helped, and she regularly took the pills: she even came to warn me when the bottles were nearly empty – I filled them once a week to check they were properly taken. It was a good time for Jayamma, as Kalle Gowda also reduced her workload: he took the millet to grind by machine and got Bhadramma to draw their water. He seemed a changed man. I think it was the effect of the film unit, for he saw the chance of gain; and he was shrewd enough to realise that since I cared for Jayamma, he would receive nothing while treating her badly. He was courteous, helpful, discreet, and always around when wanted. He was also disarmingly frank when Tony asked him questions: he confirmed he wanted another wife, and that sometimes he beat Jayamma; but he also explained that he had never wanted to marry her.

"There was no love," he said. "I wanted to look elsewhere, and my uncle found a girl from another village. But Manje Gowda came to know about it and said I should marry within his family, so that he could give me help. Then my mother said, 'See, son, we're all alone. If we bring a girl from outside, her family can't really help during difficult times. But if they're from our own village, they'll see you through good and bad.'

"Even so I said, 'Mother, we don't want a girl from the same village. If there's a fight, or blows, it'll reach her family. Then we'll all be on the streets to fight.' Yes, I told her that would happen. But she said that either I married Jayamma, or I married no one. I was quite happy to wait. I was too young to marry, but she brought her brother and made him persuade me to marry. After marrying, there was no point in being resentful."

Indeed it was the lack of children he minded more than the lack of love: there was no point in a family which did not grow. It was the productivity of Manje Gowda's family – both in work and numbers of children – which made him really bitter. Hadn't the old man promised to help him in his struggles. But what had they ever done? It never came to their minds to think about others' poverty.

Kalle Gowda did think about others. He got his mother-in-law, Bhadramma, to prepare a chicken stew. He carried it up to Krishnapatna and presented it to the film unit. They thought he had cooked it himself and promised to give him a shirt.

11 Birth

'No,' said Manager Nanjeswamy, 'you can't film there.' He tapped his foot impatiently and flicked his right hand as though dismissing servants.

The film unit moved from the gods' corner and set up the camera near the old man's cot.

'No,' said Manager Nanjeswamy. 'Not there either.'

They moved their equipment again, into the cattle area.

'The cattle are coming in,' said Manager Nanjeswamy, though it was midday and they never returned till night. 'Can't film in the house,' he shouted. 'Too much work to do.' The old lady and his wife were quietly sifting flour, the only ones in the house.

Outside the men were sorting millet seedlings in expectation of rain – it had rained in Sundrapura; it had flooded in Mysore; they were sure it would swing their way. The old man sat on a small bank watching the work idly, his chin propped on his raised knees, his eyelids drooping heavily. He was tired; he had hardly slept the night before, the children had screamed so much. He blinked, trying to keep awake to watch the men work.

The camera moved towards him. Its whirring made him more drowsy: he closed his eyes with the lens only a yard from his nose.

'No,' said Nanjeswamy, marching between.

'Cut,' said Tony coldly.

'You can only film my father asleep when he's lying down. That's the proper way.'

The film unit gave up and returned to Krishnapatna.

Manager Nanjeswamy was furious that Bhadramma and Jayamma had gone to Bangalore before he had. In revenge he obstructed every moment of filming. He also marched round to Bhadramma's house and abused her like a prostitute: he wanted to know what plot she had hatched to gain the film unit's favour. The old lady went there too, screaming and shouting at Bhadramma. But Bhadramma said nothing. She kept her peace and answered coldly that no one had given her anything, that some people did things for nothing. The hostility between step-mother and step-daughter was out in the open now.

The next day Tony stayed away and filmed a farm for handicapped children two miles from the village. It started to drizzle. Within an hour, Nanjeswamy came striding along the road, his head and shoulders wrapped in polythene sheeting.

'Why aren't you in the village?' he asked.

'We want to film here,' said Tony.

'You have to film our family. The fields are very wet.'

'We're trying to film your family.'

'You should film them in the rain.'

'We'll do it another day.'

'There won't be another day. You can't film any more. Not now. Not any more. Not till you've paid more money.'

He strode into the farm hut and took off his polythene sheeting, tossing it to the ground and wiping the rain from his nose. He was bursting to speak, to spill out the tensions he felt. He'd heard of another family, somewhere beyond Mysore. They'd been filmed by foreigners, but they'd been properly treated. And they'd been paid. Yes, hundreds of thousands of rupees. Who knows, perhaps it was thousands of thousands? Yes, oh yes, he'd heard. And now people were saying that *he'd* received two hundred thousand. What could he answer? He'd say, 'Yes, yes, I'm going to buy a scooter, I'm going to get a car. Just wait till the unit leaves.' What else could he say? Even when he was ill people came all the time and said, 'Give me a hundred rupees, give me two hundred, give me five thousand.' He couldn't stand it. He couldn't take any more. If he'd known it was going to happen, he wouldn't have let it happen, he wouldn't have agreed to start with. And all for what? Two thousand rupees.

Well, now he was going to change things. Thirty thousand rupees. That was what he demanded – the family needed a new pumpset. It was reasonable. The unit could easily afford it. They stood to make plenty of money. Yes, it was quite fair for all the trouble they'd taken, for all the help they'd given to film the family, film his wife, even though she was pregnant. The village talked about that. They said he'd sold his wife in return for a little money: if the child were lost, if his wife had a bad delivery, then he was the one who would get the blame.

He stood his ground, thrusting his shoulders back, and glared at those around him. He would have looked like an angry lizard if he hadn't been so intense, if he hadn't been so certain of his power, a menacing, threatening power.

Tony's interpreter took up the argument as fellow-Indian and mediator. He cajoled, he confronted, he persuaded, he tried to explain the problems. The budget was very limited, it wasn't a lavish production, no one would make any profits. The people of England had paid for it to be used to increase understanding.

Nanjeswamy didn't care who or what had paid for it. He wanted his money. He'd get his money. Thirty thousand. No less.

But didn't he realise, the interpreter argued, that he had a responsibility to the people of India to help the people of England?

Nanjeswamy laughed. In England they had money. Did his family have money?

The interpreter lost his temper. Did he think he'd attain salvation by rubbing his hands with money? How could he live as a man if all he could think of was money? Was Mother India made of such men?

Nanjeswamy spat. He'd been a man. He'd provided for all the needs of the film unit. He'd opened his home to them, given them food, given them shelter. And why should the interpreter be so concerned? Perhaps those who walked with the film unit had also received some money? Didn't they follow them round wherever they went? They must be getting millions.

The argument ran for three hours, tossing and turning in waves of bitter resentment, anger, and then cynical calm. The film unit said they could manage five thousand. Nanjeswamy laughed in high-pitched hysteria and said he'd take twenty thousand just as a special favour to help the people of England. The film unit said they could find another family; Nanjeswamy said ten was his lowest figure.

'We can go to another family.'

'But you've filmed our family already.'

'We can always film another. We've plenty of time and you seem to think plenty of money.'

'But you wanted our family especially.'

'Oh no, any family does. In fact, we've found another not very far from here.'

Birth

'Eight thousand,' said Nanjeswamy.

'Why should we pay eight? Six will buy you a pumpset.'

'Six,' said Nanjeswamy.

'And now can we film what we want?'

'Yes.'

'We can film your wife's delivery?'

He hesitated. He didn't mind, but some of the family might. And all the village would gossip.

'Not the birth itself of course but just immediately after?'

'I need a watch for myself. And two thousand cash in advance.'

Everyone shook hands. Nanjeswamy beamed.

'Very good,' he imitated in English, rolling the 'r' with relish.

'Very good,' said Kevan the associate producer. 'You little bugger.'

The unit returned to the family house to be feted and honoured: the old lady gave flowers and burned a scented stick; Thayee brought coffee; and Susheelamma prepared a special sweet.

The old man sat on his cot, withdrawn and uninterested.

'We've agreed on extra money,' called Tony. 'It'll buy you a diesel pumpset.'

'Oh?' said the old man.

'Yes, it's six thousand now.'

'How much was it before?' he asked wearily.

'Didn't you know?'

'No one tells me such things.'

'Well now you know and can tell your sons.'

'You must tell them yourself. They no longer listen to me.'

Five days later Tony and I sat on the old man's cot: Vara had gone to Krishnapatna to take a proper bath since she had started her period, so we waited alone for the meal which Nanjeswamy was arranging in honour of the new agreement. Bhadre Gowda, the husband of Thayee, was crouched over the flames singeing the skin of a chicken and plucking the last few feathers. The children watched closely and puckered their noses against the smell. The sounds of the house were timeless: the crackle of wood, the whirring of grinding stones, the repetitive thud of pounding; the light of the house was soft and mellow with pale reflection and muted shadows from burning single flames. The people were silent and calm, conscious of waiting guests.

194

Birth

I felt strange, almost embarrassed, sitting high up with Tony and receiving respect as his wife. My place as a woman was in the kitchen doing the work with the others, concealed and discreet: it was where I normally chose to be, in order to share with the women. But now I was exposed to the family stage, the open arena where men performed and women kept to the shadows. Each time I talked to Tony or shared an intimate look, I felt self-conscious and even a little brazen, so I slipped off the cot to take my turn at the grinding. My hands had hardened, though one or two places were still raw from blisters. I grasped the stick and swung round the stone with Susheelamma. Her pace was slow so I pushed round faster to finish the job more quickly. She smiled and quickened it further. There was only a little left and she trickled the seed through the stone. We spun the wheel like a top and ended gasping but happy.

Nanjeswamy placed Tony and me together and ordered the women to serve us food: rice, chicken, vegetables, more rice, buttermilk, and half a teaspoon of sugar. They gave my portion of meat to Tony since I was vegetarian and laughed with pleasure when he accepted more. The women liked Tony and recognised his kindness. They didn't think it strange that he should help me to food sometimes or let me walk through a door first; they didn't find it embarrassing that he put an arm round my shoulder – they accepted it and said once they'd like the same freedom but knew it could never happen.

There was no question however that we should share a mat. Tony slept outside on Nanjeswamy's cot; I slept in the bedroom along with the women and children. Madakka settled down in the far corner, pushing her children to one side and taking the only pillow. Then came Vara's empty mattress, long and thin like a camp-bed; then my mat, shared with Lakshmi, the youngest wife. Thayee was hugging her two daughters under a thick blanket; Susheelamma had tossed aside any cover and was panting from heat and sweat.

'Here,' I said, lifting Vara's mattress and dragging it across the room. 'You can lie down in comfort.'

Susheelamma giggled shyly and huddled against the wall.

'Why don't you use it?' I said, spreading it out beside her. She shook her head. With my arms, I gave myself a huge stomach and staggered about the room moaning and gasping. 'We've got to take care,' I said. But still she refused; I picked it up and dropped it lightly on her. The women burst into laughter.

Thayee went to her trunk and took out some leaves and lime. She gave some to me and Susheelamma, but purposely left out Madakka. They still weren't speaking. The three of us sat chewing like schoolgirls at a midnight feast, half waiting for the old lady to come in and reprimand us – but she was surveilling the youngest wife who still had the vessels to clean.

Thayee beckoned me over and showed me her treasured contents: the silver anklets worn on her wedding day, a button, some ghee, and a plastic comb. Four white pills were wrapped in a piece of newspaper; two sweets had gone sticky in yellow wrappers. She thrust something into my fingers and pushed my hand to my mouth – it was half a stale biscuit which she must have saved for days.

At 2.10, I woke to hear Susheelamma whisper to Thayee. I could not make out the words. She stumbled across the room and shook Madakka urgently.

Madakka scratched at the matches and lit the wick of a small lamp. She placed it on Thayee's trunk, then slipped back under her blanket and fell asleep again.

Susheelamma moaned and bent her body backwards, holding her stomach desperately. She doubled forward and sank to her mat gasping for breath in her pain. Then she sat quietly, waiting, waiting. Her body jerked again. Thayee helped her up to the trunk and made her grip the edge, bending her body towards it.

I sat up uncertainly, thoughts running through my head. Should I wake Tony or not? Couldn't I go on sleeping until it was too late? I coughed, quietly. Thayee turned, and Susheelamma looked under her arm while straining against the trunk.

'Tony?' I said helplessly, spreading my hands in submission.

They nodded, perhaps without understanding, and gestured for me to wake him up: he also sat mute for a moment until with determination he left the house to run to Krishnapatna, guided by Bhadre Gowda. The rest of the men went out of the house and huddled on the verandah wrapped in their shawls and blankets. One strode away to a neighbouring village to tell some cousins and fetch the midwife.

Birth

Madakka sat up.

'Hey,' she hissed and prodded the youngest in the back. 'Get up, get up, must start the grinding at once.'

The girl rolled out of reach.

'Lakshmi,' she shouted over and over again until the girl stood up and the noise of grinding began. The light in the bedroom flickered and smoked, too soft to give any shadows, but it made Susheelamma choke.

At 2.50 the Harijan midwife came, a woman of the 'untouchable' caste dressed in brown, her thick grey hair tied hastily, her face sweating from the speed with which she had come. She kept her head low, humble, and her hands tucked into her sari. She had a soft face, almost tender, with its wrinkled lines and wide eyes, but there seemed a streak of cunning. She had no land, she had no husband now, and had learnt her art from her mother-in-law, both with calves and children. The family trusted her skills, for she had delivered four of their children safely and charged only two rupees together with some grain. She seemed to suit the family and they used her in preference to the government midwife, who in any case lived further away.

"Just here?" she asked Susheelamma, feeling the stomach carefully.

Susheelamma nodded. "Bad pains, worse, worse than before."

"You've nothing to fear," she said blandly.

The old lady brought in a ragged sari: Susheelamma changed and slumped down on her mattress.

At 3.20 everyone moved from the bedroom into the hall. Thayee and Madakka hurried to fill the big brass pot, feeling their way with their feet along the steps and between the cattle, out through the door and along to the tank, backwards and forwards, backwards and forwards. Only two lights burned, one on the old man's cot, the other among the gods. The house was still, expectant.

Some cousins arrived and the old lady sat with them on the floor near the old man's cot. They reminisced about earlier births, the problems when women were weak, the birth of a son, the birth of a daughter. They did not bother to stop when Susheelamma's mother slipped in and sat by herself near the bench, not joining the conversation.

Birth

The old lady stood up and tossed back her sari over her shoulder: she took a broom and began to brush down the floor along the red cement between the pillars, muttering to herself, forgetting the pregnant Susheelamma. She swept round the grinding stones, glancing cursorily at Lakshmi; she swept round the old man's cot; she swept round her cousins and round the feet of Susheelamma, on to the end of the room, then turned and swept her way back again.

Susheelamma cried out. She clutched the stone pillar nearest the cattle area; she bent herself against it, moaning. She stood upright, her hands in the small of her back, arching, arching, whispering the pain, her stomach protruding violently. She writhed, her body circling round; she rolled her eyes; she closed them; she opened them and looked from side to side; her hair fell in strands on her face, a face which had started to sweat, which showed the strain and exhaustion, black rings, the pores of her skin stretched open. She stumbled, her leg giving way with the sway. Her mother leant anxiously forward but did not move to help: none of the others noticed.

Thayee brought a rope and throwing it over a beam gave the ends to Susheelamma on which she could strain herself, pull her body, arch her back, ease the pain slowly. One of the cousins started a fire to heat the water, snapping the twigs into kindling: smoke and flames began to rise. The old lady placed a small wooden board auspiciously painted with rice paste near the feet of Susheelamma; then she seated herself at the grinding stone to urge on the slackening Lakshmi. The cattle moved restlessly, dropped their dung with a splatter, heaved themselves up and down, fretted against the rope. The children continued to sleep in the bedroom. The fire burned strongly.

At 4.05, Susheelamma sat on the board, with her mother in front between her outstretched legs, and the midwife behind supporting her back. Together they groped through her sari, feeling their way to her thighs; together they told her to breathe, deeper, deeper, to push out with all her strength. They worked together easing the baby out, first the head, then the torso, finally the legs. It gave a soft cry.

The old lady hurried over, peered forward, pushing the legs of the baby apart. A hint of disappointment skimmed her face: Susheelamma had delivered a daughter.

Birth

The midwife lay the child on a tossing basket, its grey cord trailing through blood to its mother who sat motionless, exhausted, her head bent onto her knees. The midwife cleaned the baby, wiping away the blood with a rag; she tied some cotton round the cord, pulled it tight, and cut through with a billhook. She burnt the end with a candle and tied a rough knot.

Susheelamma sat silently slumped against a pillar disregarded by everyone. The smell of blood was almost a stench and the cattle chafed wildly. The room shook with the shadows from the flames of the fire and the door was kept firmly closed against the intrusion of men.

The old lady slipped outside. Manager Nanjeswamy sat glumly against the wall, the old man asleep beside him, his brother awake but unconcerned. Susheelamma's father was smoking nervously on the other side of the verandah.

Nanjeswamy looked up.

"It's a girl," said the old lady.

He dropped his head.

"God's given her to us," he said. "Let it be. When God gives, you can't do anything about it. He's given a boy, he's given a girl, what more do I want?"

He stared out into the night.

A Land-Rover stopped at the bottom of the street and the film unit came running up.

'Well done,' said Tony, shaking him by the hand.

'Bloody good, mate,' said Kevan and gave him an English cigarette.

The old lady let them in for five minutes to film. The bright lights swung over the baby, across to Susheelamma, through to the cattle and back to Lakshmi grinding endlessly on. It picked out the midwife as she carried the baby into the sunken area and poured water over it, so hot and heavy that it clutched frantically at nothing, its pink skin turning to vivid red.

When they had gone, Susheelamma was helped by the midwife into the sunken area. She stripped off her clothes and crouched shivering while water was poured over her hair, over her body, pot after pot till all the water was finished. Her hair was long and black round her shoulders; her skin was sallow and firm except for the sagging stomach. She had a fine body with long legs, wide

199

hips, a broad yet delicate back, and full breasts weighed down with
the milk of pregnancy. She stood unsteadily while Thayee wrapped
round her body a clean sari and tied a cloth round her wet head.
Supported by the women she tottered across the room and lay
down on a mat next to the old man's cot: she clasped the baby
to her stomach then put it to sleep in the tossing basket at her
head.

The old lady was soaking the blood of the birth with earth and
warm ashes, rubbing it onto the stone, then sweeping it down with
a brush, washing it well with water. Lakshmi was still grinding,
her hair from her plait trailing into her eyes. Sweat was on her
face and her eyes were narrow from tiredness; Susheelamma's
mother approached and motioned her gently to stop. She sat down
and started to grind herself. She was calm now that her daughter
was safe, was sleeping after a quick delivery. Deeply, quietly, she
began to sing.

"Oh grinding stone for *ragi*, the stone that sings a saga,
the precious, precious stone of my father-in-law's house,
the darling precious stone of my father-in-law's house,
the stone we hold now – shower the flour, shower the flour.

"Oh grinding stone for rice, the stone that grinds so fast,
the precious, precious stone of my own father's house,
the darling precious stone of my own father's house,
the stone we hold now – shower the flour, shower the flour.

"Oh mother stone, grind the millet,
drop the flour with a *jal jal* sound,
drop the flour with a *jal jal* sound,
and we shall light you a lamp.

"A fruit tree shot up outside the village,
blossomed early and bore sour green fruits;
now the fruits are nearly ripe, they laugh, laugh,
while the mother who married her daughter to a distant
    village cries, cries.

200

"Oh foolish, deluded mother,
see the picture on the sandy wall and forget your sorrow."

Dawn was breaking, its soft light creeping into the village, penetrating the house. Susheelamma's mother gathered the flour in a basket, bent for a moment over the baby, and tiptoed out of the house. The rest of the visitors followed. The night of drama was over.

No one went back to bed and the house returned to normal, unmoved by the night's event. The men came in for coffee, the women cleared the dung and prepared the morning meal. Nanjeswamy fixed round his own cot a stiff screen made from coconut leaves which he secured to an overhead beam with yards of rough twine. Susheelamma lay inert on the floor, buried in a blanket.

'Come,' said the old lady softly and pulled back the blanket from her face. Susheelamma groaned and opened her eyes, the lids flickering with effort. 'Lift your head slowly.' And when Susheelamma did so, the old lady draped some cloth about her. 'Come now, sit up.' Susheelamma levered herself painfully upwards. 'Must stand,' said the old lady impatiently, and grasping her round the arm pulled her shoulders forward. With head bent and hair tangled, her clothes heedlessly worn, Susheelamma shuffled slow step by slow step towards the cot, supported on the right by a neighbouring cousin, supported on the left by the old lady. She lay down behind the screen on her husband's hard bare cot; the old lady fetched the blanket and spread it over her, tucking it round her neck. Susheelamma closed her eyes.

The old lady took the baby and sat on the steps in the light of the open roof: its skin was deep pink, crinkled and wrinkled over the joints; its hands flapped feebly; its eyes were shut hard against the brightness. Taking a handful of castor oil she rubbed the skin with her coarse, stiff fingers poking between the limbs, smoothing it over and over. She coated its hair, wiped its mouth, wiped the eyelids and ears; the baby began to scream.

"Wah, wah," cooed the old lady, bouncing it on her lap. "Wah, wah, why are you crying like that?" She clicked her tongue and ran her palm over the baby's forehead. She tickled its stomach roughly. "Oh, yes, oh yes, isn't it nice to have girls? Girls will look after their mothers, ask after their mothers, come when their mothers are ill. Will sons ever do the same? They just come and go, take their food, sleep, and go out to work."

She had six granddaughters now. She said it would cost twenty thousand rupees to get them all married, so perhaps we should take the new baby back to England.

12 Manly Revelations

After the birth, everything seemed flaccid, even the bursts of rain which dampened the soil spasmodically. I don't know what the family felt – they probably felt nothing, accepting the pattern of life in its inevitability, continuing their work in order to sustain themselves. I felt sad that fate had brought no answers, but then I had hoped for a boy, and hope brought disillusion. It was better not to hope, not in a life where chances were small, and choice did not exist. For the family, resignation was better, it brought less pain and trauma.

The film unit also sensed the climax of birth and the lack of result it had brought, but they felt that something strong had developed in sharing such an occasion. They were no longer much in the village, for they were filming another story elsewhere with one of the handicapped children, and perhaps wisely they understood the need to be far from Nanjeswamy. Not that he openly blamed them that his wife had borne a daughter, for he was the one to be taunted for selling his wife to the strangers. His demands were still as persistent, for watches, cloth, cash, and as Tony was rarely around he transferred his requests to me, adding more to the list, of female paraphernalia: a shawl, some white bread, some whisky as medicine, all for his wife; a bangle for his new daughter; a dress; some diamond studs for her ears. And in order to make his demands more effective, he claimed that I was the baby's new mother who had the means to look after her. He touched a raw spot, for I often felt guilty at the freedom and privilege of my life when compared to theirs.

The child's future was fairly predictable. Suckled till two, she'd have her mother's attention; once weaned, her aunts would increasingly help to look after her, and subject her to greater discipline; at six she'd start her own jobs, such as tending sheep or filling the animals' water-trough. From then onwards, also, she'd learn her domestic duties, to cook and sweep and wash – skill came from observation and error rather than any direct instruction from her aunts or mother or grandmother. She'd certainly learn where authority lay, but also quickly assess the possible sources of affection – her mother, a favourite uncle, the grandfather – and those areas of rivalry best to avoid.

And then she'd be ready for marriage. A girl was born to be married, to enter another household, and any relationships formed in childhood would have to be broken abruptly. But Susheelamma's child was the daughter of Nanjeswamy: she might have a chance of change, of marrying a richer husband who didn't require his wife to work in the fields. It all depended on dowries, and the alliance the Manager fixed. He was bound to work something advantageous for his daughter, for it would bring advantage to himself.

It was slightly different with boys. They still had the same restrictions of freedom in childhood while learning the tasks of men: but they could copy their fathers in assuming authority over younger people and women; and of course they stayed at home on marriage. I think they had one disadvantage, however. A son was released to his father from five or six years of age to be trained in work and self-sufficiency and isolation from others: there was not the chance of natural affection which women could have for women, such as Bhadramma and Jayamma, or Madakka and her mother. A boy's bond with his father was based on work and the needs of everyday living; and a boy's contact with men was filled with mistrust and suspicions. 'When boys are born, they are brothers,' Nanjeswamy had said, 'but when they grow into men they become cousins with equal yet opposite interests.'

But first a baby had to be named, eleven days after birth. For a girl it was usually a small ceremony; but because the unit was filming, and because word had got round that the foreigners were leaving soon, the house was packed with neighbours. All the family had come, including those from town.

A name was not yet chosen. The priest in passing had said it should start with 'S' as defined by the position of the planets, but the old lady could not make up her mind. It was she who made the decision, once the men had given their views. The mother was not consulted. The priest had also said the ceremony should start at six o'clock in the evening; but at eight, the women were still preparing food: the family was giving a feast as farewell to the film unit. Not that they had done the things which were meant to

be done to mark the end of eleven days and the pollution brought
by the birth: traditionally, the whole house should have been
cleaned, the walls whitewashed, the floor redone, and the gods
worshipped with offerings and prayers. But all the family had
done was to have their baths – men, women, and children – and
to light a scented stick. That took time enough, along with all the
cooking.

It was an occasion for women. They crowded round the empty
cradle which hung from a central beam, while the men sat in the
shadows on the outskirts of the room. Eramma from the town
distributed *kunkuma* to the women, thumbing the red powder on
their foreheads and thrusting into their hands a flower, a banana,
a betel leaf. Her daughter helped, dressed in bright new clothes
with an ostentatious pendant swinging round her neck – the envy
of the women.

The old lady carried the baby into the room and laid her in the
cradle. The women started to sing and to rock the cradle roughly.
The old lady bent over the baby.

"Shardamma," she whispered, "Sharda, Shara, Saramma."
She struggled to find the pronunciation and kept interchanging the
words. "Sharda, Shara, Sara."

Susheelamma leant from her bed to peer round the edge of the
screen, her head still wrapped in red cloth to prevent her catching
cold. She had ventured out that morning to take her first bath and
to crack a coconut on the steps of the house as offering to god. The
pollution was nearly over: for the past eleven days no one had
touched her or her clothes, no one had been to the temple, no one
had done any worship even within the house; she ate from her own
dishes a special diet of coffee, rice, and salt, with no fruit and no
curds – her body had to heal, there shouldn't be harsh foods to
aggravate her stomach.

Jayamma was also there, squatting beside Susheelamma's cot,
gazing into the crowd, a forlorn figure separate from the ceremony.
Together they formed a bond in their isolation from others,
purposely unwelcome, purposely neglected. And yet they seemed
unconscious of each other and were lost in their own thoughts,
each with a separate problem that had no ready answer.

I went to the cradle and placed on the baby's finger a small
gold ring from the film unit. Everyone looked to see its value, and

205

then the baby was returned to her mother. It was time for her to suckle, and time for the guests to eat.

A sense of fulfilment came from the sharing of food between the family and the film unit, heightened by an awareness that the partnership – or bargain, whatever one wanted to call it – was coming to an end. The men sat on the verandah smoking, telling stories, enjoying a moment of unity.

It was shattered the following morning. Manager Nanjeswamy and the old lady gave back the gold ring. They felt it wasn't good enough, that more should have been spent on diamond earrings or silver anklets. They were huddled together in the dark store room where Vara and I had been called. They consulted together in whispers, then told me it might be better to get instead a gold necklace for Susheelamma, in thanks for all the trouble she'd taken, all the filming she'd done . . . No, not possible? Mother and son conferred together again. Then couldn't the unit buy the necklace and pay for it from the money still owed to the family? There was no need to say who had thought of it, just deduct the amount and tell the family that something like two thousand rupees had been spent on some gold for Susheelamma and her baby.

The audacity of it stunned me. Until that point, I'd accepted the demands of Nanjeswamy as the demands of a man who was driven by poverty, who wanted to get out of the spiral of peasant conditions, whose boldness I almost admired. I'd also felt guilty at my intrusion and the havoc of the film unit. But now he had gone too far: it was predacity succoured by selfishness. I lost my temper and shouted at them with anger. It had a disastrous effect, for they started to sneer and ridicule, offering back the cash the unit had paid to the family which was locked in the family trunk. What would they want with money? Didn't they have their land? Of course if I felt they had too much, if I needed it for myself, then I should take it back. They thought I'd *want* to give something to Susheelamma and the baby. They even took out the money and waved it in front of my face, knowing I would not take it; and when they had finished their mocking, they took the ring from my lap and locked it in the trunk.

On reflection, the incident was revealing not for their materialism, given the conditions of life, but for their collaboration. Mother and son seemed Machiavellian in their partnership, and on several nights over the last few days I had woken to hear the old lady whisper to Nanjeswamy. It puzzled me why they should be so close. He was probably her favourite but why should he bother with her since he had power himself? It was hardly an Oedipus complex, though mothers in Hindu mythology have sexual and sacrosanct power. Perhaps she was a useful servant to him, and he was the means of power to her. They both had similar characters.

The relationship of mother and son intrigued me, but I had no evidence of its nature. The old lady refused to talk about her feelings; the men were inaccessible. I could speculate only from observation. With her other sons, the old lady seemed more cautious, particularly with S.M.B. She probably knew that as a woman she had always to show respect, and though the son had to do the same to his mother, and to make sure she was properly cared for, in the end it was he who had independence. Power for women in men's affairs required careful calculation.

Bhadramma was free of intrigue with her sons, since she controlled the household. But she clashed with her eldest son, a man of twenty-seven, who lived and worked in the town. He was kind, and responsible about his family, returning to work the fields at weekends. He had also spent a lot of money trying to help Jayamma. But Bhadramma said she felt he could do more, and though she accepted quietly his advice and always followed it through, she seemed disillusioned. I suspect she felt subconsciously that sons should stay at home to look after their mothers. That was how it had been, and that was how it should be.

The rain came at last. Bursts of sun and torrents of rain, one after the other, soaking, drying, soaking, drying. At first, with its hot hard crust and defiant dust, the soil rejected the rain; but the earth turned darker, richer, redder, and mixed itself into mud. The trees dripped, and the leaves were runnels directing the water downwards for capture in cracks and furrows. As the rain sank into the earth, the smells rose like steam, pungent, sweet, heavy. The scent of vegetation escaped as only the rain could release it, a temporary release before the sun came back to burn it dry once more.

There was no sudden joy on people's faces though for months

they had prayed for rain. They started to work intensively and to watch the clouds with quiet acceptance.

Bhadre Gowda, the husband of Thayee, was ploughing a millet field, up and down, up and down, turning the soil to catch the next torrent of rain: the bullocks pulled and he pushed as the wooden plough shuddered through the ground. We watched from a bank, and when he stopped for a rest he came and sat beside us. The sun was hot on our backs.

He was a handsome man with the fine features of his sister Bhadramma – the same straight nose, the same delicate eyebrows over bright kind eyes, the same wide mouth expressive of thought and feeling. Small earrings studded his rounded lobes, crystal glass set in a gold trefoil; and tucked on top of each ear was a single pink blossom plucked from a flowering bush.

'Yes, we worship the land,' he said. 'It's our life. It's beautiful, it's always beautiful. But the most beautiful is when it's green, when the crops are large and fruitful. Then it's like a woman. How much more beautiful it is when she wears her jewels, does her hair, wears fine clothes. And when she takes them off, how empty we feel.

'Yes, when we cut the crops we feel empty. But then we know we'll be starting to plant again, controlling the land, making it bear fruit. And then we feel happy. We feel satisfied in working the land where we grow our life.'

He unwound the small torn scarf from his head and wiped the sweat from his face: his chin was black with stubble, his skin dry and dark from the constant exposure to sun. He looked poor, almost beggarly, with a shirt ripped at the shoulder, and most of the buttons missing.

'You see, we *feel* the land, just as we feel the rain. We don't *see* it, splashing down on the paths: we feel it cold on our backs. And the sun – we don't see it, a beautiful sunset as you say. We feel it in the morning when it's cool, when it gives us light to work by; we feel it when it burns our backs and we want the shade of the tree; we feel it in the late afternoon softened by a breeze; and then when it goes down and takes away our light, we feel we've done a full day's work. Then we can sleep in peace.'

He sat quietly, his forehead puckered, his eyes half-closed, and his body began to sway.

"We have great affection and trust for Mother Earth. When we're alive, it's she who gives us rice, gives us food. It's she who takes us in when we're dead. If we don't work the land how will we get food? If we trust her she'll always give. See, this year there was no rain. But now it's come, now we can live and prosper. We should trust her. We should trust her more than our own mother, the mother who's given birth to us."

He closed his eyes; his body was silent now.

The women had a feeling of freedom because of the rain. They were excited as we went to wash the clothes: Thayee, Lakshmi, Madakka, and the old lady's cousin. We passed through the dripping mango grove and came to the top of a stone staircase where the land slipped into a small ravine: the water was thundering through – red water, the colour of bricks and thickened with soil from the banks; it gushed over rocks and tore at the sides, carrying off mud and pebbles. Upstream we found a calm pool surrounded by rocks. The women squatted down in separate parts, and spread out the bundles of clothes which they rubbed with sand water. They flicked each garment against the rock with a quick twist of the wrist, beating it and beating it. When they came to the lengths of saris, they stood up: gripping one end of the cloth, they swung it into the air and brought it hard down against the rock, up and down, up and down, hissing at the effort. Finally they rinsed the clothes in the pool, the saris spreading out across the water in billows, to be drawn back in by the women foot by foot till every inch was free from sand and dirt. They spread out the garments on bushes to dry in the burning sun: they smoothed and pulled them to remove the creases.

Within an hour they were dry. Black clouds were gathering so we hurried back home. We made it just as the storm burst and torrents of rain came down.

In two days time, the unit was due to leave, and still I was no closer to understanding the men. I was getting almost obsessive about the problem, partly, I think, because I did not know what to look for. It was easy, as a Western woman who was influenced by and had benefited from the concepts of female liberation, to condemn the family men as classic examples of selfish oppressors, especially Nanjeswamy and Kalle Gowda. But then I had to admit that the men themselves were oppressed, by debts, by decisions, by work, even by life itself, for all of which they had to be responsible. And men like Bhadre Gowda, the old man, and Madakka's husband, seemed to contradict the theory of male oppressors.

The problem was finally solved when Tony decided to interview the men, one by one, so that their taped voices could be used as commentary over the film; he also did it for my sake, for he knew that only a man could talk to a man in any intimate manner. And so he drove to the village with the male interpreter, and parked the car away from the road in a secretive place near some bushes. S.M.B. was invited first to sit in the car and talk, while I stood guard in the distance to intercept any inquisitive passers-by. Then the old man was enticed from the fields without the family knowing: he sat erect on the back seat with his stick held upright in front of him while Tony sat in the front. Finally that day, Rame Gowda, the husband of Madakka, agreed to talk but he stayed for only an hour. The day was gone in any case.

The next day, since the male interpreter had hurt his ankle and had to lie in bed, it was agreed that the men should come to the Travellers' Bungalow in Krishnapatna. I was despatched to fetch Bhadre Gowda, but he refused to come unless Nanjeswamy gave permission. Nanjeswamy refused, sullenly. I pleaded and cajoled. He must have known that he could do nothing now to stop his family talking, so he acceded at last with a nod and an angry glare.

Bhadre Gowda talked for three hours without inhibition, then immediately returned to the fields to continue the work he had left.

That afternoon, Nanjeswamy insisted on coming to Krishnapatna for he wanted to tell his side of the story: he was furious and yet he was slightly fearful, for he did not know what the others had said. If he denied something they had revealed, then Tony would know he was lying; if he talked of something they had not revealed, then he was exposing himself unnecessarily.

Some of the things the men had to say were startling, but some revelations only confirmed what we already suspected. I don't know why they were so frank: I think they found it a relief to tell at last the true story, and since the old man started the rot, why shouldn't the others tell their side of the story? They had nothing to lose now that the unit was leaving. I suspect also that one or two of them hoped they might get extra money on the side.

Manly Revelations

I shall give only key extracts from the hours of taped interviews done by Tony.

S.M.B.:
(Unfortunately, after half an hour, the cassette tape got stuck. But perhaps it was fortunate: with skill and great diplomacy, S.M.B. managed to reveal nothing new.)
(*of the joint family*) "Freedom? Everybody has freedom." And, "If we're all together, we can improve even more." Finally, "There isn't much free independence within a joint family."

THE OLD MAN: (*of Nanjeswamy*) "He doesn't work. He keeps loafing around all the time. Therefore I said, They work hard, and he can't, let him loaf around and look after the management. You all can work in the fields. I said this. It could have been a good arrangement. But that Nanjeswamy. He's a bit of a crook, not honest with money. He never looks after others.''

* * *

(*of the managers*) "S.M.B. and Nanjeswamy spend money on this and that. We never know anything. Yes, they're in league together."

* * *

(*of the joint family*) "It's nice, but it's not working well. If we aren't united, if we don't cooperate with each other, how can we do anything? There should be unity if anything is to be done. Instead they fight with each other."

* * *

(*of his second wife*) "Yes, she was very nice. Even if the old lady beat her, she wouldn't say anything. She never fought with anyone. She used to do all the work outside, and then come home. She was very gentle. She wouldn't talk back, she wouldn't argue whatever happened."

* * *

(*of the old lady*) "Yes, she is rather harsh."

* * *

211

Manly Revelations

(*of Nanjeswamy again*) "He does whatever comes to his mind, and keeps everything to himself. Look, there are four brothers – I know you won't go and tell Nanjeswamy this – there are four brothers in the village, and yet Nanjeswamy is paying insurance in his wife's name. Now where did he get the money from to pay for this insurance? So we all asked him, 'How could you do such injustice when there are four and you are the head. You must buy policies for the others. What you did was wrong.' He retorted, 'Oh, my father-in-law gave me the money.' "

*   *   *

(*of his sons by the second wife*) "Poor things, they don't even have their mother. They have nothing. Nothing. And they have to work all the time. At least while I'm alive, I can do something, and look after them. No one else bothers. They say to me, 'While you're alive, do something for us. Divide the family and finish everything, whatever happens afterwards.' "

*   *   *

(*on division*) "There'll be injustice because of the way the managers have written the loans. Who knows what the loans really are. The managers will say, 'You must all take your share in the loans if you want your share of the land.' "

*   *   *

(*of his two sons in town*) "Those two are educated and can do something. They know all the tricks. But what will the others do?"

*   *   *

(*of Nanjeswamy and the old lady*) "The mother and son – they just look after themselves. If they feel like bringing us food in the fields, they'll bring us food in the fields, but if they can't be bothered, they won't do it."

*   *   *

(*of the old lady*) "She's the one who says, 'Why do you want any food? Shouldn't the children eat it? It's a waste feeding you. Why do you want it?' She's the one, she's the one."

*   *   *

212

"Yes, the old lady likes her own children and grandchildren better."

*   *   *

(*of his sons by the second wife*) "Yes, I have most affection for these two. But I don't have anything to give them."

*   *   *

"Nobody gives me anything. I don't even have any money to buy a packet of *bidis*. And yet everything came from me – the land, the crops, the work."

*   *   *

(*of the film unit*) "You might ask why we didn't tell you earlier. I wanted to say good things about the family, so I told you, 'Yes, we're getting along very well, there's nothing wrong at all.' " (He laughs ruefully.)

*   *   *

"I feel sad. I feel so sad. Sad. That it should happen right in front of my eyes. I feel sad about the family."

RAME GOWDA: (*of the managers*) "We have to stretch out our hands for whatever they give us. Whatever they bring, and buy, we have to accept it as good. We even have to pick up what they throw away. If we want to do business ourselves, we must do it through them as managers, while we work in the background. But we shouldn't go against them. We don't want any bitterness in this house. So we keep them in front, and obey them without any argument or complaint."

*   *   *

(*of Nanjeswamy and Bhadre Gowda*) "They had a terrible fight with each other. It was when we were building the second house. Bhadre Gowda called Nanjeswamy: 'Come, let's go and fetch some water for the walls.' But Nanjeswamy said, 'I'm not coming. You go.' Then Bhadre Gowda yelled, 'Why not, you son of a widow?' And just for that they started fighting. It

213

reached such a pitch that all the people said, 'It's finished today, the family can't continue.' It must have been six years ago.

"My father spoke for Bhadre Gowda, and that made things worse, they went on fighting. And my mother spoke for Nanjeswamy. It made them fight all the more. She said, 'That's just how he always behaves.' And the old man said, 'Why blame him?' And the fighting got really violent.

"After it was over, I said, 'Whoever can work and feels he shouldn't be sitting, must work. Whoever can't work needn't do it. He can just sit and watch. But we won't have this fighting in the house. If we can't work, we'll get some labourers to do it, or we'll manage and do all the work ourselves. Let it cost me anything, I'll do anything, but let us stay together as a family.' I told them this. Then I made Nanjeswamy eat. We fried some salt, put it on some cloth, and applied it to his bruises for warmth. The old man said he'd been hit also, so we warmed his bruises. Bhadre Gowda hadn't been hit much – somewhere on the leg, with a whip.

"And so things carried on. Otherwise it would have been over that day. All the people said, 'They won't stay together any more, they're bound to divide now.' But what do they care whether we live or are destroyed?"

* * *

(*on division*) "I say that if the people who manage do it well and honestly, then we should stick together for another ten years or so. But it's only because we're slogging here that they have anything to manage. And they can save money from what they handle."

* * *

(*of Nanjeswamy*) "He's improved a bit now. After he had his children, slowly his mind has settled to business."

* * *

"We planted too much sugar-cane last year: and what happened? We didn't have enough millet. It was S.M.B. who decided that. Normally all the agriculture is our responsibility.

They don't argue with our suggestions. And when they make small suggestions, then we don't argue with them."

*   *   *

"I leave everything to Mother Earth: if she gives, then she gives; if there's ruin for the crop, then there's ruin. It's her will. Through her, you can prosper, and have storeyed buildings, or cover your body with gold. Through her, you can lose, and have nothing. If you show kindness to her, and hard work, she will return the same. She'll never hold back your wages. That's my experience."

*   *   *

"You see, I can go on weeding the whole day without getting bored. I can work in the fields all day. But Nanjeswamy can't do it. He's the kind of person who wants to talk to many people. If he sees four people, he has to join them. But we can't leave it half done."

*   *   *

(*of Chikke Gowda, the bridegroom*) "He should realise it himself, in his heart. He should say, 'I'm not young any more, I'm grown up, I shouldn't eat what they've earned. I must do some work. Or at least I should do some agriculture.' But it doesn't come to his mind."

*   *   *

(*of S.M.B.*) "He's put his four children into a good school, so he could have put one of mine there also. Alright if my son doesn't study, that doesn't matter. At least my mind would have been satisfied. I would have felt, 'See, my brother did for my children what he did for his own.' But he doesn't do such things. Instead, if he wants a pair of sandals worth twenty-five rupees, he just goes and buys them."

*   *   *

(*of the two wives*) "The family wouldn't have stayed together if both of them were alive. I'm not lying. It wouldn't have been together today. When she was there, we were all still very small. But there used to be lots of fighting."

*   *   *

"I'm not boasting, not exaggerating. Just the truth. If I hadn't worked all the time, even when the managers weren't there to supervise, we'd never have reached this level. Even if I'm dying, without food, I don't leave till the work is over."

*   *   *

"Only if a man goes through hardship can he attain happiness. If you kill yourself with work, then you can get happiness."

BHADRE GOWDA: "Yes, it's true, the 18,000 rupees debt is true. I can confirm it, they're not lying to you. We borrowed 3000 rupees for coconut plants, 5000 for the well, 5000 for the pump-set, 2000 for other things. It's just that the managers don't pay back the interest, so the debts are never paid off. Nanjeswamy must have saved more than 2000 rupees for himself, and the manager in town must have saved much the same. I myself have got about 300, and Rame Gowda must have about 500. My younger brother hasn't managed to keep anything."

*   *   *

"This morning I drew two hundred pots of water before nine o'clock. But no one brought me anything to eat in the fields. After so much work, if no one brings us something to eat, how can we go on? Wouldn't a man get angry? So I strode back to the house, I shouted lots of things. I thought, 'I won't eat *rotti* today, I'll just have my lunch instead later.' So I sat down and refused the food. Five or six people called me to go and eat, so finally I went and finally there was peace. What else could I do?"

*   *   *

(*of his mother*) "She was tall and fair in complexion. She used to work really hard."

*   *   *

"It would have been nice if I'd studied. It would have made life more convenient. But I wasn't destined to study, so I didn't study."

*   *   *

"I feel the family should continue. If everyone behaves properly, it will, but if they don't, then it won't."

*   *   *

(*of Nanjeswamy*) "There's no consistency. Sometimes he's nice, but other times he isn't. His mind isn't stable. Very fickle."

*   *   *

(*of Nanjeswamy's management*) "We have to accept it, otherwise the family wouldn't last."

*   *   *

(*of his own management*) "I used to do it before, about eight or ten years back. I managed for four years. After that they stole some money. I had sold an ox for a thousand rupees and locked the money in the trunk. When my brother came from the town, I took out the money and gave it to him to count. A hundred rupees was missing. Someone must have broken the lock and taken it. No one knew who'd done it. It must have been somebody in the house. Who else would steal it?

"Then the others in the house said, 'You must be the one'. They made me the thief. I said I'd kept the money in the box and someone had broken the lock. But no one believed me. They said, 'You've taken it, and now you talk like this?'

"Then S.M.B. said, 'Nobody need handle the money, I'll do it all myself,' and he snatched the notes. After two or three months were over, he said, 'I can't come frequently to handle the daily accounts. Anyway, Nanjeswamy, you don't go to the fields with the others or do much work. You can supervise the labourers, keep the accounts, and do small jobs.'

"So he handed over the management."

*   *   *

"Either Nanjeswamy or Rame Gowda must have stolen the

217

money. Rame Gowda is a good man when it comes to work. He's a good man in everything. If it wasn't for him, this house wouldn't go on. But sometimes men do such things. They might be good in other things, but will money let anyone be good?"

* * *

"I have this shirt and one more. I have one pair of pants, and a sheet. Also this one towel. I have only one vest. He hasn't even stitched me another – see, this one's all torn. I don't have a blanket for when it gets cold. They promised to get me a blanket on the feast of Hemagiri Ratha-Septhami, but it wasn't bought, and I didn't ask them to buy it. I said, 'Let my sheet last as long as it can'."

* * *

"There's nothing more to say. What else can I say in my present condition? This is how it is. Nothing more."

NANJESWAMY: "What did you ask Bhadre Gowda? Tell me. He's the one who causes the trouble. Let the others be."

* * *

"Just tell me what Bhadre Gowda said, and what the old man said, and also what Rame Gowda said. Whatever complaints they've told you about me, just tell me. Don't worry, I won't tell them."

* * *

"I'm not going to answer any questions. I'll go."

* * *

"Now if everyone wants to be like me, the head of the family, and if everyone wants some shirts stitched, how will the family get on? I've come here; I might go and see an official also. I'm the one who has to manage the family affairs. I have to go out often. If you want to get on in the world today, you should have good clothes, even if you don't have enough to eat. Nowadays,

218

if you go to an official, and you're wearing rags, he'll say, 'Who's that? Throw him out.'

"I'll buy my brothers working clothes, quite cheap. But if everyone wants to be like this, if everyone wants to be fashionable, what about the land? Or let them manage affairs, and I'll take whatever clothes they get me. One can't be equal. If I feel like it, I'll say, 'Alright, you can have some new clothes, but you must work to deserve them'. See, if they get new clothes, they'll stop working because their clothes get dirty. It's different with me. I wear my smart clothes when I go out, but I take them off when I get back, and go to the fields for a while. But they have to work there twenty-four hours a day, whether it's raining, or whatever."

*   *   *

"It's *I* and my brother who manage everything. The others should do as they're told. They ought to say, 'Let the managers do what they want, let them put us either in milk or water,* while we do the work.' "

*   *   *

"*I* can get the work done, even if everyone else should leave. I'd hire labour to do it. I even told them one day that I wouldn't be frightened if they all left. Let them go off and earn their own living, and let them return when the debts are paid off. I'll suffer the difficulties. I'll also have the good things, but let them leave everything to me. But they won't accept it. So let them suffer, let them work and pay back the debts themselves."

*   *   *

"When it comes to ploughing, Rame Gowda is the best, he does it very thoroughly."

*   *   *

"I'm not going to stitch any more shirts for myself, I won't wear any of them. Let me just wear whatever the others get me. I can't stand their jealousy. See, my eldest brother got edu-

---

* i.e. 'let them do good or bad as they wish.'

cation, and the youngest. But can we all demand the same because of that?"

*   *   *

"Look here, if I could only use a pen and write, I'd have started a mill for grinding flour: I'd have accepted every contract I could get. But now I have to manage without education. What can you do?"

*   *   *

"There were some teachers in our village. I used to go to their room every day. Our children used to go and study there. The teachers said: 'Nanjeswamy, buy an insurance. Do it. After all, you only have to pay 127 rupees a year.' All three teachers said this. I said, 'Alright, sir.' There was an agent among the teachers, and he just went ahead and arranged it. He did everything. He sent the bond, and paid the first instalment. Later, I gave him the money. The bond came. Then I started thinking. 'I listened to them and got caught. When we are four people, I alone have bought a policy. What should I do now? Let me waste the money, I'll tear up the bond.' Then people like you said, 'Don't, don't tear it up.'

"I thought and thought. I'd made a mistake. I could get caught. What answer could I give if they asked me? I thought, if they ask me, I'll say, 'Look, I didn't lose it in gambling, I didn't eat up the money, I just did it that day. If you think it's wrong, I won't have it, I'll throw it away. Let it be wasted, if it has to be. Will you cut me up because I've made this mistake?' I told them that. And I've gone on paying: I've paid for the last three years."

*   *   *

(*on insurance for his brothers in the village*) "I've bought the policy. But is it possible for everyone to have one too? It can't be, I say. Why should we peasants want an insurance policy? If they do want it, then they should buy it themselves from the money they've earned themselves."

*   *   *

"Let's say I committed a theft. But how can you do anything

without cheating at all? You might say God is just, but even God . . ."

*   *   *

"Yes, I had a fight with Bhadre Gowda. He asked me to fetch water with him. I said, 'I'll come, carry on.' Again he said, 'How many times do I have to call you?' I was still sitting. He came and hit me with a big stick. I got really angry. I thought, I've done nothing wrong, he's beaten me for no reason. I got up and said, 'Let someone fuck your mother.' And I gave him a good beating. That day I wanted to divide. But our Rame Gowda said, 'Don't worry, even if he's beaten you, it's over. But if we behave like this now, the house will be ruined.' After that Bhadre Gowda and I never spoke to each other, just a few words now and then. Such things happen. What can you do?"

THE OLD MAN: (*on division*) "There is nothing definite yet. When the proper time comes, it will happen. How can you say it now? Division depends on the stars. The right time will come."

At 6.30 the next morning, some of the film unit gathered in the main hall of the family house. They waited for the men to come in from the fields, for Nanjeswamy to come from the second house, and for S.M.B. to dress himself in his new pale blue tweed jacket.

They gave three thousand rupees to the old man. The old man gave it to S.M.B., who handed it over to Nanjeswamy to put in the family trunk.

In return, the unit received garlands, betel leaves, and bananas; everyone shook hands.

"Goodbye, you buggers," said someone almost inaudibly, "God bless your greedy hands."

As they got into the Land-Rover, the potter came up for his payment for half an afternoon's filming.

"My terms," he said with gravity, "must be one ox." He hesitated. "But a cow would do." He bowed obsequiously. He was paid fifty rupees: twenty times more than he'd get for an afternoon's labour, but a tenth of his expectations.

The film unit also gave me two thousand rupees in secret for Bhadre Gowda and his brother Basave Gowda. They also left me some money to buy gifts for all the family.

13 New Elements

I spent three days in Bangalore with Tony and then returned to Krishnapatna alone. I still had research to complete, but more I felt that I wanted to see the family without the film unit, to make my peace and try to establish some form of friendship which had nothing to do with bargains. But for two days I could not gather the courage to walk down to Palahalli. At first I thought I was ill, and then I started to cry on and off for several hours. Partly it was because I missed the support of Tony; partly it was the sudden fear of returning to the family.

It is hard to show in this book – without becoming boring and therefore losing the reader – the obsession and repetition of the family's daily life, and the difficulties I felt in trying to become part of it. So far, perhaps, I have included too much action, or at least made it seem as though exciting events were part of the family's life. They were, and yet they weren't, for events were quickly engulfed by routine. It was often the static event which assumed the greatest significance, like the loss of a basket, or burnt food, or the repair of a broken plough.

It wasn't so much the routine I feared, for I had learnt to cope with the physical hardships, as the tentative quest for understanding. Certain barriers always reminded me that I was an alien interloper: the language, the customs, the religious beliefs. The worst was the meaning of language, which sometimes eluded even the interpreters, with its rambling, repetitive nature, and I knew I should face again days of black depression when I'd feel I was getting nowhere. It was like a huge jigsaw puzzle, taking hours to complete a tiny section only to find that it doesn't fit into the whole; and as the sections build up, the overall picture changes with alarming and frequent inconstancy. I still have no idea whether I've got close to completing the puzzle. I still don't know what the final picture should look like, though there's no definitive answer since it depends on interpretation. Take Kevan, the Associate Producer of the film. He read this book in typescript:

he liked it, I think, but felt I had missed the grinding monotony which dominates peasant society. He also felt differently about the men, since he himself is a man.

In a sense this book is dishonest in that it is a distillation of the family's speech: everything in the book *is* what they said, but it frequently leaves out the tortuous route by which we got there. My endless questioning and the catalyst of the film unit helped crystallise the family's ideas, but our presence itself was unreal. And of course this book leaves out my own inadequacies – the tiredness, the anger, the lack of patience, the failure to lose my own identity. I still felt hurt and annoyed every time the women mocked my sari and hair, or asked for money or silver – they went on and on and on and on, and on, and on, and there was never any escape.

With Tony gone, I had lost my anchor – no one with whom to discuss, to help interpret events, to put things into perspective. And no one to ask questions, the best prompt of all for making one think and find answers. I would have to think up my own questions, and be certain of what I was looking for in the answers. Venkamma, the new interpreter, was to prove a superb ally.

All this made me fear my return, plus the chance of rebuff from the family. They had probably had enough of me.

I was wrong: they gave me a wonderful welcome. Word spread that I had come back and was ill. Within an afternoon, Nanjeswamy came to visit me, and then Bhadre Gowda. They asked for nothing, they said little, they were only surprised to see me: they had thought I would go with my husband to England and forget all about them, whatever I might have promised. I gave the two thousand rupees to Bhadre Gowda in secret, and he shook me by the hand – the first time one of the men had touched me.

The next morning, Venkamma and I walked down to the village. The old man was sitting near the pumphouse idly harvesting millet. Madakka, Thayee, and three grandchildren worked in a field nearby. They all rushed towards us, shouting and grinning their welcomes; they were also concerned for our comfort, especially the old man.

"Don't be scared," he said gently, "we're here to look after you. We'll do whatever you want. If you'd asked for it, we'd have sent the cart to fetch you. Poor things, why did you have to walk?"

They were also concerned for Venkamma, since she was a high-caste Brahmin. They offered to let her cook for herself, to provide her with special foods, and even to fix a special place for her bath. When she refused, they were happy, and even a little proud that a Brahmin had come to their house.

The euphoria soon faded, and it was back to the old routine: the endless requests for money, the engrossment in daily tasks, the arguments and orders, the cursing, the silence, the work.

Even Jayamma's enthusiasm for our return was quickly lost in repetition. I shall include the conversation to show the pace and thought-process.

"Oh, you've walked down in the hot sun!" exclaims Jayamma on our arrival. "Oh, it's so hot!"

"Yes, I had work this morning, so I couldn't leave before," I explain.

"Before, you had a bus – I mean a car. You used to come, it was easy. Now you have to talk to your legs to get them to come."

"My legs are very strong."

"Why is your face looking a bit dull now?" asks Kalle Gowda.

"Why am I so dull? Because I've been ill."

"When Tony was here, you used to laugh and talk a lot. Now even when you came to Krishnapatna, your face was a bit dull."

"Your face is a bit dull," repeats Jayamma.

"No, no," I protest, "I've just been ill. I'm very tired. I'll be bright later."

Some women approach from the neighbouring fields to see what we are doing.

"Are all these people from your neighbouring fields?" asks Venkamma, the interpreter.

"Yes," says Jayamma. "Can you see those fields over there? They belong to them. And those trees there? The land beyond is theirs."

"Oh, she's walked in the hot sun?" asks one of the women.

"Yes, she's come in the heat of the day," says Jayamma.

"I believe she had fever," says the woman.

"Look how she's become!" says Jayamma.

"You can't get away with anything," I say.

"It's too hot," says Jayamma. "Can't do any more weeding. How to go on in this hot sun? Ayapah! Can weed if it's cool. I just can't do it today, sister."

"Do Tony and you have any children?" asks Kalle Gowda.

"No, next year maybe," I say.

"Someone said you had a son, they said it before we became so friendly with each other. It was in my mind to ask you about it, but when I was about to ask, I used to forget what I wanted to ask. Somebody in our village said it."

"So no rain yet?" I ask, wishing to change the subject. "What are you doing in the fields?"

"What can we do in the fields if there's no rain? See, there are the weeds here. They grow with the *ragi* crop. We keep removing them. If it rains soon, it will be good. If we don't weed when it's dry, it's very difficult to do it after it's rained. Then there'll be too many weeds."

Jayamma picks some flowers and gives them to Venkamma. "Will she wear them?" she asks her, nodding towards me.

"No, she can't. She doesn't have a plait."

"Why doesn't she have much hair?" asks Kalle Gowda.

"She's cut it. On their side, they all cut it. Nowadays they do it even on our side."

"Even in our villages they do it for small girls, till they're three or four. After that, they don't do it. [Pause] How many brothers and sisters does Tony have?"

"One sister, that's all," I answer.

"Is he the only son?"

"No brothers, no father."

"What about Kevan?"

"I don't know."

"Aren't you from the same place?"

"He's not from our village. He lives far away."

"It's very hot," says Jayamma. "The *ragi* is wilting."

"See, now we have this much land," says Kalle Gowda. "After it rains, we plough once. We've transplanted some *ragi*, and for the rest, these neighbours will help us. We also go and do it for them, when it rains and their land is ready. Because we worked on their land, we can bring them to plant on our land. It

225

goes on like that. And also, if it's very difficult, and we can't get any labour from our village, then we can go to another village and get people for two rupees a half day. Then you can get the planting done, if there's plenty of land. A lot of work can be done – rain is our only problem, all our troubles come from that."

"Come on, sister," says Jayamma to the woman who still stands staring at us. "What if we can't weed now? If it rains, then we'll get more people and finish it. You've finished everything. If you pull a weed out once, on our land you have to pull it out four times."

"Because we work hard, it's nice," says Kalle Gowda.

"Where do you learn these methods from? Talking to other people?" I ask.

"I learnt all this. No one taught me – not my father, not my mother. My father died before I was four. Then my sister – the eldest one who's married to Silnare – and her husband, they came and worked our land for three years."

"Did you have any land when your father died?"

"This land? It's come down to me."

"So this was your family's land from your father's time?"

"Yes. This was our land from my father's time. So my sister and her husband used to cultivate it. I was very small, you see, only four years." He scolds Jayamma for not getting back to work. "So I was very small, and then they took me to Silnare with them. There they started teaching me to plough the field. So I kept learning. I was there for four or five years. I stayed in their house doing everything they told me to do. They used to come and cultivate our land for us. So if we didn't carry the plough from one village to another, we couldn't grow even fifty seers of *ragi*. No, we could haven't done it."

And so the conversation continued for more than an hour, until reluctantly Kalle Gowda and Jayamma returned to work.

Everyone who could was working the fields up beyond the sugar-cane where the groundnuts had been harvested. Four square plots – stony, uneven, far from the village – had been terraced out of the slope to catch the rain and hold it. Beyond, the land pulled away to a spine of rock which stretched to Krishnapatna. Far in the distance, the size of a sharpened finger nail, was the temple perched on its bouldered hill. The clouds were low and heavy, moving across the sky like hanks of natural wool; a slight wind touched the trees and started to dry the topsoil.

Bhadre Gowda and Rame Gowda were ploughing one of the plots in preparation for planting. Each with a pair of white oxen, they followed the other from end to end, turning the soil, turning the soil, until it looked like a striped deckchair where the upturned earth was red and crumbly, and the unploughed earth was packed and shiny. A labourer cleared the stones behind them, heaving them onto the bank.

Basave Gowda, the youngest son by the second wife, fetched the millet seedlings from behind the family house, piling them into a flat basket which he brought on his head to the fields: past the stone tank and down to the river bed which was gushing with muddy water; past the trees and high bushes which guarded the neighbours' fields; over the thick clay which stuck to his corn-covered feet; past the patel's fields and under the jack-fruit tree, whose large fruits hung like breasts, sinister in their skins of coarse nippled shagreen; past the sorghum, which was ready to harvest, its wispy heads white in the vivid green; through the sugar-cane and out onto the plots. He dumped the seedlings on the ground and turned back for more.

The old man divided the plants into bunches of fifty or so. Since the stalks were fragile and the delicate roots interwoven, he shook away some of the soil and carefully, slowly, prised them apart: his eldest grandson distributed the bunches over the plot at intervals. Manager Nanjeswamy had traced a grid on the soil with a huge wooden rake. He ensured that the women were planting properly: the old lady, Thayee, Madakka, two cousins, and a labourer. They each worked three lines vertically, moving forward inch by inch on their haunches, thrusting in the plants and patting the soil to secure them: the younger children ran backwards and forwards collecting plants whenever their mothers needed them – even Thayee's youngest daughter had come to the fields.

"Look at that," said the old lady, "even the last one's here."

"Who? Who?" called the old man, unable to see.

The child played on the edge of the plot: she wanted to capture a leaf, to pin it down with a stone, but whenever she left the leaf to find the stone, the wind blew it away.

"Hey, sing about rain," called the old man. "That would be nice, sing, sing as you work."

"What shall we sing?" asked Thayee.

"Sing whatever you know."

"They sing well of the rain," said the old lady.

"Sing of the rain," said the old man.

"Rain, rain, the rain has . . ." started one of the women.

"Sing slowly," shouted the old lady.

> "Rain, rain, the rain has gone away –
> it's twelve years since you went, brother,
> and the cattle have no water,
> the land is all dried up, brother,
> see this and be kind.
>
> "We've worshipped Shiva,
> we've worshipped Krishna,
> we've worshipped all the gods –
> every month we worship,
> asking God for rain."

The rain brought new tensions: it was a crucial time for planting, yet the family was short of free labour, particularly of women. Susheelamma was still confined to the house; Thayee did little work, being so heavily pregnant; Lakshmi, the youngest wife, had been away for three days getting hospital treatment.

Nanjeswamy was irritable, pacing up and down behind the women, goading them on to work. When Basave Gowda gave up fetching seedlings from behind the family house because his corns were hurting, Nanjeswamy lost his temper.

Basave Gowda stood his ground, stubbornly refusing to work. Strong arms, hollow chest, fragile legs, he was a strange mixture of pugnacity and impotence, a helplessness which angered him and others. He could have been handsome if his knees hadn't knocked, if his ears had been flat and his hair less curly, if his nose had been less of a beak as it tipped over his nostrils. The family normally thought him a simpleton and accepted his weakness in work – they gave him the children's tasks of herding the sheep or tying up bundles of millet – but when pressure was on they lost patience.

Nanjeswamy stepped forward, threatening him with a large stick. Basave Gowda stepped back and stumbled on a stone, stubbing his corns painfully. He flared up with anger. But Nanjeswamy kept the stick raised: either Basave Gowda went back to work or he fetched his wife Lakshmi to help plant in the fields. Basave Gowda turned and marched off the field, shouting over his shoulder that he'd send back his wife but he himself would never return to the house.

'Go,' shouted Nanjeswamy after him. 'Go and look after yourself. You'll only get blows from us.'

I followed Basave Gowda back to the house where he packed up a shirt and towel, and marched out of the house. I watched him leave the village, hobbling over the rough stones, like an old man.

In the house Susheelamma was by herself, still on the wooden bed behind the screen and cut off from contact with people. She sat there all day, all night, never leaving her bed except to wash and go to the lavatory when no one else was about. She was given the same plate, the same tumbler, the same food each day: rice and coffee, milk and curry, day after day. She said she was meant to have eggs and herbs and even a bit of bread but no one had got them for her. She was also meant to have moved to the bedroom after the naming ceremony but no one had thought to mention it, and she certainly wouldn't ask: they wanted the bedroom as a store for harvested millet.

"It's such a nuisance here," she said. "People keep coming and going. It's like a gypsy's tent. There's no privacy at all. But then I suppose it would also be bad if no one was around. If people come and sit with me, then I don't feel bored. Alone, I'm always bored."

She wasn't sure how she felt now that she had no work; but she had resigned herself to the birth of a girl, not a boy.

"What can you do?" she said with a soft sigh. "Whose will is it?"

She had found the delivery hard, but weren't all deliveries difficult? At the time, you think, I'll never go through this again, but then when you're pregnant again, then it's different somehow.

The cradle hung over Susheelamma's bed, leaving her little

space to sit in. At least the baby seldom cried, and when she did, Susheelamma simply gave her a breast to suck on.

The new baby was already being subjected to living with so many people: she was handled by aunts and uncles, she was washed by the old lady, and teased by the other grandchildren, including her sister and brother.

That evening, the old lady passed a burning wick in a plate of red water above the baby's cradle to burn away the evil which anyone might have left. She stooped to look at some red marks on the child's legs.

"What's happened?" she asked.

"That?" said Susheelamma. "Nothing. Just some marks. Must be due to heat."

"It must be the mosquitoes," said the old lady and pulled up a cloth on its legs. But the child kicked it away.

"See how she kicks it away!"

"Yes, she'll kick it away till she goes to sleep."

The old lady rubbed some turmeric as antiseptic into the baby's stomach: the last piece of the cord had come off and was tied to the side of the cradle. When Susheelamma was stronger she would throw it for luck into running water.

That evening, also, Lakshmi returned to the house. She slipped in without a word and sidled towards the bedroom in an effort not to be seen.

'You fool,' said the old man from his cot as she passed. 'You think you're so clever but what do you know?'

'Better to be a fool than wise in this house,' she retorted. And when Manager Nanjeswamy hurried towards her, she pulled her sari over her face like a cowl. Her eyes caught his. 'Do you think my husband's a baby?' she cried. 'To be beaten and threatened and bullied?' She walked into the bedroom and slammed the door shut.

'Lakshmi, Lakshmi,' said the old lady scratching at the door. 'Let me in, Lakshmi.'

'Leave her alone,' said the old man.

The family left her alone and got on with the evening chores. It was midnight before I slipped into the bedroom: Lakshmi was lying on a mat staring up at the ceiling. Her eyes were red from crying, her nails chewed, her hair loose about her shoulders. I sat down beside her: we always shared a mat at nights and shared the same blanket. I had felt a desolation in her and had tried to share some feeling. Not that we had spoken much – she was always watched and guarded. Only once in a whispered rush she had said she wasn't happy: she had no children, her husband was illiterate, she wasn't used to working in the fields.

"Oh this atmosphere, it's so different from home," she whispered, her eyes roaming across the ceiling. "After I came here . . ." She stopped, listening, her head on one side. She dropped her voice further. "It's hard. I wasn't used to it. Here we have to work all the time. At first my hands were red, raw from grinding and husking rice. They bled. See how rough they are." She turned her hands over to let Venkamma and me see the coarse skin, the deep cracks, the overgrown cuticles.

"I've moved around in so many places, I've talked to so many people, and look what education I've had – how much I've studied, how many exams I've taken. In the debates, the Saturday debates in school, I used to be first. Whichever boy joined the debate I'd still come first. I used to be first in class. When we had our school-day, then my lady teacher used to put my name in for everything. We didn't call the teachers by their names, we just used their initials. R.P. put me forward for competitions – skipping, tennis quoit, pushing the counters, I got first prize in them all. Exercises, dumbbells, running races, breaking the pot: in everything I'd come first. Even for regular attendance and neat handwriting. I was always top of the class. Now I come here . . ."

She turned to face us and leant on her elbow stroking her hair in luxuriant strokes, sweeping it up from her neck and curling it through her fingers. Her sari had slipped off her shoulder to show her tight-fitting blouse over full firm breasts – not the village blouse but one buttoned up the back, with short sleeves and scooped neck.

"But there's this thing called fate," said Venkamma. "You may be first in school but last in this house."

"I don't know," said Lakshmi. "Maybe. It's about four years back, in the middle school. There was a teacher called Ninge Gowda. I used to be with him all the time, for he lived next door to us. The room was actually ours, it was part of our house. When I had my lunch break, I'd wait and walk behind him. The minute we'd finished our meals, we'd go to this house. We'd call him, 'Come sir, come sir.' He'd say, 'Why do you rush me like this?' And then we'd say, 'What sir, how much do you want to eat?' And then we'd walk with him. We'd be with him while coming from school, going to school, we'd be together all the day. Even in the evening.

"One day he got sick; he died. When I was still in school he died. He jumped down a well. He'd lost his mind. And then he . . . he was still the age of my husband. Is that the age to die? He became a spirit, and his spirit came into me."

Her body had stopped all movement, her hands grasping the mat, her toes clenched. She relaxed a little and brushed her hand over her eyes.

"Now it's slightly better but even so I haven't had my periods for ten months. That's why I went to the hospital, to take an injection for bleeding. I don't know what it is. God only knows. I can't work and all kinds of things haunt my mind. I don't tell anyone."

She cracked her fingers one by one and stared at us as though pleading with us not to tell anyone.

"What happens when the spirit's on you?"

She shrugged and flicked the hair from her shoulders.

"I don't know what happens. How can I? It's on me then. They did all kinds of things, only God alone knows. See, I haven't had my periods, and my mother says . . ."

Thayee came through the door, stretching and yawning.

"You should have helped," she said. "There's so much work."

"Why should I help?" said Lakshmi. "My husband's not here, and I've taken no food."

"Then you should stay with your husband. If you're here, you're part of the family."

"Whose family?" said Lakshmi. "Does anyone let me cook, does anyone let me alone?"

"It's worse when you have children."

"Who wants children?"

Thayee sat down on the mat, leaning against Lakshmi. As the two youngest wives, and as the wives of the two step-brothers, they had some understanding. Thayee liked Lakshmi. "When I'm pregnant," she said, "all the work is difficult. But she doesn't find it difficult." She looked at Lakshmi, smiling. "If it wasn't for her – see, I feel close to her – if she's not there to help, it's hard for me to cook. Why weren't you there these last few days, Lakshmi?" She said it softly with kindness. But Lakshmi did not answer.

Thayee stretched herself out with her head on Lakshmi's lap, laughing. "I always laugh," she said. "I don't cry. I'm always laughing."

"What do *you* feel, Lakshmi?" I asked.

"I don't feel anything."

"It's easier for Lakshmi," laughed Thayee. "Because she's alone it's alright for her. No children . . ." She looked coyly at me. "Why don't you have children?"

"We've only been married a short while," I said.

"It's two months since you came, but you haven't slept . . .?"

"How do you know?"

"Weren't there many people in the bungalow?"

"We had our own room."

She nodded. "Do you . . . *like* your husband?"

"Yes," I said. "Very much. And you? Do you . . . do you want your husband?"

She laughed, coyly. "If we had such desires, would we have gone on living in such a house? We don't have such things on our mind." But then she admitted that yes, perhaps there had been some desire to begin with, before the children had come.

"And do you find your husband handsome?" I asked.

"When we're married, won't we think our husband's handsome?" she said. "My husband's handsome."

"Is my husband handsome?" asked Lakshmi.

"But say you weren't married, what would you hope for?"

"If a girl is tall," said Thayee, "then he also should be tall; if a girl is dark then he should be dark also. They should match each other well."

"Light-skinned," said Lakshmi, "and tall."

"And what qualities?"

"There should be patience on both sides," said Thayee. "Without patience, then it's difficult."

"He should be educated," said Lakshmi, "and clever. His wife shouldn't need to work." She looked at me for support. "And you, Saramma, what do you think?"

"I think kindness and understanding."

Lakshmi played with the chain round her neck. "In such a place as this, where will you find such things?"

"And before marriage did you know about . . ."

"Will we know such things?" said Thayee giggling. "When we get married we learn. Our mothers don't tell us."

"And men?"

"They'll know won't they?"

"Wouldn't you learn from others?"

Lakshmi laughed scornfully. "In such a village there's no such thing. I learnt from my friends." She pushed away Thayee's head and turning over curled up on her side. I lay down too and pulled the blanket over us.

"Let's sing," said Lakshmi. She had learnt some nursery rhymes in school and could still remember the English.

"Solomon Grundy, born on Monday . . . married on Thursday, died on Sunday, buried on . . . Friday."

She giggled and we took up the chant together. "Baa baa black sheep, have you any wool? Yes sir, yes sir, three bags full."

"Goodnight."

"Goodnight."

Education was seen by the family as something advantageous, but as usual reality did not match their expectations. The primary school in the village was more closed than open: the elderly teacher had five miles to walk to the school each morning, and the children argued that since he didn't bother to come much, they needn't bother to go. The secondary school at Devarahalli, two miles away, had better teachers and facilities. The village children wanted to go there, but many did not make it. Either they had insufficient primary schooling, or their labour was needed at home in the fields.

As they always did, when there was no chance of fulfilling their hopes, the family accepted the situation with resignation. If their children could have no education, then they would work in the fields. After all, they were born peasants, and so they would continue as peasants.

Perhaps in a way it was better: the system of education had so little to do with their needs, leading, as with Chikke Gowda, from useful productivity in the village to redundancy in the town. Not that the family was seduced by the prospect of urban life, for they understood its economic problems; but they were seduced by the chance of increased status, like S.M.B. had achieved. To them, it meant success to be able to recite by rote, to them it seemed important if a man could write his name even if he could not read the document which he'd signed. They had become part of the text-book system without understanding why.

Take Lakshmi and Basave Gowda. She felt she was superior because of her education, and when he returned after five days' absence, she showed no welcome. She was planting millet in a slow bored manner, and when he came to the edge of the field, calling quietly, she bent her head pretending not to hear; he called again and when again she ignored him, he limped away.

He had spent five days in Mysore and then had run out of money. Besides, he realised that people would mock him for running away and so he had come back by bus. All the family ignored him except for Bhadre Gowda, who was ploughing more plots for planting. Basave Gowda took over for ten minutes: his frail arms could barely turn the plough and his legs jerked like a puppet's on the furrows. Lakshmi looked up once or twice and glanced at him: her mouth was set and her eyes were hard with contempt.

Black clouds had gathered and it started to rain heavily. Some of the family took to the shelter of trees while others ran for the pumphouse; but the rain went on and on, and the clouds closed in. The order was given to go home. The women and children left first, without any covering. Thayee carried a bundle of fuel on her head and her youngest child in her arms; her sari was soaked and so weighted with water that it clung to her body like a wrinkled stocking. Her eldest daughter, Prema, followed behind, sliding at first with glee along the muddy paths, then sobbing with tears when she slipped and muddied her dress.

The children ran up the street jumping over the currents of water which had flooded from the gutter. Umesha dripped from his head, his nose, his arms: he looked dejected and cold, trailing a sodden lamb behind him. Saroji burst into the house and stripped off her clothes at once, leaving them in a heap, not wanting to put on dry ones. Sudhamani stood shivering, waiting to be dried with a towel: she demanded her pale blue dress with the tinselly thread and the flouncy skirt.

Thayee and Madakka changed their clothes and hurriedly collected all the pots they could find. There was no sign of Lakshmi; Susheelamma was asleep. Madakka scrubbed a small cooking vessel: she wiped the soot from the base, cleaned the rim, and stretching an arm into the rain to gather a handful of water swilled away the dirt. She balanced the pot on a step under the open roof to catch a stream of water. Thayee did the same with another pot and soon they had a line of vessels strategically placed to catch the clear, fresh water. The rain was sheeting down, pouring into the central area, white, silver, luminous, carrying the outside forces into the home, into the mind.

The men came in one by one, almost dry from the sacks and polythene sheeting that were hooked over their heads: Manager Nanjeswamy rubbed his hair and neck, he took off his shirt and strutted with pride to show off a new vest; Bhadre Gowda entered and his eldest daughter rushed to help, clasping him round the legs. As he dried himself he bent to wipe her hair and to remove the mud from her face; she looked up, resting her chin on his knee; he pinched her cheeks roughly.

A scuffle at the door announced the old lady along with her eldest grandson. Cloaked in a sack which trailed to his feet he ducked in front while she drove in the cows, struggling through the door with a bundle of green fodder bigger than herself. Her teeth were chattering with cold – she looked like a starving coypu with her thin grey hair dripping in strands down her neck.

As darkness came no one moved to light a lamp. The central washing area had filled to the second step, for the outlet was too small to cope with the volume of water. The noise of rain was like a kettle coming to boil, and we sat, mesmerised, staring.

'Nine years ago,' said Rame Gowda, 'we had so much rain that the cattle were swept away – the small calves were drowned. We couldn't cross to our fields, we just sat at home waiting, waiting for the water to subside.'

They weren't worried this time, for the land was unlikely to flood. They were just happy. It was always good to have rain, to let your clothes get soaked, to have the cool nights.

Venkamma and I were to eat that evening at Bhadramma's, so

Bhadre Gowda escorted us through the village beneath a black umbrella. He was proud for he sported a new blanket and a new pair of shorts: he had picked a whole field of pumpkins and taken them into Mysore without telling the family. He'd sold them for two hundred rupees, then bought himself the blanket, the shorts, and a shirt, and the rest he'd spent on fertiliser. Obviously his discussions with Tony had given him greater courage. And he chuckled with deep delight in remembering Nanjeswamy's reaction: an attempt at self-control and the angry comment, 'We should have grown millet instead of the pumpkins, and then we'd have seen some profit.'

Bhadramma's house was warm and welcoming: the shutters were tightly closed, the red, polished floor was glowing from kerosene lamps, and the mats were spread out in welcome. She herself was relaxed, and, making us sit down, she brought us peanuts to shell. They were hot and crunchy.

'We never get these at our house,' said Bhadre Gowda, tossing a handful into his mouth. 'Not hot anyway.'

Bhadramma gave him some sugar for them. 'You never get anything there,' she said.

'True,' he said with his mouth full.

The door opened slowly to let in Bhadramma's husband: he blinked at the lights and ran a quivering hand round the back of his head, over his eyes, and down the sides of his nose to wipe away the water. He was shivering so Bhadramma gave him a towel, a change of shirt and wrapped him up in a blanket. He sat against the wall staring across to the opposite wall; once he whimpered before breaking into a wide smile.

Bhadramma made some coffee and sat beside us; we clutched the tumblers in our hands and bent our heads to caress our cheeks with the steam.

'They never fry things at our house,' said Bhadre Gowda, taking a handful of deep-fried *vade*.

'Only at times of festivals,' said Bhadramma.

'And then do we ever see them?'

'No, you never see them.'

'So where do we come for fried food?'

'You have to come here.'

'We have to come here.'

She pushed the plate towards him.

The door opened and in came the old man, tapping the floor with his feet and shaking the rain from his shawl. He took up his seat on the cot with his stick across his knees and his back propped with a pillow. Bhadramma gave him some coffee. She stretched up to the ceiling where a basket hung from a beam, a wicker basket woven with pink and green in zig-zigs round the base. She took out a lump of brown sugar, crumbled it with her fingers, and added it to his coffee.

Jayamma also came in: she sat with us cracking peanuts, undeterred by her uncle's presence. She was looking better now, less anaemic, and her cheeks had become more plump. She wasn't working much, and her husband had stopped the beating, though he made no effort to provide any food for his wife. That's why they ate at Bhadramma's almost every evening. Her husband came after half an hour, and the moment he entered the atmosphere changed. He strode up and down the room, peered into the cattle shed, and asked the old man rudely whether he'd worked that day.

'When's food?' he demanded. 'I'm hungry. If you have to work alone . . .'

Supper wasn't ready, so he decided to fill in the time by telling a story. He leant against the central pillar, chest out, arms folded. 'Coffee,' he called. 'Coffee for the storyteller.' He cleared his throat. 'I struggled so much to learn this story. I used to go to his house – the storyteller's house. I asked him to repeat it and repeat it. In the village of Gadahalli. I used to go at harvest time: throughout the night people would go to listen and to learn.

'Nobody learnt stories like I learnt them but I've forgotten most of them now. After that, I took the cattle out to the fields, and the boys of the village asked me to teach them the stories. So I told them to look after the cattle and I sat on a rock and taught them. After that, I never looked after the cattle for a whole year or more.'

The story was a Gadahalli version of Ali Baba and the Forty Thieves, with village variations of intrigue and entertainment: the younger, clever brother managed to get all the fertile land on division, while the older, stupid brother received only barren land and debts; the entrance to the cave was in the trunk of a peepul tree; and the dhobi lent his twenty-one donkeys to carry the sacks

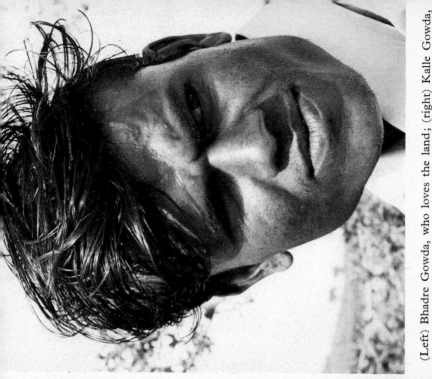

(Left) Bhadre Gowda, who loves the land; (right) Kalle Gowda, husband of Jayamma,who wants a second wife

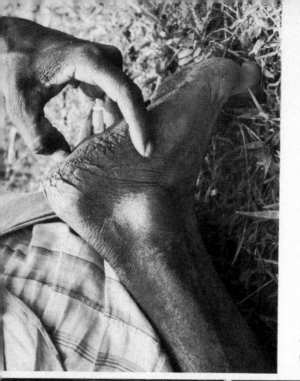

(Left) Lakshmi, the goddess of wealth and prosperity, overlooks the family's symbols of success; (right) the cost of success

of gold. Of course the younger brother was cut into pieces and tied in a sack; while the elder brother killed all the robbers with burning oil, then lived happily ever after in his large multi-storeyed house.

Bhadramma called us to supper. The men sat in the main room, the women stayed in the kitchen. It was a feast: fried pancakes stuffed with jaggery and crushed beans, all covered with milk; lemon rice which Jayamma had prepared especially for me; rice and curry; chutney, buttermilk, ghee.

Kalle Gowda shouted through to me as he was eating.

'Do you know much about machines?' he asked. 'What's good, what's bad?'

'What kind of machines?'

'Watches.'

'Not really.'

'I sold the flowers for fifty rupees. I thought I might buy a watch.'

'Why do you want a watch?'

'Oh, I just want one. It looks good.'

Watches were the latest status symbol, and yet they had little function. 'What's the time?' the men with watches would yell to each other. 'Four o'clock', or 'Six o'clock' came the answers. But what did four o'clock or six o'clock mean to a community which had no schedules, no buses, no fixed meal times, nothing which had to be done at a certain time. The cock's crow and the sun were the main commanding factors of time. And rain. Rain meant speed and organisation.

'And if you had more money, what else would you buy?' I asked.

'Some good cloth,' he said without hesitation. 'I may be poor but I don't like being in rags.' He thought for a moment. 'And a transistor radio.'

'And then?'

'An automatic watch.'

'And then?'

'What more? Oh. Some lands I think.'

'And then?'

'What more? Isn't that enough? Where does the money come from?'

'And your wife?'

239

'She'd have what I had. She and I are the same thing.'

Jayamma laughed loudly. 'That's why he's got a good clean shirt,' she called, 'and I have this dirty sari.'

'Would I walk down the street,' he said sourly, 'for all the world looking proud and rich while my wife walked behind like a beggar?'

When the men finished their food, they lit up their *bidis* to smoke. The rain was pounding down outside and its noise hushed any talk. The old man sunk his chin on his chest to sleep, and Bhadre Gowda contemplated the floor. Kalle Gowda stalked off to his own house.

We closed the kitchen door so that the women could eat in private. Thayee had also come, slipping away from the family house without the old lady's permission. Bhadramma, Thayee, and Jayamma were served by the youngest daughter: the sisters shared a brass plate, the mother used tin. They ate millet in great hunks, then squelched the rice with liquid curry into a sticky paste.

'Child,' said Bhadramma gently to Jayamma, 'you should take care of your tongue. Should a wife answer her husband?'

Jayamma hung her head.

Thayee taunted her. 'Have you been causing trouble?'

Jayamma looked surly. Thayee taunted her further. Then Jayamma burst into sudden anger, cursing and screaming at Thayee. I was startled: I had never seen such rage, and certainly not from Jayamma. It certainly helped to explain something of her husband's treatment.

Bhadramma frowned at Thayee, who pushed the plate towards Jayamma. 'Come, sister, eat. I only meant to joke.'

Jayamma calmed a little and sulkily took some food.

'She rises and drops so quickly,' said Bhadramma, and filled their plate with more food.

Bhadre Gowda was singing in a low melancholy voice, so we opened the door to listen.

> 'Two sisters, two sisters were married
> into another village:
> they stood on the bank of the river,
> they stood and looked across,
> they tried to see their mother's house
> on the other side of the river.

"We've been given to a family here,
a family with much money,
We give shade to their house now,
our leaves protect their faces.

' "Look, there is a jasmine creeper – go,
go to our mother's house;
climb onto her walls,
and give your flowers to her.
The tree will be like a python
creeping round her house –
then when we go to see her,
we'll wear the flowers for her.
We've been given to a family,
A family with much money,
We give shade to their house now,
Our leaves protect their faces."

'The flower vendor comes,' said Bhadre Gowda, speaking now, 'and goes to the house of a woman who cries out in anguish, "Why do you bring these flowers here? I am only weeping. Take them to my daughter, she's the one to wear them – she will wear bright flowers for she's gone to her husband's house." '

Bhadramma closed her eyes and nodded her head at the words; Thayee stood up and leant against the kitchen doorway.

'A girl came to her mother's house for delivery,' chanted Bhadre Gowda, still looking at the floor. 'But soon it was time to go back to her husband. She took with her a buffalo, a lamb, and a cradle for the child, and as she walked, she counted her steps. At forty she stopped and looked back at her mother's house; at eighty she turned again; and then when she turned a corner, she could no longer see it.'

He was silent for a moment, taking in his words. "It's hard for a woman sometimes," he said reflectively. "But it's written on their forehead, what can anyone do?" He looked towards his wife. "It's easier for Thayee. She can come to her mother's house whenever she wants, she needn't count the steps. It's always been that way.

"We married very young." He seemed to be addressing me now, but barely spoke louder and did not look towards me. "We wanted her to stay within the family. There was also another daughter – this one we called Jayamma. We wanted her in the family too but some of the brothers objected. I said, 'Why should we bring in an outsider? Let our girl come to our own family.' But they wouldn't listen.

"See, there's a custom in our village to marry the girls young. They say it's nice if you get married young. They somehow like it in our villages. If you get married older, people laugh at you and say, 'Look at those two, they're as tall as poplars, and so heavy they'll break the wedding board they stand on.' They say it's nice if you marry young."

It was late, so Bhadre Gowda got up to go and told his wife to follow soon. It was still raining outside, so he put up his black umbrella and hurried out of the house to disappear in the darkness. Thayee helped clear the dishes, then slipped out also, borrowing the old man's umbrella. Jayamma left without protection.

The old man stayed behind on the cot. He was still sleeping, so Bhadramma spread a blanket over him. Then she spread out two mattresses: Venkamma and I were to sleep in her house that night. We were warm, comfortable, and quiet: we slept till eight o'clock and spent a leisurely morning chatting and sipping coffee. Thayee's eldest daughter tied some bows in my hair and pretended to look for lice: it had been my game to find them on myself and to feign disgust and horror. The children thought it a great joke and repeated the action endlessly.

"Awah!" she cried, "I've found a louse, I've found a louse."

But this time it was real.

Bhadramma pulled me in front of the door where she could get better light.

"I'll comb out your head for you," she said.

"Kerosene's probably better," I said lightly.

"Only if there are many," said Venkamma.

"Head, head, tiddly head," cried the child dancing around.

"Oh, I've nothing to remove the nits with," said Bhadramma. "Child, fetch one from the neighbours."

I bent my head forward till my hair nearly touched the ground. Bhadramma started to comb, working from back to front right through to the ends. She tugged and tugged till I cried out in pain, for I'd not combed my hair for weeks.

"Lice! Lice! They'll all fall out if they're there."

"Look," I shouted. "Here's one."

"Here, look, another," said Bhadramma.

"And another."

"And another."

"So many?" said Venkamma. "My god."

"We'll kill them," said Bhadramma with cool efficiency. "Leave it," she ordered as I picked one up in fascination. "You don't know how to do it."

"Quick, quick," I said, "I don't want them in my clothes." The lice were moving across the floor towards me. She picked them up and crushed them between her nails.

She started to comb me again, peering through the strands of hair. "Can't see the small ones."

Venkamma came to look. "There's a small one."

"They're the babies."

"See, there's one here in the middle. How could you bear them?"

"I didn't know I had them. I couldn't feel them."

"Oh! Oh!" said Bhadramma. "They're huge. Look at them!"

"What karma!"

"Ayor, don't move. Come on this bit of the floor. You can see them better when they drop."

"Have I got more than most people?" I asked with some pride.

"Oh Rama, there aren't a few you've got. And you're asking me if you've got them!"

Bhadramma showed me a tiny piece of white stuff.

"What is it? My dandruff or an egg?"

"I can't see the dandruff, but there are plenty of nits."

"Can't you put something on them to kill them all at once?"

"If you do all that, it's not good for your health. We don't do anything. We only comb and remove them. We get them out like this. It's safer that way."

When the child came back with the nit-remover, Bhadramma went through every inch of my hair with the tong-like instrument. Snip, snap, snip, snap, the nits stood no chance.

After that I went regularly to Bhadramma's for her to clean out my hair. But now that I was aware of having lice, my head itched constantly.

14 Lakshmi Possessed

Manager Nanjeswamy still dogged my footsteps, partly to ensure I caused no trouble nor got into further secrets, partly because he had fresh demands: he didn't want a watch, he'd have a transistor instead. And brown terylene – it must be brown for his shirt – and brown for his wife's cardigan. And the trip to Bangalore. The unit had promised a trip but when had they ever taken him? He must go to Bangalore, he would go to Bangalore.

I was happy to arrange it by hiring a car, and waved them off for two days with relief – Nanjeswamy, his father, his mother, his father-in-law the patel, and the eldest grandson. But within an hour Chikke Gowda, the youngest son, arrived from Sundrapura to take over as manager and to follow us round the fields.

Early next morning, before Chikke Gowda had stirred or was likely to stir, Venkamma and I set out for the fields to try and find Basave Gowda. The women had recently risen and would be in the house for some hours; the village and fields were silent. The sun was pushing into the sky and easing its pale rays into the strands of mist: everything seemed fresh and green but the soil was sticky and heavy.

Basave Gowda was waiting by the pumphouse, almost as though he had known we were coming. He showed no surprise, and we did not question him. He led us into the pumphouse and told us to sit on the cot: Venkamma and I at one end, he at the other facing us. We were like actors, with set movements and practised speeches. Basave Gowda cleared his throat.

"My brother, Bhadre Gowda, said the film unit had paid some money." He leant forward enquiringly.

My heart sank. Was that all we had come for? I said:

"They gave a thousand for you, and a thousand for your brother."

He nodded. "He said . . . he said, 'If they come and ask you, tell them we're one as brothers.' " He picked at a thread in his shirt.

244

"But you don't feel the same?"

He shrugged. "As things stand today, he says we're both one. But that day may pass. In the future he might not think such things."

I felt sad. If even Basave Gowda and Bhadre Gowda could not find unity in opposition, then what chance did they have if the family were to divide?

Apart from Chikke Gowda, Basave Gowda was the only man in the family who had not talked to Tony – it was clear that he wanted to tell his story now. But he rambled on about Bhadre Gowda and the problems of the family in almost a perfunctory manner, barely mentioning Nanjeswamy as if he were unimportant. Then suddenly, without a lead from us, he switched to the subject of Lakshmi.

"See, my wife is always going away. She'll work for three days and then for three days she does nothing. She'll just lie down. She shouts. She goes off. Strange. She's a strange girl. No love for her husband. She isn't very clever – thick, uncooperative. She *is* educated, but she's got no knowledge. She doesn't know that if you do one thing, something else will happen. She still hasn't learnt to behave properly, after four and a half years – to show respect and love to her husband; to smile; to behave in a willing way. If only she'd behave like I do, and follow my example, things would go well."

But just as quickly as his thoughts had turned to Lakshmi, he moved onto something else: he spoke of division, he spoke of the wish for children, he switched from money, to corns, to the film unit. He was not always clear what he wanted to say, but through it all, like a death-knell, were long descriptions of Lakshmi and the spirit which possessed her.

He wasn't sure why the teacher had killed himself – something about how the teacher borrowed a jewel from his best friend's wife, pawned it for some money to pay back a debt, and then could not redeem it. In the end, the friend made an evil charm against him, which turned the teacher mad.

"The villagers tied him up: they tied him with chains to a pillar. but he broke the chains and threw himself into the well. And so he haunted that place. When my wife got her periods she used to wash her clothes in a tank on the edge of the village. Once when she went there, that evil bastard must have been sitting under a tree nearby. It went up to her and moved into her.

"It erupted the third time I went to her after the nuptials. I'd slept with her the first time – as husband and wife – and I'd slept with her the second time. But the third time, do you know what it did? It tried to strangle me, and then it bit my hand and made me bleed. I got very angry, wild. I gave her a blow. There, on the cot. Then the spirit said, 'If you want to stay here, stay quiet. Otherwise get out. I'll cut you up and throw you out.'

"After that, on certain days it would be alright; but on other days, if it came, I couldn't do anything. She wouldn't let anyone near her when she lay down. No one could talk to her. I was tired of all this. Disgusted. I almost felt like leaving her. We'd spent 4000 rupees on the wedding. It was like buying some sheep and then they die.

"So I told my eldest brother in town. We got a witch-doctor, who came and did a puja. He made her sit on a board, he put black paste on her forehead, and drew some mandalas round her. Then he held her hair tight, and took a stick in readiness. But that spirit was impossible. They're meant to come to the surface, speaking everything, but some of them are so stubborn they'll never talk. Then you can't catch them. Only if their time is up,* then they say, 'I'll go of my own accord.' But some are so stubborn they never leave.

"That day, when the spirit came to the surface, the doctor grabbed its head. Immediately it kicked and kicked. So the witch-doctor said, 'Let it be,' and left it. He went away quietly. He couldn't do anything that day.

"Then he went to the graveyard, and got a hole dug, very deep. He made her stand in the hole, and filled it up with earth, up to her shoulders, leaving the neck bare. And that day, the spirit said, 'I'm caught in your hand today. If it hadn't been today, you'd never have caught me. You chose this place well. Till today I've never been caught. Today I'm in your hands. You've won.'

"We spent more than 200 rupees."

Although she was meant to be cured, Lakshmi was still not

---

* The family believed that some evil spirits came from people who had committed suicide, and that they had a definite life-span until the suicide's natural death would have been.

right. She would lie down for days at a time, refusing to work, refusing to eat. The family was very fed up.

" 'Why can't she work?' they say. 'She's got no children. Has she ever been helpful in our house for even a single day? She's always complaining that she's got some sickness or other. What sickness?' That's what they all say. Oh god, help me, I've reached a pitch where I can't go on."

Basave Gowda hung his head in despair. Once he'd nearly battered his wife to death. He just couldn't help himself.

"It was about a year after the nuptials. She hadn't eaten for three days, and she wouldn't get up either, whoever told her. Everyone was talking about it. I couldn't stand it.

"I was warming myself over the fire, heating a handle to put in the axe. They'd prepared some gruel for her, and the old lady was calling, 'Come, Lakshmi, come and eat. Lakshmi, Lakshmi.' But she wouldn't move. Suddenly I got very angry. I was livid. I started choking with rage. I took out the stick from the fire and gave her some blows. I had the axe in my hand. She screamed and fell down.

"Then they brought some milk from the coffee house – there was no milk in the house that day. They put it in her mouth, took her, and laid her down. Even then, for two hours she didn't breathe. No. No one could talk to her. After two hours, slowly she came back to life. She was clenching her teeth; she wouldn't even open her mouth to drink more milk. So it all happened. Then my mother, my father, everyone scolded me. They said, 'You bastard, you son of a shaved widow, how can you do such a thing? This is the last time. Don't ever touch her again. If she doesn't eat, her stomach will suffer, not yours. Look out. Don't touch her.'

"After that I felt, What a bastard I am, I beat her, I beat her just like that. I felt bad – I'd hit her but could that girl hit back? Curse my anger. Since then I've never given her a single blow."

But more than anything, more than his wife's evil spirit, more than her strange behaviour, his shame lay in their lack of children. The old man had said he should adopt one of his brothers' sons, but it was one thing to bring up another's child, and another to have your own. What he really wanted to do was to find another wife, but he knew it wouldn't be easy.

"She won't leave that easily. If she'd come without a marriage ceremony, she could have gone easily. But where will she go? She'd go only when she'd got her share of the house and the land. Oh do you think she'd go? She won't go. If I say, 'Get out, there's nothing between you and me, you go your way and I'll go mine,' that'll make it worse. She'd go round saying, 'He left me and married another.' Even if she died it would still be difficult. Suppose her spirit came to haunt us, it might say to my second wife, 'These people killed me, they did this and that.' You don't know what she might do, you can't predict such people. But if she suggests it, if she says, 'I don't bear any children, so do whatever suits you, get a girl up to your level', then I can do something.

"My wife doesn't care," he concluded. "If she was stable I could say what she wanted, but her mind flits in four or five directions. Isn't it natural to want children? But who knows with her, who knows what's in her heart?"

Later that morning, we found Lakshmi washing clothes in a pool that was hidden from view by trees and a steep bank. We scrambled down and sat near the water to watch her: she had no energy and moved her arms in slow motion through the air down to the surface, on into the water, carelessly rinsing each garment before feebly wringing it out.

"Hello, Lakshmi," we said.

She seemed barely to recognise us and closed her eyes for a moment with a slight frown. She was beautiful with her wide face and full mouth, her skin firm and fresh; her body was rounded but youthful.

"Have you started your periods?" I asked. "Have the injections helped?"

She shook her head.

"Is it the spirit which stops it?"

She dropped her hands to her side. "The spirit's been taken out," she whispered and stood for a moment with mouth open. "But I still get some pain."

"Did it come on you often?" I whispered.

"It didn't come on me here, not in my husband's house – I just felt it pressing me, squeezing me round the neck. I'd scream out, scream, scream. It called me. It said, 'Come with me, let's go. Come, let's go, go with me.' It just squeezed my neck, that's all, it didn't take me over.

"When I was at my father's house – oh, when I talk about it, my eyes fill with water and everything grows yellow." She wiped the back of her hand over her eyes, over her forehead, and over her eyes again. "I can't even see you sitting there. You look like a mass of saffron. My eyes are full of water, I can't talk about it at all. I don't know why. See, if I'm sitting alone I feel he's coming. I can see his trousers and hear his sandals, tread, tread, I feel like turning, turning to look. Even today it comes like that. What can you do? Can I give anyone else this life I've brought with me? Why should God give me such a life at this age? Tell me."

She sank onto a rock and let her hand trail through the water till the bangles clinked on her wrist. Birds sang in the background and the water lapped gently against the bank.

"I'd matured," she said, "and married. It came on me then, so that when we had our nuptials it didn't let my husband come near." Her voice had risen and her body tremored. "It would say, 'I'm here, aren't I? I'm here inside you. If you try to sleep together as husband and wife, I'll carry you away to another place.'

"My husband used to come once in eight days during the time of the nuptials. But even if we slept in the same room, I wouldn't be conscious. I'd lie by myself and he'd lie by himself. Whatever he did I wouldn't be conscious. If he spoke to me I wouldn't speak. He'd scold me, beat me, and go to sleep. We didn't have sex then so how could we get children? That's why they say there are no children. Now there's nothing wrong. We're alright. We sleep together. Everything."

She stared at me, a distant blind stare; but in it somewhere was a hint of passion.

"His face was just like yours," she said. "The one who died. He was pink just like you but a bit more pink. His nose was like yours. The same face also. The same height. He wore his watch the same way on his right wrist. Everything the same. Same build, same height, a face like yours. If I suddenly see you I feel, 'Oh Ninge Gowda is coming, he's here, he's come to me.' When you came now I heard the noise of footsteps, walk, walk: I wondered what it was. I looked this side first and then I looked that side. And there you were, just like him. My heart went bang. What's this, I thought. And then I saw it was you – I got so scared.

"He was thirty, maybe thirty-five. He was very fine featured,

249

very nice looking. Taking games, specially singing – there was no one else like him. He was very good and wrote down songs for me. I've still got them but why do I want them now? Even a cuckoo's voice wasn't like his. He'd sing so well. He was like a king. Human beings can't be like that so that's why he had to die. What can you do? Oof, when there was the debate, he had to sing first. You know, his song could be heard so far away. People came from miles around to hear him.

"Yes, I knew him very well, didn't I tell you? And he was very fond of me. I would go and do his housework. I'd go and bathe him also. I'd pour water over him. I'd fetch water, I'd serve him food. He'd call me and I'd go. I'd go myself, I did everything for him. Yes, I had great affection for him. Very great."

She sighed and adjusted her sari till the material was tight round her body.

"His wife wasn't there, she was still at her father's house as their nuptials had just taken place. But even if she came she wouldn't stay long – she came from Mysore and didn't like the small village. Yes, he was my uncle's son – not uncle exactly but we called his father that. I was his younger sister. No, I was more than that. Even a younger sister wouldn't have been like that. He'd say 'Lakshmu, Lakshmu, come and eat, why are you sad today?' I was twelve, thirteen, at the time.

"I used to wash his clothes. He wouldn't let anyone else do them. Only me. He'd say. 'Nobody washes them well, Laksh-mamma. You must wash them yourself. I want you to do them. If you don't I'll beat you.' I ironed his trousers and everything.

"If he'd been alive today the school would have been so active: he used to smile all the time, and the whole school was bright. He was so good. Never lecherous. He'd talk to everyone in such a gentle way, so friendly. He'd say, 'Come now, let's come.' "

She rested her head on her knees and closed her eyes in sorrow.

"But why do you think it possessed you? If he cared for you, why would he give you such trouble?"

She lifted her head and smiled wanly. "He said, 'I wanted to do it. I felt affection for my sister so I came into her. I felt love for her. I wished to come.' "

She sat silently staring into the water, rippling its surface with one finger; then she looked up at the sky.

"It might rain," she said slowly, "I'll just finish the clothes, but you go straight to the village."

"No, no, we'll wait for you, we'll go with you."

"Why do you want to do that? Does anyone wait for me?"

"Just like that. What work do we have? We want to be with you."

"It'll rain on you."

"We don't mind. It'll rain on you too."

"What do I matter? Your clothes will get wet."

"Then we'll change into one of your saris."

"As if you'd wear our saris."

She looked down at her own, a maroon sari, not the green or blue of the village. It was her last symbol of superiority, an effort to defy the family.

"The other women are different," she said. "They say all kinds of harsh things, they all scold me, saying, 'This life isn't like studying or loafing around like you used to. If you ask for that, will you get it here?' Oh, what's it matter. Whether I feel sad or glad I have to be here. It's only the work which is too much. I'm not used to it: when I was in my father's house I'd never go to the fields, I'd never go near them. I'd go to school and when I came home I'd go to my father's shop. I'd help him keep the accounts of what we'd sold and bought – biscuits, sweets, matches."

She loosened her hair and stroking it flat plaited the strands again. She pulled the plait forward over one shoulder.

"See, my husband can't even sign his own name," she said. "One day I had to get something, I had to put my signature. He didn't even know how to sign. I felt very sad. How could I live with such a man? Have you seen him? If you see him, you'll know. It's very difficult to live with a man like that."

She lolled her head on a raised shoulder and tightening her sari round her waist she picked up her basket and climbed to the top of the bank. She stood with a hand on the top of her head and her hip swung out to support the basket, waiting for us to follow.

The next evening Manager Nanjeswamy and the others returned to the village. He was disappointed, he hadn't liked Bangalore, it didn't have much character, not like Mysore with its Maharajah's palace and the big cathedral and the gardens with all the lights by

251

the dam. No, Bangalore was nothing. It was big but nothing much had impressed him. They'd seen a statue or two, they'd seen the white building, they'd even been to the airport. It had all seemed a waste of money, it could have been better spent on an automatic watch as well as a large radio.

The old lady was thrilled: she kept thanking god and the film unit that she'd achieved her life ambition. To see Bangalore! She could tell everyone about it. Oh, and she'd been given such nice food, she'd never had anything like it. And all their expenses paid. Thank god, thank god.

Nanjeswamy distributed the spoils of the trip: oranges, sweets, puffed rice for all the family; white bread for Susheelamma; a cardigan for his daughter, two cotton bed-spreads for the family to use: he handed one to his wife and wrapped the other round himself. He'd spent more than a hundred rupees.

The old lady stood in the corner before the gods, her hands raised to her tired old face, a joss-stick smoking through her fingers.

She called her youngest son to her. 'You haven't been out in the fields have you? You mustn't go in the sun, you mustn't get your skin dark. Have you been well today? Have you eaten, Chikkanna?' She bowed to the pictures. "If we pray to the gods, they'll protect us."

"Who are the gods, Ajji?" I asked.

"What does she know?" said Chikke Gowda. "She doesn't know anything."

"What do I know?" said the old lady with shame.

"Don't you know?" said Chikke Gowda.

She pointed to one of the pictures and thought for a moment. "This one is Rama."

He laughed scornfully. "It's not." *He* knew all the gods, he knew all their stories, he'd learnt them in school.

"Come on, Chikkanna, tell me who it is."

The old lady knew the gods by name and vague attribute, but she could not distinguish between their pictures, though she'd seen them for most of her life.

"It must be Lakshmidevi," she said in desperation.

"It's not Lakshmidevi, it's Murugendra."

"Murugendra, Murugendra," she repeated. "What do I know?

I fold my hands and say, 'Lakshmi, do us good. Rama, Arjuna, Bhima, Suryanarayana, Ishwara, Nanjundeshwara, Parvati, Parameshwara, do us good.' That's what I say. Am I educated to know other things?"

Nanjeswamy did not pray that night. He had better things to do than to thank the gods for a trip he didn't enjoy: he spent two hours trying to make me agree that he needed a transistor more than he needed a watch. Of course it wasn't for him, the whole family would benefit, they could listen to the radio and so improve their knowledge.

"We listen to the radio with interest," he said. "Which way things should be done, which way the plants should be cut, how deep the manure should go, how deep we should plant, what seeds we should choose. They announce all these things on the radio. If they say half the things, we follow at least a quarter of it."

It was like the film he had seen once called The Golden Man. It was all about a poor man who had made himself very rich by digging a well, planting out special crops till many acres were green. Nanjeswamy had learnt from that and implemented the ideas. All he needed now was a proper labour force.

He was angry with the women, he was angry with his brothers: what work had they done while he'd been away? They hadn't even finished cutting the patch of millet, only a tiny patch, not half a morning's work. What good was anyone without him to act as manager?

15 Irresolution

Lakshmi started her bleeding: she lay in the bedroom beside a pile of harvested millet whose dust made her cough. She was pale and inert, for the bleeding was heavy and her stomach ached. But within a day she had disappeared. The family said she had gone to her own village to give her parents the news since they had paid for the doctor, but they glanced at each other surreptitiously when they said she'd be back in a day or two.

I felt something was wrong, so Venkamma and I decided to visit her village: it would also be an opportunity to understand her background and the crisis of her mind. The village was called Rampura and was only six hundred yards from the main tarmac road which ran from Krishnapatna to Sundrapura: it had electricity, a post office, a shop, and two coffee-houses; there was a feeling of muted achievement because of the green fields and the men we passed with bicycles. The primary and middle schools stood prominently at the entrance to the village, with cream walls and green shutters; the classrooms were full of chanting children.

Lakshmi's house was small: it was poor and neglected with only a small square hall and two adjoining rooms. Some sheep were penned in one corner, and clothes hung in another. The dung still lay in the cattle area, the mud floor was unswept, and the ashes beneath the water pot were piled high – it was an ordinary village house belonging to a Gowda family, without grandeur, without pretence, with no sign of sophistication or any perspective other than rural life.

We sat in the empty house till Lakshmi's mother came in from the fields: she was a big woman with flat splayed feet and a slow walk which made her seem weary and cumbersome; her eyes were quick and distrustful: she showed no curiosity and did not ask who we were.

'Where's Lakshmi?' I asked.

'She lives in Palahalli,' she answered.

'But where is she now?'

254

Daughters-in-law of the house: Thayee (left) cleans her daughter's hair; Lakshmi (right) was said to be possessed by an evil spirit

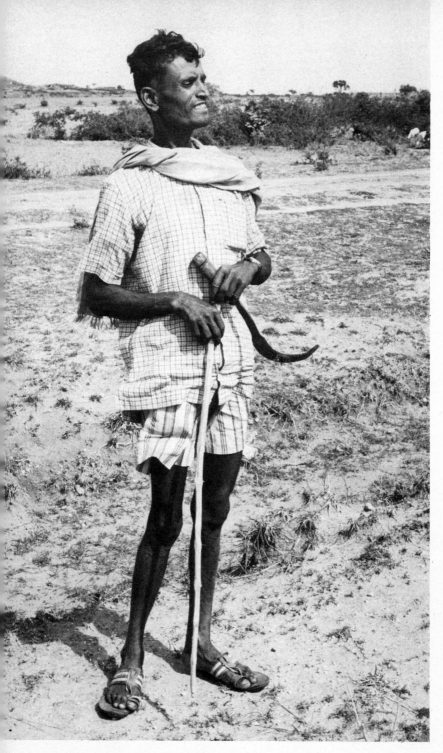

Basave Gowda, the husband of Lakshmi

'She's at her husband's house.'

'We've just come from there.'

'Then you must have seen her.'

'She left two days ago. They said she'd come here.'

The mother was surprised, but when we explained about Lakshmi's bleeding, she nodded her head.

'Then she's gone to the hospital in Sundrapura. She must be with her in-laws.'

'She can't be,' I said. 'S.M.B. was in Palahalli also. He didn't mention Lakshmi. He said she'd come here.'

Her mother sat down. She was worried, unable to work it out. 'Where do you think she is? Where's she gone? She's not been here at all.' She scratched her head distractedly, and as relatives entered the house to find out who the visitors were, she whispered to each in turn that Lakshmi couldn't be found.

The news spread through the village and soon a group of women was crouching in the house.

"Didn't she tell anyone? She must have told someone," said one woman.

"If she went anywhere," said another, "she should have gone to Sundrapura. Or here. Where else could she go?"

"If she goes to strange places and hangs around, how can her family take her back? They'll have to tell her to stay away."

"Why did she go away?" asked her mother. "Where did she go? Why is she always like this?"

"Who knows where she's gone?" said a woman with contempt.

"Who knows what she's doing?" said another with a jeer.

"Oh, your Lakshmi, she hasn't learnt to behave yet."

"Each one's nature is different, and if all the girls were like this, what would we do?"

But they quietened as Lakshmi's brother entered the house: he was a heavy man with one earring and a close-cropped fringe over squat eyes and thick chin. He glared at the gossiping women. "She must have gone off," he said coolly. "She's always going off. What can we do?" Then he pointedly turned to us. "You've been filming the family," he stated.

We nodded.

"Why didn't you come to this village? We're educated people, we could have helped you more. See, there are many graduates here. The middle school has a strength of two hundred. Yes, this village is grand. We have a well, too, we dug it about four or five years back. We've got to fix the pump."

He ignored all further mention of Lakshmi and gradually those who had entered the house filtered away discreetly, leaving him, Lakshmi's mother, and Lakshmi's younger sister – a plump girl in a lush pink sari who had just delivered a daughter and was resting for a while before she went back to her wealthy husband. She had an easy life, for she had only to cook and to wash the dishes, for there were labourers to work the fields.

Lakshmi's brother shut the door firmly against other visitors.

"Why can't Lakshmi be like this younger sister?" he said angrily. "This one gives us no trouble. She said she wanted to marry an educated man where she needn't work, so we found her such a place. But Lakshmi? What has she done? We married her to that family – we thought they were fairly prosperous. Someone in the village told us about them. They all came. The one from the town, he came and arranged everything. What's wrong with it? There's no problem for food or clothes and what work does she have to do? They hire labourers for everything. Fetching water, cooking, sweeping – that's all she has to do. Weeding and planting and other things. Not much. We're peasants aren't we? We have to do all this, don't we?"

Peasants they might consider themselves, but they had a wider knowledge than most. They knew that the English came from England and had come before, long ago, to do business with scales. They knew the English had conquered India and ruled for many years; they knew of dollars and pounds which could not be used in India, so wondered how I paid for anything; and they were explaining the difference between import and export when Lakshmi walked through the door. Her head was bare, her chin was lifted defiantly beneath a thinner, tighter face. Her brother swung round.

'Where have you been, Lakshmi?' he challenged.

Lakshmi ignored him and moved towards us. 'They said you'd come,' said Lakshmi. 'I came here to see you. I'd have stayed away otherwise.'

'Lakshmi, Lakshmi,' said her mother.

'Where have you been?' asked her brother.

Irresolution

She turned her back on him.

'You saw what pain I had,' she said to us. 'But do you think they'd leave me alone? And when S.M.B. came from the town, they cursed me all the harder. That Eramma tried to strike me – she told me I came from darkness, she told me I brought evil on the house. Did she know how I felt? Did she know the pain I had? How could I take her words? I ran out of the house, I ran into the night, I had to leave that house.'

She walked into the bedroom to change her sari. Her mother tried to follow but her brother stopped her.

'Why should she have help?' he said.

'No one wants to help me,' called Lakshmi coldly. 'Does anyone care whether I live or die?' She banged round the room trying to find a sari. 'I don't even have a sari, I gave them all away, I gave them to my sister who sits idly at home. I had such fine saris but I've given them all away. I have to wear the village sari, I have to wear what they tell me.'

She stripped off the maroon one and moving behind the door changed her blouse also. When she emerged, she looked magnificent in solid cream silk over a lime-green blouse, which gave her an elegant grace. She moved with sophistication, a bright figure in a dark house where mud walls predominated. She combed and plaited her hair and fastened a flower in the nape of her neck.

'Lakshmi, you should have come home to us,' said her mother. 'Can you behave like that? Can you wander about strange places?'

Lakshmi lit a scented stick and waved it in front of the gods: she was pale; her hands shook.

'Do my family understand?' she said in a tight voice. 'What have they ever done for me?'

'Lakshmi,' said her brother. 'You should learn respect for your parents.'

Lakshmi swung round.

'Do my parents care for me? Do they try to help? They do nothing, nothing to help.' She bent and shouted into her mother's face. 'Do you do anything? Can I come here? Where can I go when I'm troubled?'

'You can come here,' said her mother.

'Can I? Can I? Oh god, why should I be alive?'

'You can come here,' said her mother.

257

'At least my cousins look after me: they took me in this time. But do you care where I go? Do you help, do you care? You send your daughter away.'

Tears were pouring down her face but she proudly wiped them away.

'What do you mean, Lakshmi?' her mother asked with be-wilderment. Her face had softened with concern.

'You can come here, Lakshmi,' echoed her younger sister.

'And that's why you send me a message never to come here again?' Lakshmi was turning in circles staring first at her mother, then her brother, then her younger sister. She could barely speak without choking and kept tugging her plait in anguish.

'Never to come here again?'

'That's what they said my father had said.'

'Who?'

'They. My husband's family.'

'No one has said such things.'

'Is my father here?'

'He's gone to sell horsegram.'

'Perhaps he said such things.'

'He's never said such a thing. He was hurt you didn't come last time.'

Everyone stayed silent, avoiding each other's eyes. Lakshmi's mother tried to take her arm but she stepped back quickly.

'I . . . I must get back to my cousin's house,' she said. 'They're expecting me at once.'

Her brother got up and stood in her way.

'You must go back to your husband,' he said.

Lakshmi lifted her head and stubbornly confronted him.

'Why should I go back when they treat me so badly?'

She tried to step round him but he moved to block her way.

'You must go back to Palahalli. All the village is talking.'

She tossed her head. 'What do I care of the village?'

'Lakshmi, Lakshmi,' said her mother, beginning to cry. 'What will your father say?'

'I'll see him when he gets back.'

'Lakshmi,' said her brother with sudden anger, 'you stay here in this house. You've brought shame enough already.'

Lakshmi sat down abruptly and stiffly arranged her sari about

258

her; then noticing our concern, she moved towards us and took my hand.

'You can help,' she said. 'You must advise what should be done. You're educated like me, you know more than all my family. I'm like a sister to you, you'll tell me what to do.'

She looked at us expectantly and I felt a sudden sense of despair, of uselessness, and treachery. What could we advise except to return to the family? There was nothing she could do elsewhere except become a prostitute: at least with the family she had some security, some protection, with food, shelter and clothing. Above all, she had respectability – when that was lost, few would help or protect her.

I stayed silent but she kept urging me to answer.

'You must stay with your husband, Lakshmi,' I answered finally. 'It's the only way to survive.'

'I must?' She dropped her hands to her side. 'Couldn't you . . . must I . . . oh, what's there for me?' She covered her face and started to cry.

None of us looked at each other.

'I'll . . . I'll take you back to Palahalli,' said her mother gently. 'It'll help if I come back with you.'

'Yes, let your mother go with you,' said her brother.

Lakshmi nodded glumly. Her body heaved with a few more sobs and then she quietened.

'Maybe I'll go tomorrow,' she said.

'We'll be there tomorrow,' I added.

She smiled weakly. Yes.' She picked at the cloth of her sari. 'Yes, maybe I'll go back tomorrow.'

Her mother made coffee and then it was time for us to go in order to catch the bus before dark. Lakshmi was eager to take us, to show us the high school where her teacher had been. She held our arms and guided us through the village: she was confident now and recalled the day of her marriage. Her father had paid three tola of gold and nearly four thousand rupees. She laughed, a brittle laugh. Four thousand rupees, just for an ugly husband who couldn't read, who couldn't make love, who gave her no children. She hadn't seen him before the marriage, not one glimpse. Would she have agreed if she'd seen such a man? No, they brought Manager Nanjeswamy and showed him as the bridegroom. They cheated her and her family. On the day of the wedding – she nearly died that day but what could she do about it? If she'd refused, it would have brought shame on her family.

Her walk slowed as we passed the school, she slurred her words and widened her eyes, tilting her head on one side. She had been so popular at school, she had known a lot of the boys, they'd been her friends and fellow classmates, but with marriage she had left them behind. There was one boy, her cousin, whom she saw whenever she returned to the village. He was there today, following us to the bus-stop. I found him classically handsome in a youthful virile way, but Lakshmi said he was too dark-skinned and not very intelligent. She treated him like a servant.

'They need coffee and food,' she said as we reached the village from where the bus would leave, so he hurried to order some from an eating-house nearby. But after a few minutes, she grew impatient and followed him inside. 'We'll eat here,' she ordered and sat at one of the tables. He sat at another facing her: with timid respect he kept glancing at her, watching her mouth as she ate, watching her hands clasp the metal tumbler, watching her shoulders move. He did not himself eat but kept lifting the sickle from his lap, placing it on the table, then returning it to his lap.

Another youth came and sat beside him. He had curly hair and wide shoulders, which were contoured through sky blue nylon: his shirt was undone to the vest.

'He was in my class,' whispered Lakshmi. 'He used to come top after me.' She called across to him. 'Have coffee and *idli*.'

He nodded. 'Have you come home, Lakshmi?'

'I've just come for a rest.'

'Can you still write your alphabet?'

'Can you even recite it?'

They both laughed.

She stood up and tossed the end of her sari provocatively over her shoulder.

'The bus will be here soon,' she said. 'You must take my friends to Krishnapatna.'

And when the bus pulled up, she pushed him in behind us with easy familiarity. She stood in the road waving and waving as the bus drew into the distance.

Irresolution

By learning about the story of Lakshmi, I knew I had filled in a major gap, but I still had more to learn and more that needed confirming. Yet if I stayed on, how much could I achieve? So much in their life was predictable given the restrictive conditions; so much of their life repeated itself within the terms of authority; nevertheless nothing was ever the same, especially their emotions and the content of each crisis. Perhaps if I stayed six months when work on the land was reduced, I might find signs of joy which seemed too harshly absent; perhaps if I stayed a year I would understand better the cycle of life and the continuing rhythm of their survival. But I didn't have a year and the family wouldn't want me. One thing especially worried me: I cared for the family and believed that our relationship would continue into the future, yet still I didn't know what they really thought of me, whether there was any caring, or whether they would brush me aside in their memory as an unwelcome intruder. It was true they had grown used to me, but did that mean any commitment? Perhaps acceptance was all I could ask for: there was no reason for them to trust and believe in my own feelings for them. Even Bhadramma was sceptical. "Because you've come to our country," she said, "you've done everything like us. But when you go back to your own country, you'll take off your village clothes and forget us quickly." I suppose she was right, for she had no proof of my sincerity. And for me to stay on would prove nothing further unless I gave myself permanently to their way of life and became part of the community.

In the end, as with the family, I had no choice: I had to return to England to be with Tony and help with the film, since schedules were very tight. I told the family I would leave shortly. No one seemed to mind, no one was surprised: they knew I must join my husband, that I could not stay by myself. Some of the family were more concerned with the presents they'd been promised than with the thought of my departure; and even the women did not seem to mind. The only difference it seemed to make was to prompt lethargic curiosity about where I would go, how I would get there, the sort of house I would live in. But even so, the questions were soon used up.

I spent a day in Mysore buying the family presents. When I returned, S.M.B. had come from the town and was sitting on the verandah checking accounts with Manager Nanjeswamy: he seemed angry and ignored me; Nanjeswamy was unshaven, he wore an old shirt, and sat like a frightened schoolboy, biting his lower lip and peering nervously at his brother from beneath his bowed forehead. Apparently he had made a bad deal which although it brought him some status was not financially lucrative. S.M.B. was salvaging what he could.

I had bought something for everyone in the family but there was no sense of ceremony in their distribution: saris and mirrors to the women, a wool jacket for the old man, money for the old lady, shirts and torches for the men, clothes and toys for the children, a clock for S.M.B., a watch for Nanjeswamy. No one said a word. The old lady stuffed the envelope unopened into her blouse; the women peered timidly into their parcels, then locked them away in their trunks; the children grabbed each other's in jealousy; the old man stroked the fabric and put on his jacket with pleasure. Bhadre Gowda and Basave Gowda were still in the fields.

S.M.B. was angry – he'd expected a pressure cooker; Chikke Gowda was indignant – what would he do with a pen set, he'd got two already? He'd wanted a camera at least. Someone with his education could handle a camera well. Manager Nanjeswamy was the only one who grinned: with a flourish of humility he offered the watch to his eldest brother who slipped it on his wrist.

Jayamma was in her fields when I went to give her a green silk sari: she had covered her face with a rag to stop the dust blowing into her eyes while she crouched painfully to prune the millet seedlings. Her stomach was heavy at seven months.

She stood up to take the present and smiled wistfully. Then she started to cry silently, turning her face to the wind, turning away from us.

Her husband had started to be cruel again. He'd told her to get out of the house unless she got on with some work, so now she was pulling water once more, grinding, pounding, carrying manure to the fields. And still he provided no food.

I was frightened. With the film unit gone, and myself leaving, there was no restraint on his actions. Although she was stronger from all the pills and had sufficient to last her until the end of her pregnancy, if he beat her again she could easily miscarry. Seven months was the critical period.

Irresolution

I insisted we go to a hospital – Jayamma, Kalle Gowda, Venkamma, and I. It was pointless returning to Bangalore for it was too far away to follow up visits, so we went to another hospital, about forty miles by bus. I had an introduction to an efficient female doctor who thought I was part of the B.B.C. She examined Jayamma and said she must rest till delivery. Kalle Gowda said that of course she could rest – at home. I argued that she'd find no rest at home. The doctor offered to let Jayamma stay in hospital until delivery; Kalle Gowda said it wasn't necessary; I said it was. No decision was reached. Only when we got home and consulted with S.M.B. and the family did Kalle Gowda grudgingly agree: she could go in a few days. I therefore gave her the money for medicines, and asked her uncles and brother to ensure she went into hospital. I wasn't certain whether she would go or not, whether her husband would let her once I had gone.

During my last two days, I felt in a dream at departing, though everyone else was suddenly spurred into action: the neighbours invited me in for coffee; Jayamma cooked us a large supper and begged us to stay the night; Bhadramma cleaned a bagful of millet and cut her largest pumpkin for us to take away. The old lady said we could leave only on Tuesday: Monday was inauspicious, nobody left on a Monday.

The women stayed up most of Monday night preparing sweets and biscuits, and early the next morning Thayee served me breakfast with samples of their cooking: delicate whorls of fried rice flour; crisp, spicy biscuits; warm, sweet *obbittu*. The old lady wrapped the bulk of the cooking in polythene and newspaper to make four huge bundles – one for Tony and me, one for the film unit, one for Vara and Venkamma, one for my mother and family.

We visited everyone's houses to say a last farewell: we sat in Jayamma's house on the low mud wall which divided the cattle from humans. She made us drink some coffee; she offered auspicious powders, dabbing them on my face; she placed in our hands some bananas, flowers, and betel leaves. As we left, she thrust in my hands a small bundle wrapped in white cotton.

'Take them,' she said. 'I know how you like them. You can use them straight away, I've cleaned them all of grit.'

She had given me her entire stock of sesame seeds which she'd cleaned and roasted herself.

263

Irresolution

We went to Bhadramma's house and sat on the red floor. She gave us some coffee, she offered the *kunkuma* and turmeric, adding it to my forehead; she placed in our hands bananas, flowers, and betel leaves.

I left Venkamma and walked to the fields alone – out through the village, past the square tank, down to the river and up past the trees; along the winding path which led through others' fields, up a small bank and into the sorghum. I clanged the metal plate to scare off the birds; I tapped the gross jackfruit and brushed through the sugar-cane; I peered in the well and ran down the steps to wash my hands; then I went into the millet fields. I touched the soil and lifted my hands to my eyes. Mother Earth, the protector and destroyer.

There was no answer to anything. The rain had stopped and started for two weeks, but now it had definitely stopped and the sun was burning the soil again. Would it return in time to revive the millet seedlings which drooped in their lines? There was water enough in the well to keep the sugar-cane growing but would it last till the crop could be harvested and then could the debts be paid? Or would the family divide?

Lakshmi was emptying the dung by the pumphouse. She had come back to the village the night before, and no one had said a word, and no one had spoken to her since. She had come back alone, for her mother had started her periods and her father had paid no interest: she had come only because we had said so. We stood for a moment together, holding each other's arms.

'Go,' she said, 'and come back.'

'I'll come back,' I answered.

I returned to the family house. The old lady gave us flowers; she put *kunkuma* on my forehead and offered us betel leaves. She arranged my sari and smoothed back my hair. She tried to touch my feet.

I burst into tears. I couldn't stop crying. I cried as we left the house, I cried as we walked down the street. The old lady kept clutching my wrist in surprise.

'Why do you want to cry?' she said. 'Why do you want to cry?'

'Don't cry,' said the women as they followed behind.

'Oh ho ho,' said Manager Nanjeswamy. 'Saramma's crying at leaving.'

I bowed to the old man with my hands raised to my forehead; I bowed to the old lady. I shook hands with Nanjeswamy and touched the women's arms. I hugged each child. Then I got into the car which the film unit had hired in advance for me. The family stood at the gate of the village to watch me leave: I turned to wave often, with the tears running down my cheeks. But it was worse when we stopped at Jayamma's fields for she was waiting for us at the roadside with an armful of chrysanthemums and a basket of freshly picked eggplants.

'Don't cry,' she said, squeezing my hand hard. She wiped away my tears. 'We'll see each other again when I have my child.' And she told the driver to take me to Bangalore.

I stared out of the back window at the receding village, the flat fields, the acres of scrub and rock, and the diminishing figure of Jayamma, stone-like on the road, her head erect, her shoulders square, as she watched the car intently, her eyes screwed up against the sun.

Two of the family came with us to Bangalore – Rame Gowda and Bhadre Gowda. They wanted to escort us, to give their guests a proper farewell and of course to see the big city. They sat in the car while I delivered messages, collected parcels, visited one or two people. Bhadre Gowda apologised, the town wasn't for them, they were only peasants without any money.

'See, we're a little dull. Just like you when you first came to the village. But now you're our mother, you're the one who's closest to us.'

At the airport they shook my hand with genuine warmth; they stood at the barrier and watched me cross the tarmac; they watched me enter the plane. As it sped down the runway, I could see them waving and waving and waving, and then they were lost as we shuddered into the sky. I stared down at the brown land crossed by hundreds of tracks, dotted with brown villages whose fields covered the ground like an intricate patchwork. From this height, it was a landscape empty of humans, without detail, without intimacy; and yet I knew what it meant, I had my own commitment.

16 Division

Three months later in England, I received a letter from Jayamma, written by her brother.

All safe here.*
Jayamma's greetings to my dear Saramma. By god's grace I am keeping well. I hope you are well and I pray to god that he should give long life and health to you who have so much love and affection for me.

On ———** I was operated on in Mandya hospital. At present both the child and I are well, but even now I can't walk. I am staying with my brother in Sundrapura.

In the same way that you looked after me, the lady doctor in Mandya hospital and a nurse called Jayalakshmamma looked after me day and night like they would their own daughter. My elder sister Thayee has had a son. She too is well. Because of the doctor's treatment and your kindness my child and I are well. Here my father, mother, and everyone is well.

I forgot to tell you the most important thing, that is, I didn't tell you what the child was. I want to tell you now. It's a 'girl'. I would have given you sweets but I don't know how to give them to you. Now you do one thing. *You* buy some sweets yourself in my name and eat them and give them to Tony and your friends; when they ask you what the sweets are for, tell them that you helped a poor sister when you went to India, and that now the poor sister has sent you some sweets.

I feel that if a person like Saramma had been born as my elder sister or mother, I would have been floating through the skies. I found the love I hadn't found in my father, mother, brother, mother-in-law, or husband, in a gem that came from

---
* A formality to indicate that the letter contains no news of death.
**The day and date are not given, only a blank underlined – presumably to have been filled in before the letter was posted.

the sky, stayed with us for three months, and flew back in the sky.

You say it's raining a lot there. If it's raining a lot there, there's no rain at all here. In some places here there is no water even to drink. It's very cold here also. I await your loving letter giving me more news.

Your dear sister,
Jayamma

Four months later, a letter came from Lakshmi.

All safe here.
My dear Sarah,
Here our health is in the same condition. There doesn't seem to be any improvement.

About a week ago our family divided. Basave Gowda and Lakshmi have set up separately and are immersed in debts of Rs. 7000.

God alone knows what kind of life we are going to lead. I don't know in which direction to turn. Bhadre Gowda and Basave Gowda are together. I don't like it. Basave Gowda says to me, 'If you want us to stay together, stay. I can't till the land so I have to stay with my brother. If you are happy about it you can stay; otherwise you can go away to your father's house.' Therefore I am staying at my father's house for a while.

I am in great trouble now. There is no solace. I hope that you will help me as soon as you see this letter. You must help me. They have put us in great trouble. They haven't even given us cattle to plough the fields. Till now we haven't even got children: God has not opened his eyes to see us. We don't know when he is going to show mercy on us. Our family is in greater trouble than theirs. They have kept the money also. We are troubled for want of money. They have given us the loan taken for marriage expenses; they have given us the debts made for the pumpset and well; they have given us the debts to purchase land.

My health is not very good. The hospital expenses are being paid for from my father's house. I feel deeply grieved. I still have no children. You should not at any time or in any letter tell my husband's people that you are helping me. Basave Gowda punishes Lakshmi a lot. Therefore I feel sad. They haven't even given me back my jewels.

I am incapable of writing anything more to one who knows much. You must write about everything. Do not ignore us. We are sitting in great sorrow with no cattle to till. I hope you will write as soon as you see this letter and send whatever help you can with it.

Your dear sister,
Lakshmi

Almost a year after I had first met the family, I flew back to India. I dreaded my return after the calm and comfort of England – the physical hardship of blistered feet and sweating body in harsh oppressive heat, the ruthless adjustment to inadequate diet and lack of privacy, the hard floors and noisy nights. I also dreaded a new invasion of lice and parasites which I'd only just managed to clear from before. But more, I was frightened of seeing the family again, their jealous demands, their fixed relationships where no one could choose affection or friendship, where few had choice of anything.

I wanted to see Jayamma, I longed to see her again, but I also feared what I might find – a daughter and a caesarian? And the family – shouldn't I be blamed partly for hastening division? A heightened consciousness of their problems which activated the split must have come through all my questions and through conflict with the film unit. Would they want to see me? Perhaps there would not be the same involvement, the same memory that I had retained for them.

My body adjusted in preparation: I noticed the cold in England, though it was mid-summer; I felt repulsed by food except boiled rice and potatoes; I did not want a bath. And the moment I got to India, everything seemed tangible: the bustle of people, the bodily contact in buses, the pungent smell of *bidis*, the sickly smell of jasmine flowers, sweet and claustrophobic; the sour smell of urine in the heat. Dust. Heat. Sweat.

Then the cool of Krishnapatna, aloof on its rocky promontory where the priests still chanted and the trumpets wailed and the streets were empty of devotees; along the valley where god resided with lotus blossoms and ponds; out on the plain with the pimpled rock and the tinkle of bells on sheep. And there, there in the distance was Palahalli, a squat clutch of roofs reduced to insignificance by the trees and fields and scrub.

It was nearly dark when I reached the village and walked up the street to the house. Nobody was about. I climbed the two granite steps, took off my shoes and went in. In the far corner where the gods had their pictures, the old man was saying his prayers, a spiral of smoke wafting up to the roof as he clutched a burning joss-stick. Susheelamma was grinding with her back to the door; the rest of the house seemed empty.

One of the children saw me and came rushing up to clutch me round the knees.

'Saramma's come, Saramma's come,' he cried. I picked him up in my arms.

Susheelamma turned and smiled with delight; Thayee came out of the kitchen, pinched my cheek hard, and thrust her new-born son into my arms. The old lady came out of the storeroom.

'Saramma. Saramma. Our daughter Saramma's come,' she cried.

Others emerged from the rooms and everyone surged round.

I hugged each child in turn, I shook the men by the hand, I laughed and laughed with the women, my eyes filling with water. We held hands, pinched each other's arms, passed the children and babies from one to another, one to another.

The old lady grinned and clutched my arm. She wanted to show me her 'house'. She lived in the storeroom now, for on division, she and the old man had decided to go their separate ways. The storeroom was used by S.M.B. and his wife whenever they came from the town, and also by Chikke Gowda and his bride Bhagyamma. The old lady was proud housekeeper for them all.

Thayee called me into the kitchen, which she shared with her husband, Bhadre Gowda, their three children, Basave Gowda, Lakshmi, and the old man. He'd decided to support his sons by his second wife when division finally happened. And these two sons had decided to stick together.

The old bedroom belonged to Madakka and her husband and their five children; the old tool room belonged to Susheelamma and Manager Nanjeswamy and their three children.

Division

Each room was divided in two by a low partition to mark cooking and living areas, so that each new family group had two dark sections not more than seven by eight feet. Each room had its pile of clay pots stacked in a single diminishing tier, some mats strung from the roof, and a bare dung floor. The cattle remained outside, the furniture stayed in the hall with the gods and the big brass pot. Bhadre Gowda, in a fit of liberation, had painted the walls bright turquoise.

Madakka pulled me into her room and thrust her baby into my arms. It was a boy, her fourth son. He looked healthy, with no deformity from all the drugs she had taken in her attempt to abort. She had also had a tubectomy. She seemed more relaxed.

Manager Nanjeswamy came in.

'We're glad you came,' he said softly.

'I'm so happy to be here,' I answered.

'We thought you wouldn't come back.'

'Could I forget this family?'

He fingered my village sari.

'Did you leave it in Krishnapatna?' he asked.

'I took it to England and brought it back.'

'It's the same, the same sari?'

I nodded.

He looked down at his mustard-coloured shirt which once had been so smart but now was worn and faded.

'When you came last time,' he said, 'I was very bold. Now I'm sweeping the floors.' He grinned ruefully.

He looked older, much older, with lines of stress on his forehead and a tight, thoughtful mouth; his hair was no longer sleek, his hands had coarsened with work: he had lost his jaunty arrogance.

'Your watch?' I said with surprise, noticing his empty wrist.

He shrugged. 'S.M.B. is wearing it.'

'Haven't you asked for it back?'

'He says I gave it to him.'

Everyone gave me something for supper, which I ate in the old lady's room: Susheelamma brought the rice, Thayee the curry, and Madakka the millet. The old lady supplied a dollop of ghee and a cupful of creamy buttermilk.

Then I gave out the presents I had brought from England. Everyone seemed pleased. Nanjeswamy even thanked me.

Division

'You've remembered everyone,' he said.

'I feel this is home, so shouldn't I bring presents after my long absence?'

'But what have we got to give in return?'

'You give me your food, you give me your roof, what more do I want?'

'You're our sister.'

'I've no brothers but you.'

We stared at each other and were glad for the peace that was made. He took me to his 'house' and said I should sleep there. It was my house to live in.

The room was beautifully neat. He must have spent months preparing it, for rows and rows of shelves lined the walls; wood was stacked in the roof, each piece cut to a matching length; and the floor was even and smooth right into the cooking area. Susheelamma laid out a mat and motioned for me to lie down. Then Nanjeswamy brought in their baby Saramma and laid her at my head.

'See, Saramma and Saramma are now together again!'

I tried to sleep but interruptions were constant: Thayee came in to chat, the old man bowed from the doorway, the children ran in and out. It must have been two o'clock when Lakshmi crept in. She flung herself down on the mat and whispered with urgent intensity.

Things had got no better; things were worse now. What could her husband do? Why should he stay in this house? They'd only be given four acres of land with debts of five thousand rupees; there was no cattle, nothing with which to plough. Only three sheep. That's all they'd got. What could they do with that? But she'd had to come back from her parents, for her father had left her mother, and how could she stay at home?

She tossed and turned; she groaned; she brushed the hair from her face. She couldn't stay here, no, not with these ignorant people. Her husband was so ugly. She was going to leave to-morrow, she'd leave the house at once: she'd go to Mysore and finish her education. Her parents – yes, they'd help her, they knew they'd made a mistake, they'd pay for her education. She was going to Mysore. She'd heard from her teacher, he'd sent her an invitation, she was going to see him married. Yes, he was getting married. He was so handsome, so kind. But her own husband, what could he do? What could he do? What could he do?

Her words slurred: she turned on her side, folded her arms round her head, and closed her eyes.

The next morning I went to find Jayamma. Her house was locked, so I went on to Bhadramma's.

'Bhadramma?' I called.

No one answered. I went in. She was sorting some dried chillis. I threw open my arms in greeting. She stayed passive, not moving.

'Bhadramma?'

She smiled, sadly.

'Where's Jayamma?' I asked.

'She's here.'

Jayamma came out of the kitchen. We held hands and smiled. I took the baby from her arms, a small beautiful thing with thick black hair, huge eyes, and an uncoordinated head which flopped and jerked like a rag doll. Her name was Manjula.

Jayamma had lost all brightness: she seemed without hope. She said she should have died. There was nothing for her now.

When she had started her delivery pains in hospital, things had got very bad. The doctor wanted to operate to try and save the child and maybe also Jayamma. But her husband wasn't there to give permission. By chance in the evening her brother came. He didn't know what to do, and though he knew it would cause trouble, he finally gave permission. The doctor performed a caesarian and wrapped the baby in cotton for three days. Jayamma hadn't been frightened, for she knew if she died then her brother was there to take her body away.

Her husband was angry, she said. 'Why did you have the operation?' he'd asked. 'If you had to die, you should have died.' He was making her work now in a way that might easily kill her because of her weak condition. He didn't care for the child, he took everything for himself – the child's oil, the child's food, he'd even broken her trunk and stolen the hundred rupees which I'd left when I went to England. They had nothing in the house now. Nothing. He'd sold the few sheep, he'd spent all the money, he'd spent it on drink and women. He went off for days at a time. And though Jayamma had pains in her stomach, her husband insisted on sex.

Her life had changed and in some way I was responsible. My wish to help had only worsened her life: I had intruded without understanding the rules of her society, without anticipating the change which might result, without providing alternatives and support.

We had little else to say, and our gloom was only broken when the baby I was holding wet herself and a warm stream ran down my leg. We burst into laughter, and smiled at each other.

The family's fields looked neglected, since many of the plots were now uncultivated. Most of the sugar-cane was harvested and nothing was planted to replace it; the sorghum field was bare; the jack-fruit tree had lost its largest branch, struck down by a storm; the onion field was empty and the hand-lift dismantled.

The family had divided in March. Some said that a bill had come for a loan with three years' interest unpaid: a thousand rupees loan, a thousand rupees interest. Others said that S.M.B. had tried to buy more land in his own name while charging the loan to the family. Whichever it was, the three who worked in the fields – Rame Gowda, Bhadre Gowda, and Basave Gowda – went on strike for a month and refused to do any work. Unable to find a solution, the brothers had all divided.

More than twenty people had supervised the division for more than three days, in the house and the fields. The elders, the patel, the panchayat, and the old lady's brother had all paced the lands to measure the plots and study the soil: now each son had nearly five acres in eight or nine fragments, some cultivated, some barren, some irrigated from the well. Each brother had three mango trees, three coconut trees, and an equal number of banana trees and sheep. The cattle had been divided, the contents of the house, and the agricultural equipment. Only the onion field had still to be done.

The family all had different versions of the distribution of debts: the old man could not distinguish between loans and the interest due; the women quoted figures from three to seven thousand rupees which each son received; the men ranged from four to five thousand. According to Bhadre Gowda, each brother had 4000 rupees in debt to pay back: the three who had gone on strike were given private loans to look after; the two managers had government loans to their name; and Chikke Gowda was given the debts from his wedding. Each would be responsible for the interest due on his loan, but no one knew for certain how much it would be. The managers who had government loans would obviously pay less.

Bhadre Gowda seemed the most reliable source of information. He led me towards the onion field and found a small hollow where no one could see us together. He told me to take a pencil and write down what he said. He gave me the breakdown of division as though reading a roll-call; he had memorised every detail down to the last pot.

Cattle: 1 ox to Rame Gowda; 1 buffalo to Chikke Gowda; 1 pair of working cows to Bhadre Gowda; 1 milking cow each to the old man and Bhadramma; 1 calf to the old lady. The black oxen and cart were given to Nanjeswamy on the condition he'd pay 700 rupees each to S.M.B. and Basave Gowda. Each brother's portion was worth 700 rupees.

Sugar-cane: Some of this had still to be harvested, so was put up for auction between the brothers. S.M.B. bid highest, at 4500 rupees, which he promised to pay to his brothers – 900 rupees each. It still had not been paid. The crop itself was valued at 7500 rupees.

Ploughs and iron-levellers: 1 plough to S.M.B., to be shared with Chikke Gowda; 1 plough and leveller to the worker Rame Gowda; 1 plough to Nanjeswamy; 1 plough and leveller to be shared between Bhadre Gowda and Basave Gowda.

Grain: 370 seers each.

Vessels and cooking pots: 4 each.

Plates and tumblers: 4 stainless-steel to S.M.B.; 4 brass to Rame Gowda; 3 each to Nanjeswamy and Chikke Gowda; 2 each to Bhadre Gowda and Basave Gowda.

Bhadre Gowda felt that division was fair, but only because of the old lady's brother – the teacher who'd reared S.M.B. He had known the problems, he had protected the step-sons' interests and made sure they'd had their share. Consequently he and the old lady didn't talk now.

At the end of the day, with a few sheep, a few pots, a plough, a cow, and heavy debts, each man had little to show for the power and prosperity the family had once represented. Why had the men received no cash on division? There must have been some left over. And where was the film unit money?

Of all the brothers, Bhadre Gowda and Basave Gowda seemed the worst off. The others had grown-up sons, or salaries, or savings, or cunning, or education. They had none of those things: instead they had eight people to look after with only one able worker. Yet Bhadre Gowda said that whatever the worry, whatever the stress, he would never go back to a joint family: they would struggle alone without cheating.

The old man was glad about division. His best memory was the fury of the old lady when he'd sided with his two sons by his second wife. She'd said that *her* four sons should get all the property, but he'd told her to shut up, for now he would do what he liked.

He was happy. He had no thoughts for the future.

S.M.B., Rame Gowda, and Chikke Gowda, would move in time to the second house and pay for its completion. Nanjeswamy would stay in the old house under the watchful eye of the old man and Bhadre Gowda.

'At first Nanjeswamy wanted to be in the new house,' explained the old man. 'But now he's not so sure. He's getting help from his in-laws – the patel who lives opposite.'

S.M.B. was bitter that his brothers had gone against him. His main problem was how to manage the lands while living in the town. He felt his wife should move to the village to act as his manager, aided by Nanjeswamy. She was thrilled at the thought of leaving town.

S.M.B. summoned me to his room the day he came to the village, presented me with a flower and told me to join him for lunch. It was a sumptuous meal: we ate off stainless steel and drank from cups with handles. Behind us was evidence of wealth in the pots and vessels which lined the walls.

He was not reticent about the land he was trying to buy – twelve acres for which he'd put down a deposit. Nor was he slow to show me the details of all the accounts from which they'd worked out the division. He set them out on the wooden cot for all the family to see: bundles of odd receipts, notebooks filled with figures, loose pages of jottings and calculations. There was no monthly breakdown, no running totals, nor any form of balance. It didn't prove he'd cheated but it certainly showed that he hadn't bothered to do his book-keeping properly, and that no one else would be able to check his figures.

He called his wife to his side and put an arm round her shoulder. She blushed and looked at him with anxiety.

'Ah ha, Mrs. S.M.,' he said, patting her hand. 'This lady's mother will come to cook for me in town, and though she's a village woman, she can help look after the children. Fine Indian ladies.' He said it again in English.

It took me several days to adjust to the heat, the food, and sitting cross-legged in a sari; but once my sunburn had faded I felt completely at home. My relationship with the women had changed subtly so that we accepted each other without alienation. They had been curious at first: they'd hoped at least I was pregnant, and Thayee said with a laugh that soon I'd be too old – or at least my husband would be. They asked a bit about England, then lapsed into reminiscence about my previous visit. They'd been so worried then, for I'd got so thin and looked so ill, and it was all because of their village life. We remembered the grinding, we remembered the planting, and the birth of Susheelamma's baby.

'We'd been grinding the evening it came,' I said.

Susheelamma giggled. 'And you dropped the mattress on me.'

'And Tony fetched the film unit.'

She nodded.

'Did you mind?'

She shook her head. 'I was worried at first, for all the neighbours were talking. I was frightened for my delivery. But then when it came so easily, I knew it was alright.'

This time, I felt I had more of a function. The women asked me to hold their babies, to rock the cradles, and they said I helped time go quickly. I was still inept at their work but I swept a bit and collected water, and no one protested. Thayee was even grateful, for she had little help from Lakshmi. She asked me to name her son: she'd been waiting all this time especially for me to do it. We chose Sadhashiva, but shortened it to Sadha.

I was happy and I also felt great relief that I no longer carried a tape recorder.

The women regretted division: it meant more work, it meant each must do every job without help from others – the cooking, the grinding, the sweeping, the work in the fields, the washing and feeding of children. They recognised a freedom of decision now that each was the female head of her household, but it meant little beside the loss of cooperative action. They had protested at division until Manager Nanjeswamy had said that if they wanted to stay together then they could leave the house and find a place of their own.

All the women were thinner and though with babies they had time to sit while feeding, they knew it would be harder once the planting season began. Now was a moment of ease in newly found freedom. The children also had lost their plumpness, and two had sores all over their bodies: they had to work as they could and the older boys were learning to plough. School took second place.

The women did in fact help each other in little ways by sharing the grinding, by lending water, by cooking extra food for each other; they entered each other's houses freely but discreetly, avoiding the old lady.

All her former energy seemed to have left the old lady. She wandered round the house almost without purpose, mumbling to herself and sweeping the hall occasionally. Sometimes she called her daughters-in-law to give her a hand with something, but often they ignored her: then she screamed and cursed, but without the same intensity.

I moved from room to room to sleep and eat in each 'house', but mainly I stayed with Thayee and Susheelamma. I felt freer with them. They cooked nothing special but gave me what they gave their families; they let me sit in peace and did not question where I went. Thayee was more authoritative now: she ordered more, she answered back, and because of her initiative, she and Madakka were speaking again at last.

I preferred to sit inside in the small dark rooms where the smell of cooking and bodies was mixed: I felt secure and protected, I felt the warmth of human contact. The hall outside seemed bleak,

277

a cold room where men fought out their roles – men who proudly refused to enter each other's homes unless by invitation. Only Nanjeswamy and S.M.B. went where they wanted to: the others stayed in their rooms.

Rame Gowda and Madakka kept themselves to themselves: they worked hard and were training their sons to work with them. Neither expressed much feeling about the effects of division.

My relationship with the men was also more relaxed: they no longer saw me as the messenger of money. They still asked for help – a tractor, some land, a loan – but more from habit than hope. Yet when I gave Bhadre Gowda four hundred rupees to cure his brother's corns he threw it down in rejection. He'd expected enough for an ox at least. My tears and rage startled him, and he never again asked for money.

The women also asked for things – a blanket for the baby, a plastic comb, some bangles, some oil – and they accepted my refusals passively, though they knew I had money for such small items. It distressed me, the difference in our lives, both material and mental: I had freedom and opportunity, I had comfort and choice. And yet the differences faded. I had returned; they had taken me in. I showed emotions of tiredness, anger, discomfort; they accepted and helped. They showed impatience and anger; I accepted and helped. They shared, I shared, and no one tried to change the other. I learnt from them things which changed me – to use my body more functionally, to cope with others patiently, to accept without fighting those things which could not be changed, to know what the fundamentals were. I think my presence also affected them.

As a gesture of unity, I let them oil my hair and scrape it back in a bun. At first they thought it beautiful but then they decided it didn't suit me, that I was more me with short unruly hair. Some even admitted that I wasn't born for a sari.

It rained while I was there. Once more the earth released its scent and the dry soil greedily sucked in the water, turning itself to mud.

All the families went out to their separate plots to work their tiny fragments. Even Nanjeswamy. And, of course, his fields were the greenest, the neatest, the best of all the brothers. It was true: he had worked and worked and worked, determined to prove he could manage. He seemed irrepressible.

He still had plenty of schemes: he was organising the cultivation of some acres on behalf of the patel; he worked for S.M.B. and he arranged the irrigation for his brothers, giving them each two days of water in turn. He also controlled the electricity bill, dividing it into six, he said.

I was sure that Nanjeswamy would always be alright, however tough the conditions; and so would S.M.B. Both were bold enough to continue growing sugar-cane or to experiment with new techniques. But the fate of the rest of the family seemed less certain. They might have lost the tension of living together, but they had also lost some security and possibly the chance of any further improvement. If they could reduce their debts, and manage to use the well in a productive way, then they might keep on top. If not, they'd probably return to the patterns which have dominated rural India for hundreds of years – debts, work, hunger, hope, harvest, death, birth. With land they would always be reasonably safe, but within three generations, their holdings could fragment into half acre plots.

It is easy to foresee the future, given the old patterns: the chance of change is limited to only a few alternatives, where the village and land and the preservation of family define each man's activity. Yet change on a wider scale is encroaching slowly on India, particularly with a swelling urban society. Who knows what or where the family will be within three generations.

Poor Lakshmi was an enigma without a solution and I feared for what might happen. Her mind was completely confused. She wasn't going to study, she'd start a shop in the city. Her cousin could help with the goods, and she'd do the selling all day. She didn't have any money, but she'd taken a loan already. How could she stay with her husband – he was so small and she was so big, they hadn't had sex for a year.

Her teacher was getting married. There had been another teacher, the one she had wanted to marry. He'd told her to tell her father but her marriage was fixed already. There had also been a third teacher who lived in her family's house. She would definitely set up shop, she only needed some money. Perhaps she could get her jewels back which her husband had taken away.

Her cousin still followed her round whenever she returned to her village; and her father said somewhat sadly that although his daughter was difficult he would never desert her while she suffered, for he had arranged the marriage. I was glad she had at least some protection. I myself felt hopelessly inadequate, for there was nothing that I could do. Lakshmi knew it, and grew more aloof.

Her husband, Basave Gowda, had given up with his wife and the idea of having children. To make it worse, Chikke Gowda's bride had got pregnant only four months after the nuptials. She was living in town with Eramma and rarely came to the village. Chikke Gowda had still not found a job.

One thing more depressed me: I had not seen much of Bhadramma and Jayamma, nor when we met was there the warmth and certainty of before. Perhaps they sensed that I was making my peace with the family. Certainly Bhadramma was despondent in a way I had never seen, but then she had massive problems. Her father and brothers had suffered division and so could give her no help; an ox of hers had recently died, and she could not afford to replace it for ploughing; the well she had recently dug hadn't filled up as it should have done; the pumpset she had installed had just burnt out and would cost more than five hundred rupees to repair; and her family's total debts had now reached thirteen thousand rupees.

Jayamma's life was no better, and her husband was even insisting that *she* should find him a second wife. He was openly callous now, admitting to me without inhibition that if only his wife had died, he could have taken another.

It was Jayamma's daughter, Manjula, who made us forget our depressions. We spent hours in Bhadramma's house at last, just playing and laughing with her. At first she was fat and dopey, but then she started to liven as we tickled and cuddled and swung her. It was the first time Jayamma had played with her daughter.

Jayamma loved her baby. She was so happy, oh, so happy, she couldn't express it at all. To have lost three before and now to have this one.

Bhadramma also loved the baby: she dressed her and washed her and cradled her; she held her on her lap with an ease and protectiveness which Jayamma seemed to lack. And she seemed to accept with happiness that because of the situation, the child would spend more time with her grandmother than her mother.

We also returned to the hospital for Jayamma to check her scar: she rushed round the wards expectantly to see the nurses and doctors, but they were busy and had little enthusiasm for her baby: they had dozens of others to look after now. We got some ointment for Jayamma's pains and bought some contraceptive pills so that she would not get pregnant too quickly again.

That night we stayed in Sundrapura where Bhadramma joined us in her son's house. We spent the evening eating and talking and feeling comfortable together – I knew then it was alright, that our friendship was still secure.

This time, I had no problem in deciding when to leave: I had come for only four weeks, and had to get up to Delhi to complete some business there. Besides, I knew now that I'd often be back to see them.

There was little specific left to do: some photographs of each family, and pictures of all the babies; a walk through the village to take in again its intensity; a night spent in each part of the house with each part of the family. Once, when the men had gone out for some ceremony, we took our baths at midnight in the central washing area – all the women and I. There was no coyness in our nakedness, nor curiosity: we scrubbed each other's backs, poured water, combed out our dripping hair, dressed ourselves in clean clothes, and lay down to sleep.

The following night the women worked till four o'clock preparing sweets and biscuits. They got up at six to start breakfast, and I went from room to room for coffee, food, and a whispered goodbye. I went to Jayamma's house but the door was locked; I went to Bhadramma's house and sat peacefully for an hour. She had prepared a large parcel of food for me to take to England, for me to give to my husband and family.

When I came back to the house, S.M.B. sat me on a chair in the corner of the gods: the men, the women, the children, came and stood before me. They offered flowers and betel leaves, they put

kunkuma on my forehead, they placed a garland round my neck.
S.M.B. gave me a small box. Everyone told me to open it. Inside
was a gold charm, showing Lakshmi the goddess of wealth and
prosperity. The old lady tied it round my neck: it was from all her
side of the family. Bhadre Gowda stepped forward and gave me a
stainless steel plate inscribed on the back, 'From Bhadre Gowda
and family'. The women presented their parcels of food.

Nanjeswamy's bullock cart was waiting to take me to Krishnapatna, so we walked down the street of the village. I didn't cry
this time. Before climbing in, I took off my shoes and walked to
the old man: I bent and touched his feet three times. He touched
my head like a daughter-in-law, staring silently straight ahead. I
turned to the old lady and touched her feet also: she accepted
without resistance.

As the bullock cart rolled away, I noticed Susheelamma crying.
'Don't cry,' I called, 'I'll come back with my baby.'

Outside the village I saw Jayamma hurrying along a distant
path, a basket of dung on her head. I climbed down from the cart
and ran after. She turned and waved, then carried on.

I climbed back into the cart.

'There's just one thing,' said Nanjeswamy, turning round on
the shaft where he held the reins of his oxen. 'My eldest brother
needs a scooter to get from the town to the village. Perhaps you
could send it from England?'

Glossary

(Words not italicised have an English usage)

bidi—a small quantity of tobacco rolled in a dried leaf

betel—the leaf of a plant, which is wrapped round parings of the areca nut with a little lime and sometimes tobacco, and chewed as a masticatory

betel-nut—the nut of the areca palm; so misnamed because chewed with betel. Stains teeth red when eaten with betel

cholu—a sand dug out of the ground and used for washing clothes because of its detergent qualities

dhobi—washerman by caste

dose—aerated pancake made mainly with rice flour and fried: a speciality of South India

ghee—clarified butter

gopuram—the sculptured tower usually found above the entrance to Hindu temples

Harijan—literally 'people of God', the name given by Mahatma Gandhi for people of the untouchable caste

idli—ground rice and lentils steamed in small round cakes: a speciality of South India

jaggery—a coarse dark brown sugar in solid blocks made locally by evaporation from sugar-cane sap

jayikayi—the nut used for ayurvedic medicinal purposes

kadige—a black paste used by women to darken the eyelids

Kali-yuga—Hindu mythological name for present epoch, considered a destructive one

kunkuma—a red powder used on the forehead and hairparting of women other than widows or polluted women. An auspicious sign

Lingayat—a caste which developed in the twelfth century from the followers of Shiva

lungi—a length of cotton cloth, usually white, worn by men round their waists and reaching their feet

Muhurtham—the astrologically appointed time when the bride is given away to the bridegroom in the marriage ceremony

obbittu—a sweet pancake stuffed with jaggery, coconut, and lentils

paise—Indian coin worth 1/100 rupee

palla—Indian measure equivalent to 100 litres

panchayat—Indian village council sanctioned by law

patel—formerly hereditary leader of the village with rights to administer justice, now a government representative usually responsible for revenue collection

peepul—a sacred tree

poori—thin flat cakes of wheat dough, deep fried in oil

prasada—offerings of food to God, distributed after worship to devotees

puja—Hindu religious rites

puri—puffed rice

ragi—millet

rangoli—linear design, frequently made with powdered chalk, as an auspicious symbol

rotti—flat circular bread made from rice, wheat, millet, or sorghum flour, cooked on a metal plate

rupee—the monetary unit of India

sapota—large evergreen tree with edible fruit

seer—Indian measure equivalent to 1 litre capacity, or approx. 2 lb. weight

Shivaratri—a feast day and night devoted to Shiva; the month in which the feast day falls

Taluk—sub-division of a district comprising a number of villages

tambura—a musical instrument usually with a single string

tola—small unit of Indian weight

uppittu—a mixture of fried semolina, salt, chillis, and grated coconut

Vedanta—one of the leading systems of Hindu philosophy